The Growth of Ranmoor, Hangingwater and Nether Green

Peter Bhan

November 2009

The Growth of Ranmoor, Hangingwater and Nether Green

Peter Warr

Northend Creative Print Solutions,
Sheffield
2009

Distributed by Mayfield Books and Gifts, 9 Orgreave Close, Sheffield S13 9NP.
Telephone: 0114 288 9522

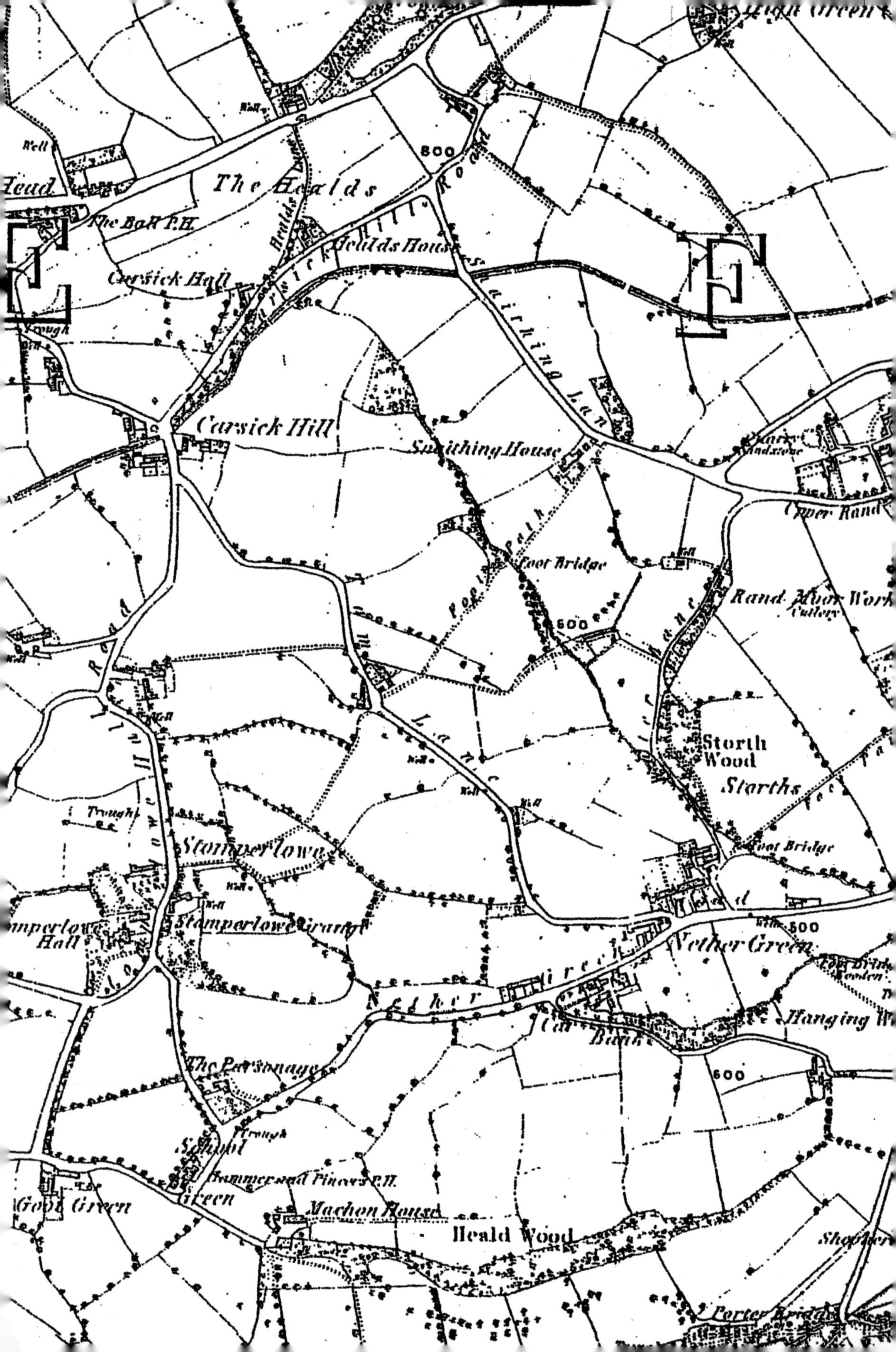
The Healds
The Ball P.H.
Carsick Hall
Carsick Hill
Healds House
Smithing House
Foot Bridge
Upper Rand
Storth Wood
Storths
Stamperlowe
Stamperlowe Grange
Nether Green
Cat Bank
The Parsonage
School
Trough
Hammer and Pincers P.H.
Machon House
Heald Wood
800
600
500
Well

**The Ranmoor
area in the 1850s**

ISBN 978-0-901100-85-6

Designed and Printed by
Northend Creative Print Solutions,
Sheffield S8 0TZ
Tel: 0114 250 0331 Fax: 0114 250 0676
www.northend.co.uk
Email: ks@northend.co.uk

Contents

Acknowledgements

Like all historical accounts, this book draws heavily on previous publications, and my first debt is to earlier authors who have contributed so much to our knowledge of Sheffield's development. However, Sheffield-wide accounts do not deal with Ranmoor, Hangingwater and Nether Green in any depth, and for that purpose I have needed to follow up many local issues in Sheffield's City Archives and its Local Studies Library. Staff in both have been unfailingly helpful, and I am grateful to both for permission to reproduce some of their material – Map 5 of ACM70 from the Archives, and photographs from the Picture Sheffield collection of the Local Studies Library.

As current custodian of the historical Archive created by the Ranmoor Society, I have also had access to an unrivalled accumulation of material. The Ranmoor Archive contains a large number of original deeds, sale plans, family histories, maps, newspaper items and other documents, providing very many details which are not otherwise available. Among the people who have kindly contributed material to this book and thus also to the Ranmoor Archive are Sophie and Jeremy Archdale, Christine Ball, Anne and Stuart Barratt, Gill Battye, Pauline Bell, John Drezet, Noel Edwards, Jill Fenoughty, Neville Flavell, Joan Forrester, Joan Garforth, Raymond Gee, Michael Gill, Judith Hanson, John Hepworth, Andy Heywood, Davida Howard, Margaret Kerry, Michael Killingley, Lambert Munro, Robert Nicholls, Pauline Oldfield, Derek Stapley, and Donald and Kathleen Thompson.

I am extremely grateful to all those people, and also (with apologies for omission) to the many others who are unnamed in the Archive's files. Particular thanks go to Graham Hague, Rita Redford and Andrew Swift for their suggestions about particular chapters, and to Gerald Eveleigh for many of the book's photographs, for Maps 1.03 and 2.03, for advice on several topics, and for his long and successful period as Secretary of the Ranmoor Society. The engraving for the front cover was created by Mike Lindley, and overall the book has gained a lot from the design contributions made by Keith Stubley and colleagues at Northend Creative Print Solutions.

The Ranmoor Archive will remain a valuable resource for many future generations. To increase still further its public value now and in the future, additional documents, information and illustrations continue to be needed. If you have any such material which could be copied, transcribed or retained in the Archive, please let us know.

Peter Warr
September 2009

CHAPTER ONE

The Region Before 1800

The 1800s saw great changes in Sheffield and around its boundaries. Isolated country hamlets expanded and became joined to the town itself. This book tells the story of one such isolated area – known then as "Rand Moor".

Hallamshire and Upper Hallam

Rand Moor was set in a region known for centuries as "Hallamshire". That had become a separate administrative area in Anglo-Saxon times – the southernmost shire of Northumbria – and from the 11th century a Norman Lordship was based on Sheffield castle (see Display Box 1 later in the chapter). Although definitions were not always clear, Hallamshire was often taken to include the parishes of Sheffield and Ecclesfield and the chapelry of Bradfield[1]. *(Notes are provided at the end of each chapter.)* "Hallun" was included in the Domesday book of 1086, and the area was covered in 1624 by the new "Company of Cutlers in Hallamshire". Joseph Hunter called his substantial history of 1819 simply "Hallamshire"[2]. Nowadays, the name is used by many Sheffield businesses and, for example, the Royal Hallamshire Hospital, Hallam University and Radio Hallam.

The parish of Sheffield itself was divided into six townships – Sheffield town and park[3], Attercliffe-cum-Darnall, Brightside, Ecclesall, Nether Hallam (roughly from Crookes to Owlerton), and Upper Hallam. The last of these, approximately between the Rivers Porter and Rivelin, was more than twice as large as any of the others, and within it lay Ranmoor, Hangingwater and Nether Green, as well as Ringinglow, Stanage, Fulwood and Rivelin.

At the time of the Domesday Survey in the 11th century, Upper Hallam was woodland that was pasturable, sufficiently free from undergrowth to permit the grazing of animals. Much of northern England had once been covered in trees (mainly oak and hazel), but those were increasingly cleared as timber was needed for heating or building and open land was required for pasturage. The name "Fulwood" and the "Storrs" of High Storrs (a Scandinavian term for a wood) point to the earlier woodland nature of the area. By the 1600s only small areas of woodland remained locally, with most fields being used for pasture and some for growing vegetables, corn or barley.

Up to the 19th century, few people lived in Upper Hallam. As late as 1819, Joseph Hunter noted that the local dialect was different from that in Sheffield itself. "There are remnants of our ancient tongue remaining amongst the rude and simple inhabitants of this remote part of the parish, which are not found and scarcely understood in the more populous parts" (*Hallamshire*, p. 380). Even by the 1850s, Sheffield street directories described the area as "extensive, wild and thinly populated".

The label "Upper Hallam" fell out of use after the Sheffield Corporation Act in 1900. This Act extended the boundary of the city (Sheffield was designated a city in 1893), and divided it into 16 electoral wards without any reference to Upper Hallam. As part of the changes, Ranmoor was placed in a newly-created Hallam Ward.

1

The Local Names

The part of Upper Hallam considered in this book, about three miles to the west of Sheffield centre, is shown in Map 1.01 – a section of the 1850 Ordnance Survey map. (A larger version is at the front of the book.) Our area of interest stretches roughly from Sandygate Road in the north to the River Porter in the south, and from Tom Lane in the west to Shore Lane to the east. The land slopes downward from north to south, with streams (now often hidden in culverts) flowing into the River Porter. In the map's centre are "Upper Rand Moor" and "Lower Rand Moor", with "Nether Green" and "Hanging Water" at the bottom. Although containing those different hamlets, the area was often known as a whole as "Rand Moor" – now "Ranmoor".

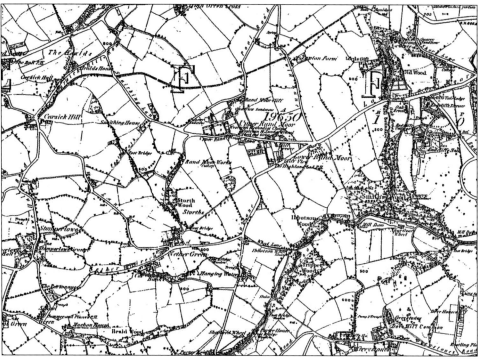

Map 1.01
Ranmoor, Hangingwater and Nether Green around 1850. A larger version of this map is at the front of the book.

The local names have been used in some form for many centuries. For example, a legal document of 1441 referred to land "near to Randfeld", a survey in 1637 included "Rann Moore", and William Beal's will of 1776 mentioned his property "on the Randmoor". Most common in the 1800s was "Rand Moor", and the current name of "Ranmoor" did not become usual until late in that century.

The first part of the name (now "Ran") probably describes a location in relation to the "moor" of the second part. The earlier title, Rand Moor, points to a "rand", which usually means an edge or border. That derives from Scandinavian languages, suggesting an early naming of the area by arrivals from a Nordic part of Europe.

2

Placing "rand" next to "moor" yields a name that might describe either an "open space [moor] at the edge" or "the edge of the open space"[4].

The term "moor" has no precise definition. Although it undoubtedly refers to an open space, a moor might be either a treeless and heather-covered area (as we nowadays think) or instead part-wooded and grassy. Frequently the term referred generally to open land, perhaps that which was common and unenclosed[5]. But what was the open space – the "moor" – in "Rand Moor"? Most probably, the partly-open forest extending between the Rivers Porter and Rivelin, including the "full wood" that is now Fulwood[6].

Rand Moor was thus probably once a hamlet in an open space at the edge of a partly wooded area, first named by Scandinavian settlers. Vikings, mainly Danish but also some Norwegians, came into Britain during the 200 years from about 865. They preferred to settle on high ground, and several sites around Sheffield illustrate their presence. Other local Viking names include High Storrs, Crookes, Grimesthorpe and Jordanthorpe.

Hangingwater seems likely to derive the "water" part of its name either from the adjacent River Porter or from the fact that it was liable to flooding. The area collects rain-water from the slopes to the north, and several north-to-south streams are shown on earlier maps. For instance, part of one (now mainly in an underground conduit) previously ran down from Sandygate into the River Porter along the lowest part of Storth Lane[7].

The first part of "Hangingwater" needs to be viewed as two separate themes, rather than as a reference to "hanging". The key idea is that of an "ing". This is a Nordic word for a field or meadow, possibly swampy or liable to flooding[8]. "Hang" often indicates that a location is sloping, so "Hangingwater" as a whole probably refers to a sloping open area that tends to become flooded and/or is next to a river.

The name "Nether Green" denotes a lower ("nether") area of common land (a "green"). A survey of 1637 indicated that land between the bottom of Tom Lane and the bottom of what is now Storth Lane was an area of common land in that year, as it presumably had been for centuries[9]. Common land (a "common") was owned by one person but was available to certain others who had "rights in common". These rights included the pasture of animals, and the removal of wood or turf. Nether Green ceased to be common land when it was enclosed by the 1805 Act described below.

Note that "common" land rights were not shared by everyone equally "in common". Rights of common were restricted to the owners or tenants of that land, and those rights were graded according to the amount held. Thus a big landowner had considerable rights to use the land, whereas (for instance) the holder of a cottage had only a very small entitlement. Non-holders had no rights at all. In earlier centuries cottages were sometimes illegally built on the edge of a common area, and allowed to remain after payment of a fine to the Manor Court for encroachment. That process may have led to some of the current Nether Green cottages, although no evidence to that effect has been found.

In addition, a "High Green" used to exist at the north end of the district, not far from the current Plough Inn in Sandygate Road[10], suggesting that Ranmoor might once have been a single area of common land between those two greens[11]. High Green was also enclosed in the 1805 Award, ceasing to be common land from that date.

3

Map 1.02
*Ranmoor and district in the map attached to the 1805 Enclosure Award.
(Reproduced with permission from His Grace the Duke of Norfolk DL and the
Director of Culture, Sheffield City Council.)*

1791 Upper Hallam Enclosure Act

Between about 1750 and 1850, local landowners throughout the country initiated
around 5,000 private Acts of Parliament to authorize the enclosure of open fields
and commons, supposedly to make better use of them. In respect of commons
(which were the focus in Ranmoor), the intention was to compensate anyone who
previously had common rights by granting them new "enclosed" land in proportion
to their loss of rights as a result of enclosure.

An Enclosure Act for Upper Hallam (extending also to some adjacent areas) was
passed in 1791. The land was surveyed soon afterwards, mainly by William
Fairbank[12], who created a map indicating which fields were commons and which
had previously been enclosed by their owners. Each field on the map was numbered,
and a separate list set out details of each one and its owner and tenant.

4

Display Box One

SHEFFIELD TOWN BEFORE 1800

In a local census of 1736, Sheffield was estimated to have about 14,000 people. By 1801, the first national census indicated a population of about 45,000 – more than a three-fold increase in 65 years.

Some notable dates:

c1130: Norman baron William de Lovetot acquires the manor and other areas. He builds a castle, a bridge over the Don, and a church on the site of what became the present cathedral; also a corn mill and other buildings needed for a town to flourish.

1200s: Metal-working and cutlery-making activities recorded.

1296: Royal charter granted for a weekly market and annual fair.

c1430: Barker's Pool, Sheffield's first reservoir, established; opened once a month to allow water to wash parts of the town.

c1510: Manor House and Lodge built outside the town within Sheffield Park, noted for its excellent hunting.

1570-1584: Mary Queen of Scots imprisoned in Sheffield Castle and later in Manor Lodge.

1624: Company of Cutlers in Hallamshire formed, building the first Cutlers' Hall in 1638.

1642-1651: English Civil War sees Sheffield castle seized by local people in support of parliament, then by royalists, and finally by parliamentary forces; it was demolished as ordered by an Act of Parliament in 1648.

1721: St Paul's Church erected on the site of the current Peace Gardens (then the south-western edge of the town), but not consecrated until 1740; it was demolished in 1938.

1736-1771: Buildings erected in Paradise Square.

1740s: Crucible steel and "old Sheffield plate" invented by Benjamin Huntsman and Thomas Boulsover respectively.

1756: First local turnpike road, through London Road and up Derbyshire Lane to Chesterfield.

1758: Turnpike to Buxton created from improved roads through Sharrow, Ecclesall, Bents Green and Ringinglow.

1773: Sheffield Assay Office established.

1784: Act of Parliament authorises a new Market Place below High Street, clearing older buildings and streets and providing space for more than 200 traders.

1786: The town's first steam-driven wheel installed to provide power for metal-working.

1794-1815: Following the French Revolution in 1789, wars with Napoleon Bonaparte close many trading markets to Sheffield goods, leading to considerable poverty.

For several years, the three commissioners appointed by the Act considered each landowner's holding and entitlement, apportioning the commons as they deemed appropriate. After extensive discussions, perhaps delayed by the death of one of the commissioners, the Award was made in 1805.

A section of the Enclosure Award map is shown as Map 1.02 on page 4. It is the earliest detailed picture available, showing roads, buildings (not many at the time),

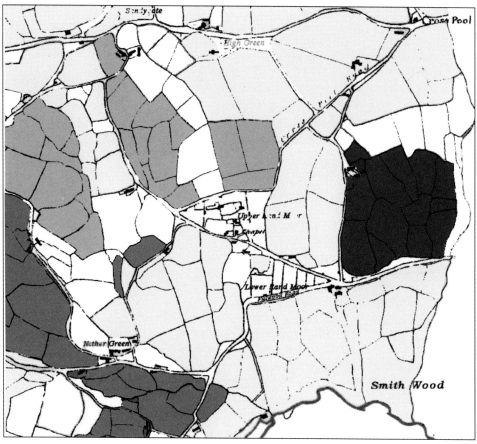

Map 1.03
Principal local landowners in the 1790s.

Duke of Norfolk; Catherine Cope; William Murray; Boys' Charity School.

and the shapes of individual fields. The map covers both the "old enclosures" (areas defined and individually-owned before this Act) and (in darker shading on the map) the commons that were now to be enclosed and granted to someone in compensation for lost common-land rights. The principal areas of common land were at that time around Ranmoor Road and at High Green, Nether Green and Carr Bank. 1790s buildings will be considered in Chapter 2.

Principal Landowners in the 1790s

The area's main landowners in the 1790s are shown in outline Map 1.03. Key individuals were the Duke of Norfolk (extensively in this and other areas), Catherine Cope (in the north of Ranmoor) and William Murray (in the south). Another large section (to the east) was owned by the trustees of the Boys' Charity School. Who were these people, and how did they come to own land in Ranmoor?

The 11th Duke of Norfolk

As Earl of Arundel, Earl-Marshal and Premier Duke of England, and Lord of Hallamshire, Charles Howard (1746-1815) owned extensive lands around Sheffield and in other parts of the country. His family held the Manor of Sheffield through marriage to a descendant of the Earl of Shrewsbury in the 17th century. He lived mainly in Arundel Castle in Sussex, was active in London society, and visited Sheffield only infrequently. Because the Howard family had preferred to remain at Arundel for some decades, their direct impact on the town was less than that of their ancestors in previous years.

In 1802, the Duke of Norfolk and his cousin, Bernard-Edward, who later became the 12th Duke after Charles's death without children, submitted a petition to parliament. This led to an Act permitting the sale of "several messuages and hereditaments[13] in Sheffield, and diverse detached parts of the settled estates of the most noble Charles Duke of Norfolk" and for "laying out the monies in the purchase of more convenient estates and otherwise", which apparently meant with an emphasis on the Arundel area. Three more Acts followed in the next decade, and a great deal of Sheffield land became freed for private and commercial development[14].

The family's long local involvement is widely reflected in 21st-century Sheffield – in the names of Norfolk Park, Norfolk Street, Norfolk Row, several Norfolk Arms public houses, Howard Street, Arundel Gate, and a variety of other references. A later Duke (the 15th), Henry Fitzalan Howard (1847-1917), became a Sheffield alderman, mayor, lord mayor, honorary freeman, and the first chancellor of Sheffield University.

Lady Catherine Cope

Another substantial landowner shown in Map 1.03 was Catherine Cope. Her father, John Law, belonged to an established Rotherham family, and her first husband John Burton had been lord of the manor of Owlerton. John, who died in 1772 aged 32, had owned a substantial amount of land in Rand Moor and elsewhere.

Widowed Catherine Burton later became the second wife of Sir Richard Cope, the 9th Baronet of Hanwell and Bramshill in Hampshire, thus becoming Lady Catherine Cope. Sir Richard died in 1806 without children, and Catherine's estate probably passed later to her daughter from her first marriage (Catherine, 1773-1855), who became Lady Catherine Burgoyne by marriage. The family's Ranmoor lands were sold at some time during the 19th century, at least some to John Pye-Smith (1774-1851) who passed them onto his own descendants.

William Murray

Around the time of the Upper Hallam Enclosure Award, William Murray was responsible for lands in many parts of Ecclesall, Ranmoor and Rotherham. He had in 1782 married Mary Murray (1759-1803) of Banner Cross, changing his name from its original Foxlowe so that the Murray name was preserved[15].

His wife had inherited considerable property from her parents – Lord John Murray (1711-1787) and his wife Mary (1732-1765). The latter was the daughter and heiress of Richard and Mary Dalton of Banner Cross. Mary Dalton had been before marriage Mary Bright, a member of the wealthy Bright family that had long been established in the Banner Cross and nearby areas.

After the death of her father (Lord John Murray) in 1787[16], the younger Mary Murray inherited local estates belonging previously (through her mother) to her Bright and Dalton ancestors. The estates were administered by her husband William Murray, both before and after Mary's death in 1803. Around 1817, William set about rebuilding Banner Cross Hall, but he died in 1818 before it was completed. The couple had no children, and the estate passed through William's sister to the Bagshawe family, into which she had married in 1798. Their Ranmoor land was later sold, but details have not been located.

The Boys' Charity School

In 1706, at the instigation of Nathan Drake, the Vicar of the Parish Church of St Peter and St Paul (now Sheffield Cathedral), a charity was formed to care for and educate boys from poor families. Money was raised from voluntary subscriptions, bequests and other sources, and the school eventually accommodated 100 boys. Most of those had been living in poverty with their mother (in the absence of a father), but a minority were parentless orphans. Accommodation and food were provided, as was religious and other instruction[17].

Premises for the new school were built in 1710, at the north-east corner of the churchyard (now 13 East Parade, on the corner with Campo Lane). These were extended several times in the next two centuries, before the school moved in 1911 to a larger site in Psalter Lane (later occupied by a section of Hallam University but now sold).

Among the School's estates was land in the east of Ranmoor shown in Map 1.03, which had been acquired either as a gift or an investment. It was expanded slightly by a new enclosure in the 1805 Award, and was rented out for farming until its sale in the 1860s. The area was advertised then as "suitable for sites for residential purposes of the highest class". That and other developments will be described in Chapter 3[18].

Notes to Chapter One

1 See for instance David Hey, *A History of Sheffield* (Lancaster: Carnegie Publishing, 1998) and Mary Walton, *Sheffield: Its Story and Achievements* (Sheffield: Sheffield Telegraph and Star, 1948).

2 The first edition of *Hallamshire* was produced by Joseph Hunter alone, but subsequent editions in 1869 and 1875 were augmented by Alfred Gatty.

3 The lord's deer and hunting park was outside the town itself, originating before 1200. It was said to be the second largest deer park in the country.

4 Alternatively, the first part of the name might in much earlier times have referred to a person or group living in the area. Thus the "ran" in Ranmoor might concern a family called "rann", "rinn" or something similar.

5 For example, the current Moor shopping area in Sheffield city centre is part of what was previously Little Sheffield Moor, an area of common land.

6 "Full wood" appears to have derived from "foul wood", although the meaning of "foul" in this context is not clear – possibly a reference to a marshy area. The Upper Hallam woodland was much prized for hunting, and a hunting lodge is commemorated by the name of Lodge Moor.

7 Presumably reflecting the presence of that stream, Storth Lane was until 1886 known as Water (sometimes Watery) Lane. The water is part of the Snaithing Brook, now in a culvert under Storth Lane and Fulwood Road.

8 A nearby ing was described in 18th century documents as "New Ing", on the western side of what is now Storth Lane.

9 The 1637 survey was commissioned by descendants of Gilbert, the 7th Earl of Shrewsbury (who died in 1616), to provide details of their Sheffield property and its likely provision of income. The survey's list of plots was published in a 1908 book by J. G. Ronksley (Survey and View of the Manor of Sheffield by John Harrison 1637. Sheffield: Arthur Wightman). However, no accompanying map was available until a reconstruction by G. Scurfield (Seventeenth-century Sheffield and its environs, Yorkshire Archaeological Journal, 1986, 58, 147-171).

10 The 1850 Ordnance Survey map (Map 1.01 and at the front of the book) shows High Green Cross on this site. The cross was also present in the 1637 survey (see Note 9), and was represented on the 1790s Enclosure Award map by a small circle surrounded by a square. An associated 1795 map (ACM S79 in Sheffield City Archives) shows this in more detail, located on the edge of the road (an ancient pack-horse route) rather than on the Green itself. However, by 1905 an Ordnance Survey map refers only to "stones" next to the road; those were still shown in 1923, but by the 1935 map had been replaced by the current letter box.

The cross was probably a way-marker, indicating from an all-round elevated position the junction between what is now Sandygate Road ("Church Lane" in 1637) and a north-south route which has since disappeared. It may have been whitewashed for better visibility, possibly inscribed with nearby place-names, and erected many years before the earliest surviving record.

Early guide-posts and crosses are known to have existed on nearby moors from the 1200s, and Stanage Pole (along the same route) was standing in 1550 and probably earlier. A 1702 Act of Parliament required the erection of a "stone or post" on every junction of main routes outside towns.

11 Consistent with that possibility is the overall description "Stockwell Green" in place of Rand Moor on a map by Jeffreys around 1770, and "Rand Moor or Stockwell Green" in a directory published by Thomas Langdale in 1822. However, the 1637 survey in Note 9 seems to site Stockwell Green north of Crosspool, so its location remains unclear.

12 Members of the Fairbank family conducted hundreds of surveys and inspections of property in the Sheffield area between the 1750s and 1848. Extensive records of their work are held in Sheffield City Archives, and a summary account was provided by T. Walter Hall in 1932 (The Fairbanks of Sheffield. Sheffield: J. W. Northend).

13 The term "messuage" is widely used to refer to a dwelling house and its adjacent buildings and land. "Hereditaments" are any kind of property, including lands and buildings, which can be inherited.

14 The register of these sales in Sheffield City Archives (ACM S431) contains 322 transactions, many involving several pieces of land. The first was dated September 1802 and the last was probably in 1812, although many entries are undated.

15 William Murray had previously lived in Staveley Hall in Derbyshire, and was an army Captain at the time of his marriage; in due course he became a Lieutenant-General.

16 Lord John Murray was Colonel of the 42nd Regiment of Foot (later known as the Black Watch) and a son of the Duke of Athol in Perthshire; he became a full General in 1770. The Scottish connexion with his family is recalled in the names of several roads in Banner Cross, including Murray Road itself.

17 Early accounts were provided by Joseph Hunter in Hallamshire (pages 320-321 in the 1875 edition) and the City of Sheffield in its Return to the Charity Commissioners of 1897 (pages 193-204).

18 The Boys' Charity School later became linked to a national network of charity schools providing free education for needy children. It was sometimes referred to as the "Sheffield Blue Coat School" (which became the official name in 1911), in keeping with the national convention that pupils in such schools wore old-fashioned blue cloth coats, buttoned up in front and cut away into tails behind, with yellow braid and brass buttons, green corduroy trousers, and a blue "muffin" cap. The boys attended church services in their uniforms, and provided drill exhibitions at events such as the Cutlers' Feast, presumably in part in order to encourage financial contributions

CHAPTER TWO

Eighteenth-Century Buildings

When William Fairbank was surveying Ranmoor in the 1790s (see Chapter 1), there were very few buildings to include on his map – less than 50 scattered around the area. What were they? Who lived in them? What did the occupants do? This chapter takes a look at these early buildings and describes what happened to them in the following two centuries.

A property often had several uses – as a house and workshop and perhaps a farm. Buildings were often sited near one of the district's many springs or wells. (An 1897 sale document described Ranmoor land as providing "a never-ending supply of pure spring water".) As they had been for centuries, some 1790s buildings were roofed with thatch, probably with locally-grown water-reeds from the many "sicks" and "carrs" in the area. Many people had their own animals – hens, pigs, perhaps a cow, and occasionally a horse. Some worked part-time as a farmer, and other principal occupations were in the cutlery and file-making trades.

The numbers in outline Map 2.01 correspond to buildings described in the text. We will start roughly in the centre of the map, and take an imaginary journey around the locality.

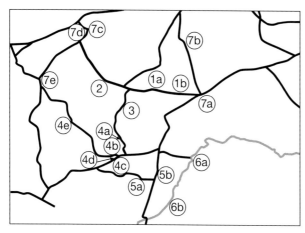

Map 2.01
1790s buildings in Ranmoor, Hangingwater and Nether Green.
1a, Around Ranmoor Chapel.
1b, Ranmoor Rise.
2, Snaithing Farm.
3, Ranmoor Cutlery Works.
4a, Joseph Hawksworth's homestead.
4b, Nether Green cottages.
4c and 4d, Cottages in Fulwood Road.
4e, Thomas Creswick's cottage.
5a, Carr Bank House.
5b, Hangingwater Farm.
6a, Ibbotson Wheel.
6b, Shepherd Wheel.
7a, Joseph Ibbotson's farm.
7b, Darwin Lane homestead.
7c, Ivy House Farm.
7d, now Stubbin House and
*   Stubbin Cottage.*
7e, Carsick Hill Farm.

1. Around Ranmoor Road

It is surprising to find in the empty space of Ranmoor a "chapel" on the 1790s map (shown as 1a on Map 2.01). The chapel had been constructed by a group of Wesleyan Methodists in 1783, and its history will be covered in Chapter 6. Associated buildings included a barn as well as a house, occupied around 1790 by Nathan Clayton and his family. He was an active member of the chapel and probably served as chapel-keeper as well as having some other occupation. The building (probably in the 1860s) is shown in Photo 2.01.

Photo 2.01
The initial Wesleyan Methodist Chapel in Ranmoor Road, erected in 1783 on land owned by the Duke of Norfolk. This was replaced in 1870 by a new chapel which was itself demolished in 1963; see Chapter 6.

Other buildings near to the chapel were occupied either by workers in the quarry being excavated below Ranmoor Cliffe Road or by people with other jobs in the neighbourhood. For example, Thomas Sampson, a stone-mason, lived on land rented from the Duke of Norfolk in what became Chapel Terrace. His 1769 will referred to "that cottage house that I builded this summer". Photo 2.02 shows part of Chapel Terrace in the 20th century.

Most early buildings around Ranmoor's Wesleyan chapel were replaced in the 1800s, but two remain in place. Across the road from the chapel was a house that

Photo 2.02
Part of Chapel Terrace, first occupied by workers in nearby stone quarries and farms. The celebrations may have been for the coronation of King George VI (July 1937) or at the end of World War Two (August 1945).

became known as Chippendale Cottage (now 73 Ranmoor Road). This had been owned since 1710 by the Free Tenants and Burgesses of Sheffield, also known as the Town Trustees[1]. A Trust record of that year refers to 13s 8d (£0.68) paid to "Chippingdale for morter, thack [i.e., thatch], leading and [other] work" as part of "repairing the cottage at Randmore".

Chippendale Cottage was rented by members of the Beal scissor-smith family from at least the 1770s. By the 1830s they had become established in Storth Lane (then called Water Lane; see Section 3 below), and grinder Joseph Howson and his family were in Chippendale Cottage. He probably rebuilt the property, since his 1838 lease required him to "make, erect and finish" "a good and substantial stone dwelling house and shop, well worth the sum of £100 at least". His workshop was probably in the separate building at the side of the house, and Joseph may have also made use of one of the water-powered wheels on the River Porter (see Section 6, below). By 1870, the tenant was Joseph Kay (1818-1907), who was a successful boot- and shoe-maker with several premises in Sheffield town[2]. He extended the property and at some time became its owner rather than tenant.

Also present in the 1790s was a "house and croft" owned by John Worrall[3], which has subsequently been extended to become what is now Ran Farm (10 Ranmoor Crescent). Further down Ranmoor Road are three more 18th-century buildings, owned after the Enclosure Award by the Duke of Norfolk and now numbered (after modifications) as 32, 34 and 42 (1b on Map 2.01). Sometimes known as "Ranmoor Rise", an 1892 legal document about the first two refers to "the workshops, outbuildings and grounds adjoining"; as in many other cases, these were places of employment as well as homes.

Photo 2.03
Snaithing Farm and haystacks around 1900. Note that houses had yet to be built on the opposite side of Snaithing Lane.

2. Snaithing Farm

Moving up Ranmoor Road towards the west, we would in the 1790s reach an isolated building (number 2 on Map 2.01) long known as Snaithing Farm (and sometimes "Snaithing House"). The present building has of course been altered over the years, but people have lived on its site for centuries, perhaps attracted by springs available for the provision of water[4]. A document in 1447 refers to "one messuage[5] and two and a half acres of cultivated land called Snayth Inge", and in the 1540s a "house" was in "a close called Snaythings". References in later centuries become increasingly precise in pointing to the current location. The farm was on its own among fields, some of which were cultivated and others used for grazing livestock.

Photo 2.04
Snaithing Farm about 1907, with the "top pond" and water-well in the field now used as gardens for houses in Belgrave Road. The "bottom pond" was lower down the field near to that road.

In the 1790s, when the Enclosure Award survey was being made, Snaithing Farm (described in the Award document as a "homestead and house field") was owned by John and Thomas Newton, and their tenant was Joshua Worrall, who also farmed the adjacent fields and some land near Hangingwater Road. The surrounding area belonged to the Duke of Norfolk (see Chapter 1), and in the 1820s the Newton family bought from the Duke several fields along the west of Snaithing Lane. The Newtons lived in Sheffield town, and were primarily employed as retail grocers, also described as "tallow chandlers" and "tea and flour dealers".

Snaithing Farm and associated land passed to the Rowbotham family in the 1840s, through the marriage of Ann Newton to John Rowbotham[6] in the 1830s. Their daughter, Ann Elizabeth Rowbotham, married George Octavius Cutler (see the West Lea section of Chapter 10), and in turn she and George's brother, John Edward Cutler, sold Snaithing Farm to Henry Herbert Andrew in 1898[7]. Following the latter's death in 1903, his lands were offered for sale. Joseph Creswick (1838-1918) was the tenant from 1866, and in the year of his death the property was bought by his son George (1874-1952).

Display Box Two

OUR 1898 CHRISTMAS AT SNAITHING FARM

Written by Nora Creswick, aged 14 in that year

This was one of my happiest Christmases. It was the last year we had our stockings filled up so we were up earlier – boy dolls and girl dolls, and animals for the boys, horses and carts, games, oranges, apples, sweets and a new penny each.

Our first duty was fetching water (which was a long way to carry) for breakfast, fetching the logs and filling the coal scuttles. Then going to meet the postman from the lower wood to save him coming across the field. What a happy Christmas Day it was.

Living in an old farmhouse with its oak beams and hanging lamps, holly and mistletoe decorations and numberless cards. The old-fashioned bookcases with hundreds of books in glass cupboards[27], and bird cases, old Dresden china and water colours. The old-fashioned grate filled with logs and coals.

Some went to Chapel Service[28] and met old friends there. Fifteen sat down to the good old Yorkshire dinner of Yorkshire pudding and roast beef, a nice cut off one of our own beasts. Plum pudding, such a monster, and nuts to crack after. The dinner service was our parents' wedding gift, so we children had to be very careful, and Father bought a lovely white tablecloth with satin fern leaves on. My Grandma's cutlery, some of the old family silver; one side [of the family] being in steel manufacture and the other side cutlery manufacture. And my Father was a farmer so we had everything home-made, and made good. After our meal the animals, poultry etc. had extra food too.

A Salvation Army band came to a large house opposite[29] in a wagonette drawn by horses, and the bugler, all complete. They played well. It was a clear frosty day, so the sound carried far away.

After dinner some of us went for a walk and enjoyed the frost-bound lanes, listening to the bands, and wended our way to the church-yard[30] to Mother's grave and two brothers and little Mary with wreaths we had made ourselves. And then back to tea of home-cured ham, home-made pork pie, mince pie, plum cakes and all the goodies Christmas brings.

Afterwards crackers and games. Father always had fresh stories to tell. We ended with supper and a real hearty sing – all the old hymns and ballads such as "Where is now the merry party", "Just before the battle Mother", "While shepherds watched", "Once in royal David's city", and "God be with you" to finish up with.

We were all together New Years Day for tea, and snow fell so the grandchild must be taken home early, with the hope all to meet again soon. But by the 21st we had buried a brother, 13, and a sister 26, she leaving a boy 13 months. We had not a thought of it, but the Lord took them.

Photo 2.05
*Snaithing Farm workers around 1910. In the background is Snaithing Grange, built in 1904
for William F. Osborn (1861-1936). He was the eldest son of Samuel Osborn (1826-1891), who
in 1852 had founded the steel company which bore his name.*

Joseph Creswick and his wife Mary (1846-1890) had 15 children, and members
of their family lived at Snaithing Farm up to 1974. In the 1870s, Joseph's invoices
described him as a "farmer, dealer in hay, coal, rock stone, peat, sand, and loam,
sod for vines, etc.", and much of his work (and that of his several employees)
involved carting materials for building and landscaping in the area, removing
rubbish, and transporting peat, manure and stone. For this work at one point he
kept at least five horses; two are in Photo 2.05. In the fields at Snaithing Farm and
also at Sandygate he had around 200 sheep and 20 cows, with pigs, ducks and
chickens kept for the family and for sale; eggs, milk and cream were made
available to customers. Crops included potatoes, wheat, oats, clover, and turnips,
and (as shown in Photos 2.03 and 2.04) hay was stored in substantial hay-stacks
next to the farm.

Joseph's wife Mary Creswick died in 1890, at the age of 43, leaving 12 children
aged between 4 and 21 (three had died young). These grew up at Snaithing Farm,
with their number gradually declining as individuals moved out or died. Joseph
Creswick himself passed away in 1918, aged 80, and four of his (by then adult)
children remained there, unmarried, for the next five decades.

The Creswick lifestyle changed little during that half-century at Snaithing Farm.
They did not want electricity, cooking and heating were from coal or log fires, and
jobs such as hay-cutting were carried out by hand without machinery. Most food
was home-grown. The farming business was continued by Frank (1875-1968, see
Photo 2.06), who worked almost to his death at the age of 92. Rose (1877-1972)
lived to be 95, helping her sister Kate (1883-1972) to manage the house and the

Photo 2.06
Frank Creswick (1875-1968) in 1963, aged 88. He worked with his father Joseph (1838-1918) before taking over Snaithing Farm himself. Frank continued working on the farm into his 80s.

Photo 2.07
Sisters Kate (1883-1972) and Nora (1884-1974) Creswick in the yard of Snaithing Farm in 1965. Kate had acted as housekeeper there for many years, and Nora had been a self-employed dress-maker.

Photo 2.08
Sisters Nora (1884-1974) and Rose (1877-1972) Creswick with the family bible in the 1960s. Both had been Sunday School teachers and otherwise active in Ranmoor Wesleyan Chapel.

small dairy (see Photo 2.07). Nora (1884-1974) worked as a dress-maker for much of her life, and she and Rose were active members of the Methodist churches in Ranmoor or Nether Green (see Photo 2.08 and Chapter 6).

Snaithing Farm was sold after Nora's death, and received much needed modernization. The "front field", between the bottom of Snaithing Lane and Belgrave Road, was at that time purchased for the houses that now stand there.

3. Ranmoor Cutlery Works

A short walk down-hill (southwards) from Snaithing Farm led in the 1790s to a property standing alone near the top of what was then called Water Lane. (It is now Storth Lane.) Shown on the 1790s Enclosure Award map (Map 1.02 in Chapter 1) to the east side of the lane, this was described as a "cottage and croft", owned by the Duke of Norfolk and tenanted by John Beal (c1763-1844). On Map 2.01 it is number 3.

Two or three buildings were located on this site, previously mentioned on a 1762 map and in the 1776 will of William Beal. William and his son John were both scissor-smiths, part of an extended scissor-making family living also in Bradfield, Stannington and elsewhere in the town[8]. In the 1790s, John Beal used the Water Lane property as a workshop as well as home for his family, and probably took materials for grinding to a wheel on the River Porter (see 6 below).

16

Display Box Three

A 1778 RANMOOR CUTLER

Excerpts from an Apprenticeship Agreement Binding John Hawksworth to Joseph Wilson of Nether Green

The said John Hawksworth of his own good-liking, and by and with the consent of his friends, doth put and bind himself servant and Apprentice to and with the said Joseph Wilson in the trade or occupation of a cutler to be taught and instructed, and with him as an Apprentice to dwell, serve, and abide . . . . for seven years . . . .

The said John Hawksworth, the Apprentice, shall and will take him the said Joseph Wilson for his Master, and him well and truly serve, and in all his commands, lawful and honest, obey; his lawful secrets he shall keep; the goods, chattels and money of his said Master . . . . he shall not misspend or waste, nor them lend or trust without his said Master's consent; fornication he shall not commit, nor matrimony contract; taverns nor alehouses he shall not frequent; at any unlawful game he shall not play, nor absent himself from his Master's service by day or night, without the consent of his said Master, but in all things as a good and faithful Apprentice and servant shall dutifully demean and behave himself during the said term.

And the said Master doth . . . . covenant and agree to and with the said Apprentice that he will teach and instruct him, or cause him to be taught and instructed, according to the best of his skill, in the said trade or occupation of a cutler within the limits of the Corporation of Cutlers in Hallamshire. And also that he will at all times, during the said term, find and provide for the said Apprentice good wholesome and sufficient meat, drink, washing and lodging, fitting and meet for such an Apprentice." (Wages were £1 6 4 for six years, and £6 1 4 in the seventh year.)

On 28 January 1785, having completed his apprenticeship, John Hawksworth was admitted as a Freeman of the Company of Cutlers in Hallamshire.

Subsequent occupants of the site included John's son Peter Beal (1787-1835) and the latter's wife Sarah (1791-1862), who were also scissor manufacturers. After Peter's death in 1835, his wife continued the business with help from their sons Joseph (1817-1878) and later James (1826-1910). They gradually enlarged the premises and presumably increased output. By the 1851 census, Sarah Beal was described as a "scissor and cutlery manufacturer employing eight men"[9].

Isolated in a rural setting, the Beal's property was described rather grandly on the 1850 Ordnance Survey map (see Map 1.01 and at the front of the book) as "Rand Moor Cutlery Works". Its several buildings provided housing for families as well as workshops, stores and accommodation for animals. By the 1850s, substantial machinery had been installed. An 1849 legal document refers to three workshops, two houses, an "old house"[10] and the "building thereto adjoining formerly used as a barn but sometime since converted into a grinding wheel" "together with the steam engine, running and going gear, grinding troughs, drums, fixtures and fastenings thereto"[11]. Such an engine required water (probably from a local well) and coal or wood (presumably brought in), as well as regular

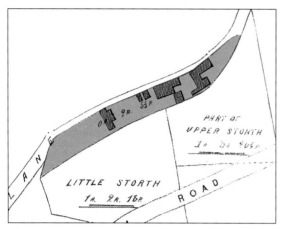

Map 2.02
Ranmoor Cutlery Works in Water (now Storth) Lane around 1860. It was abandoned at that time as the area was prepared for house-building (see Chapter 3).

operation to recoup its cost. An outline of the buildings is shown on Map 2.02 after they had been vacated around 1860.

So what happened to the Ranmoor Cutlery Works? The property developers took over. In 1853, George Wostenholm purchased a large area of land to the east of Water Lane, and prepared it for house-building by installing roads and drains; these activities will be described in Chapter 3. By the late 1850s, brothers Joseph and James Beal had instead established a company making scissors and shoe- and butchers-knives in Silver Street in Sheffield town[12]. The Upper Hallam rate book indicates that the Ranmoor "steel house and shops" were then "empty", and by 1860 their entry was crossed through and the buildings were indicated as "taken down".

4. Around Nether Green and Tom Lane

The only other buildings in Water (now Storth) Lane in the 1790s were some distance away from the Beals, southwards at the bottom of the hill. These (4a on Map 2.01 and detailed at the top of Map 2.03) were described in the Enclosure Award as a "homestead"[13] owned by Joseph Hawksworth, a farmer (and possibly also a carpenter[14]), and occupied by Joseph himself and Samuel Hawksworth (possibly Joseph's father). Joseph, who died in 1821, also owned the adjacent "house field" to the north and farmed other land in the area. After his death, the property was bought by silversmith and merchant John Eyre. It was described in an 1830 map of the Eyre estate as a "farmhouse, yard, dwelling houses and garden".

In the 1790s Joseph Hawksworth and his family lived in the house to the north, and the southern building was divided into three, presumably for farm-workers or other tenants. Joseph's son John Hawksworth started a seven-year apprenticeship as a cutler in 1778 (see Display Box 3); his "master" was another of the cutlers located elsewhere in Nether Green. The Hawksworth

Map 2.03
The Nether Green area at the time of the 1791 Enclosure Act. Note that Water (later Storth) Lane then turned sharply below the Hawksworth property; it now continues directly into Fulwood Road.

Photo 2.09
A recent photo of some of the 18th century cottages previously on the edge of Nether Green itself.

cutlery business later continued in Sheffield town, becoming linked to the electro-plating firm of Francis Howard (1837-1905). Francis married John Hawksworth's grand-daughter Martha.

The two 1790s buildings still stand today, albeit in modified form. The northern one is 432 Fulwood Road, having been extended in the 1800s. John Hawksworth (1811-1895, described in directories as a "metal-smith") lived in that house, also building numbers 9 and 11 Water/Storth Lane in 1866[15]. At that point, the three old houses became located behind the new building and were described as "Court Number 1". They were converted to a single house (7 Storth Lane) in 1977.

Close to the Hawksworths were several cottages located on the remnants of Nether Green itself (4b in Map 2.01 and shown on Map 2.03 and in Photo 2.09). The Green was still common land, but it became enclosed by the 1805 Award and allotted to Samuel Binney, described in different documents as a "yeoman" of either Fulwood or Little Sheffield (now the area around Sheffield Moor). He already owned the cottages with their accompanying barns, cow-houses, smithies and workshops. By 1812 there were eight dwelling-houses, and in 1883 the site contained 11 cottages and five workshops at the rear.

The layout at that later time is shown on the next page in an 1883 auction advertisement (Map 2.04). (Note the toilets and buildings for fuel and ashes near to Fulwood Road.) This offered possibilities that have become familiar more recently: "The present annual rental might be very largely increased by the erection of additional cottages on the land at the back without materially interfering with the garden plots, or the entire plot would form an excellent site for the erection of one or more superior dwelling-houses". Instead of those developments, piecemeal extensions were later made at the back of several cottages, and the workshops to the rear were enlarged (apparently mainly in the 1920s and 1930s).

The cottages are now listed (Grade 2) as being of special architectural or historical interest. As such, they are protected by law against demolition or substantial alteration without permission.

The Enclosure Award map also shows two buildings on the southern side of Fulwood Road (4c on Map 2.01 and in the bottom-left corner of Map 2.03). Those were both described as "house and garden", occupied by people who also rented adjoining fields. The more northern of the two buildings included the precursor of the Rising Sun public house, which is described in Chapter 8, and the other (Photo 2.10) contained cottages and later file-makers' workshops[16].

Also in this area in the 1790s and earlier were several cottages on the southern side of Tom Lane where it joins Fulwood Road (4d in Map 2.01 and in the left-centre of Map 2.03). Some of those are shown in Photos 2.11 and 2.12 just before they were demolished by the City Council in 1911-1912 in order to widen the bottom section of Tom Lane. 19th-century occupants will be described in Chapter 9.

Other buildings had also been built in Tom Lane before the 1790s. Higher up the road on the western side (4e on Map 2.01) was a "homestead and croft" owned and occupied by Thomas Creswick[17], who farmed many fields in the neighbourhood. Now modified as 105 and 109 Tom Lane, a 1920s photograph is number 2.13 on page 22. On the opposite side of Tom Lane were two houses which

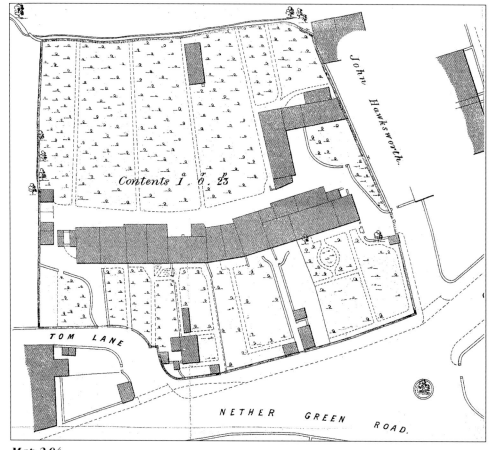

Map 2.04
Details from an 1883 Sale Plan. Water Lane has been continued southwards (compared to Map 2.03) and Fulwood Road is now in place; see Chapter 3. (Buildings to the east are incompletely drawn – not being part of the sale.)

Photo 2.10
These cottages (demolished in 1957) were near to the Rising Sun at Nether Green, before some of the ground was raised to construct a petrol station. This photograph dates from around 1900.

remained until at least the 1920s before being replaced by new developments. As in other cases, these were workshops and farms as well as dwelling-houses[18].

Photo 2.11
Seen from Fulwood Road, cottages at the bottom of Tom Lane before their demolition in 1910-1911 for widening Tom Lane.

Photo 2.12
Another view of the cottages in Photo 2.11. Joseph and Catherine Biggin had a grocery shop here around the 1880s and 1890s; see Chapter 9.

Photo 2.13
These cottages are still half way up Tom Lane (numbers 105 to 109). The photograph (probably in the 1920s) shows the Lane before this section was straightened in 1927-1928.

5. Carr Bank and Hangingwater

Behind the Rising Sun site, in the 1790s and also at the present time, a lane leads up-hill towards Hangingwater. On a sharp bend of that lane near Hangingwater Road the Enclosure Award map shows another isolated building (5a on Map 2.01).

After extensions and modifications, that has become the current Carr Bank House. From the 1780s to 1814 it was owned by Thomas Dale, who inherited it from his father. Described in the 1805 Enclosure Award as a "homestead", a later legal document also refers to "the smithies, barn, stable, cow-house and other outbuildings"; as in other cases the property was both a house and a cutlery workshop. Thomas Dale (based in Norton) was generally described as a file-smith. He employed people in several locations, and also owned several dozen other plots at the time of the Award; in later documents he is termed a "yeoman".

Although some of Thomas Dale's file-makers worked in this Carr Bank property, others used different workshops. Those were often simple lean-to sheds at the side of a house, with windows along the full length to maximize light. File-making was a very unhealthy activity, with many hours bending over a work-bench exposed to lead and lead dust; mortality in the early 1800s was as bad as for grinders, with an average age of death in the 50s for both groups[19]. Several stages in the work are described in Display Box 4.

Subsequent owners of Carr Bank House included in the 1870s Charles Thompson (1815-1897), who had operated horse-drawn cabs, omnibuses and conveyances for weddings and funerals throughout Sheffield, including on the Broomhill and Ranmoor bus routes (see Chapter 11). In 1878-1879 he built (the now-demolished) Whiteley Wood Grange on land to the south-east of Carr Bank House, with the Grange's front gate on the corner of Carr Bank Lane and Hangingwater Road. Also nearby, to the south of Whiteley Wood Grange was the Hangingwater Brick Company (between 1898 and 1916), which extracted clay for brick-making from its land behind Carr Bank House with a main entrance from Hangingwater Road[20].

Display Box Four

FILE-MAKING BEFORE MACHINES

File-making was a principal occupation in the Nether Green area. Early file-smiths were skilled tradesmen who had served an apprenticeship for several years and who could perform the full variety of tasks. However, by Victorian times specialization had evolved, with a worker usually covering only one or two of the main activities – forging, grinding, cutting and hardening.

Forging involved heating a piece of metal in a small furnace (or "hearth") and then hammering it into shape as a "blank" from which a file would be made. **Grinding** came next as blanks were worked on to create a smooth surface. A powered grinding wheel was often used, otherwise a simple grind-stone.

File **cutting** was particularly laborious, making a large number of angled "cuts" across each face of the blank and on the narrow edges. A range of different hammers and chisels was used, with a blank laid in front of a worker on a block of lead to reduce recoil and to prevent damage to cuts already made on the reverse side. Although several dozen types existed (often requiring different tools), the average file had about 1000 cuts on each side and perhaps 300 on each edge. With speeds of up to 200 cuts a minute, a file-cutter made more than 40,000 cuts a day[31]. Cutters were clearly highly skilled, exhibiting what an 1862 Sheffield directory described as "one of the most remarkable instances of manual dexterity which is to be seen in the whole round of human industry".

Finally, the file had to be **hardened**. It was raised to red heat in a coke fire before being plunged into a bath of water. Items which became bent had to be straightened, and the finished article was cleaned, oiled and wrapped for sale.

Although machines to produce files became available in Sheffield from 1865, they were strongly resisted (with a major strike in 1866) for requiring a smaller and perhaps non-union work-force. However, the work became fully mechanized early in the following century, and small file-making units fell into disuse.

As can be seen from the 1790s map, the nearest building to Carr Bank House at that time was on Hangingwater Road. This (a "house, garden and croft" – 5b on Map 2.01) was also owned by Thomas Dale. Possibly with a workshop, it remained as a farm for about a century, known as "Hangingwater Farm" and becoming owned by the Elliott family in the 1800s[21]. The Elliotts also acquired a large amount of land nearby, most of which they sold around 1900 for housing and allotments[22]. A section of the Farm then became a private house, numbered as 147 Hangingwater Road. A later photograph (2.14) also shows buildings known as Manor Farm.

6. Ibbotson and Shepherd Wheels

To the west of Hangingwater Farm the 1790s map shows another isolated building, 6a on Map 2.01. Situated on the River Porter at the end of a no-longer-existing Wheel Lane, this was a cutlery grinding wheel with a dam on its up-stream

Photo 2.14
Hangingwater and Manor Farms in the early 20th century. The site is now occupied by houses and apartments, although some earlier buildings remain.

side. It was constructed in the 1750s by Stephen Hawksworth (perhaps the occupant of the homestead in Water Lane; see Section 4 above) together with Jonathan Hall, a razor-smith. The land was owned by the Duke of Norfolk, as were the surrounding fields. By the 1790s around a dozen men were employed (or possibly self-employed) at the wheel, which provided motive power for 11 grinding troughs[23].

Joseph Ibbotson joined Stephen Hawksworth around 1760, and from 1775 he became the sole tenant. In that period, the wheel (see Photo 2.15) became named after him, and in 1817 he bought the freehold from the Duke of Norfolk. He died in 1826, and the wheel passed through several owners (including John Eyre who also owned other local property and John Elliott of Hangingwater Farm) before coming into the possession of Sheffield Corporation in the 1890s. It fell out of use in the 1920s, and was demolished around 1950.

The Ordnance Survey map of 1903 indicates "(Files)" next to Ibbotson Wheel, consistent with the fact that several local workshops were devoted to file making. On that map the dam was described as a "boating pool", and it continued as such for several decades. By the 1930s customers could rent one of about six rowing boats or take a trip in a petrol-engined vessel.

Photo 2.15
Ibbotson Wheel about 1920. It was fed with water from the dam which is still there, but the building was demolished around 1950.

Photo 2.16
Grinders at work in Shepherd Wheel around 1900. The building still contains equipment, and is being restored to serve as a working museum.

At a short distance up-stream (away from town) the River Porter powered another grinding wheel through its own dam (6b on Map 2.01)[24]. Described as "Shepherd Wheel" from around 1790 (Edward Shepherd had been the tenant from about 1750), a water-wheel had probably existed on this site from at least the 1560s.

Photo 2.17
Cottages near to Shepherd Wheel in the late 1800s. They were demolished around 1900, as the valley was prepared for greater public access. The Wheel itself is behind the cottages, nearer to the River Porter.

The building (still there and currently being restored) houses two workshops with a total of 10 grinding troughs. It was mainly used for grinding table and other domestic knives as well as pen and pocket knives (Photo 2.16). As in other cases, work was brought in and semi-finished knives were taken for final polishing and packing elsewhere.

One location for some of that subsequent work may have been in a group of cottages near to the Wheel (where the footpath now passes by). Those (Photo 2.17) probably also provided storage as well as accommodation for families. Named as Porter House in the 1850 map at the front of the book, they were demolished around 1900 as the area was developed for greater public access.

Edward Shepherd died in 1794, and the lease was later held by Anthony Thompson, who also managed three other wheels on the Porter. After several changes of ownership, it was transferred to Sheffield Corporation in the late 1890s. One long-term tenant was Samuel Hind, who worked there for several decades from about 1818; members of his family continued as tenants until about 1930, when the wheel ceased regular use.

7. Other 1790s Buildings

A few other buildings were scattered around Ranmoor in the 1790s. For instance, the Enclosure Award document refers to a "homestead, orchard and croft" immediately south of the junction of Fulwood and Ranmoor Roads (7a on Map 2.01). Those were occupied by Joseph Ibbotson, who also owned the Ibbotson Wheel (above) and farmed several adjacent fields. An 1830 map shows a substantial

Photo 2.18
Carsick Hill Farm (now Carsick Cottage, 146 Tom Lane) around 1900, before its redevelopment in 1919. The people shown are probably tenant Elizabeth Woodhouse and part of her family (with their dog).

group of buildings on this Fulwood Road site described as a "farmhouse with barns, stables, yard and gardens". Buildings were still there on the 1893 Ordnance Survey map, and those were replaced by the current properties in 1900-1901.

Further north, near the top of the eastern side of Darwin Lane, were two sets of buildings in the 1790s: a "homestead and croft" and a "homestead et cetera" (7b on Map 2.01) on land owned by the Boys' Charity School (see Chapter 1). (As in other cases, springs were available here for domestic water.) With an adjacent orchard, one of those was tenanted by James Darwin (hence the lane's later name); he also farmed other fields nearby. By 1830 the property was described as Tapton Farm, and successive maps show that the buildings were reshaped several times during the 19th century. In 1905, property on the site was called Ceres Cottage[25]; this was demolished several decades later for the construction of Tapton School (see Chapter 7).

Near the junction of Carsick Hill and Sandygate Roads were houses and cottages (7c on Map 2.01) on land owned by Catherine Cope (see Chapter 1), which were also used for farming and probably as workshops. By the 1860s these had become Ivy House Farm, which was replaced in that decade by a new road similarly named – Ivy Crescent Road. (This became Ivy Park Road in the 1880s; see Chapter 3.) Near to that homestead were other buildings (7d on Map 2.01) which remain in place, now known as Stubbin House and Stubbin Cottage[26].

At the other (western) end of Carsick Hill Road, at its junction with Tom Lane, stood another isolated farm (7e on Map 2.01). A farm had been there since at least 1620, and as in other cases it was sited next to a well. The farmhouse and associated buildings were rented in the 1790s by Thomas Creswick and later by other members of the Creswick family. Together with other land, it passed in the 19th century from Catherine Cope to the Pye-Smith family, later becoming part of the Carsick Hill Land Society (see Chapter 3). It was developed into a more comfortable home by the owners in 1919, and is now known as Carsick Cottage (146 Tom Lane). The earlier farmhouse is shown in Photo 2.18.

Notes to Chapter Two

1 The Town Trustees owned land in many areas of Sheffield, including the site in Nether Green now occupied by the Rising Sun pub (see Chapter 8). Together with the Church Burgesses and the Cutlers' Company, the Town Trust was one of the main bodies providing civic administration before Sheffield's incorporation as a borough in 1843. The Church Burgesses had particular concern for the parish church (which became a cathedral in 1914) and its officials, and the Town Trustees (numbering 13 since 1681) primarily dealt with infrastructure in terms of roads, transport and related facilities.

Dating back to 1297 and also referred to as the Burgery of Free Tenants or as the Town Burgesses, the Trustees had long been responsible for the maintenance and cleaning of Lady's Bridge, Barker's Pool and principal streets. In the 19th century they were also important in the construction of a new Town Hall in Waingate

(1808), in street widening and lighting improvements, and in supporting railway, canal and turnpike developments; in 1897 they purchased the privately-owned Botanical Gardens for the people of Sheffield.

Over the centuries, the Trust acquired property and investments which provided rental and other income. Their administrative work was largely taken over by the new Town Council from 1843, and the Trust's current activities are in support of charitable organizations in the city. Some details have been summarized by Edward Bramley in *A Record of the Burgery of Sheffield* (Sheffield: Northend, 1957).

2 An 1879 advertisement for Joseph Kay's premises in Fargate indicated that his company ("established in 1838") both made boots and shoes and also sold footwear made by others.

3 There is some uncertainty about which

Enclosure Award plot is the site of Ran Farm. The map suggests that the building was on plot 688 (a "house and croft"), which was owned by John Worrall and tenanted by John Hatfield. Next to that was plot 687 (a "house, croft and cottage"), owned by the Duke of Norfolk with Joseph Ibbotson as tenant. Although buildings are included as part of that plot's description, none are shown on the Enclosure Award map itself.

4 One well was in the adjacent field – later an open rectangle edged by flagstones. See the bottom left corner of Photo 2.04.

5 "Messuage" was the general term for a dwelling-house and its outbuildings.

6 John Rowbotham (c1799-1851) is identified in directories as a merchant and cutlery manufacturer, working in the company of Wade, Wingfield and Rowbotham. Those were described in an 1849 directory as "merchants and table, pen and pocket knife, razor, file, and steel manufacturers" at 82 Tenter Street and were also saw manufacturers in Arundel Lane. The company had been founded late in the previous century, and operated successfully until the 1890s, when it was taken over by Thomas Turton and Company. In 1833 (probably before marriage) John Rowbotham lived at 5 Gell Street, and in the 1841 census he was in that street (not numbered in the record) with his wife Ann, daughter Ann E. and three servants. By the 1851 census, Ann T. Rowbotham (1809-1878) was a widow at 17 Gell Street. In that year she was a "landed proprietor", in 1861 a "fund holder" and in 1871 an "annuitant", in all cases at 17 Gell Street.

7 Henry Herbert Andrew (1850-1903; Master Cutler in 1895) was head of the Toledo Steel Works, founded by his father as J. H. Andrew and Company in 1860. The company built up extensive American trade, including the provision of steel rod suspension cables for the Brooklyn Bridge in New York City. It became Andrews Toledo in 1928, and was taken over by Darwins in 1938.

Around the time he bought Snaithing Farm Henry Andrew also purchased land to the south including Snaithing Brook, a house built by William Wheatcroft Harrison in 1880. He subsequently enlarged that house and extended the grounds southwards to Stumperlowe Crescent Road. It is now known as Ranmoor Hall. See Chapter 10.

8 Scissors were used in many more trades and activities than now, and scissor-making required a wide range of skills, including forging, shaping, grinding and finishing. Scissor types included button-hole, cutting-out, flower, grape, garden, hair, lace, nail, pocket, tailors' and drapers'.

9 From the 1840s Peter's brother, Joshua Beal (1795-1868) lived on the opposite side of Water Lane in what is now Nether House; he was also a scissor-maker.

10 Valuation records (documents CA/VU in Sheffield City Archives) indicate that the buildings were quite substantial, all having two storeys. Two of the houses were 28 feet by 16 feet and possessed cellars and two first-floor "chambers" (bedrooms), and one was 32 feet by 15 feet. The workshops were all 32 feet by 15 feet.

11 This detail is from a mortgage with the Sheffield Union Banking Company taken out on 26/03/1849 by Sarah Beal and Joseph Beal. Other documents suggest the presence also of possibly six houses (sometimes indicated as "cottages") as well as a cow-house and stable.

12 The firm, later known as J. and J. Beal, moved in the 1870s to a large factory in Red Hill, near Broad Lane, soon employing more than 300 people and later managed by Joseph's sons. It advertised "butchers, bowie, hunting, table and pocket knives, in all their branches for home and colonial markets", and for some decades achieved considerable sales success in America and continental Europe. The company later moved to Corporation Street before closing down in the 1950s.

13 Other documents refer to a "barn" and "outbuildings" also on the site.

14 There is some evidence that Joseph maintained and repaired water wheels and associated equipment – much needed in the area at the time and requiring the wood-working skills of a carpenter. It was Stephen Hawksworth (Joseph's grandfather) who built the nearby Ibbotson Wheel (see Section 6).

15 The schedule of prices for constructing these houses included a sum for "taking down the old shop". The building had thus been used in part for metal-working.

16 A rough 1757 drawing of these buildings, owned or tenanted by John Warburton, can be found within the map on page 120 of Field Book 12 of the Fairbank Collection in Sheffield City Archives.

17 Several other members of the Creswick family also lived in the area. They worked as farmers (see Sections 2 and 7) and (until late in the next century) as landlords of the Plough Inn in Sandygate.

18 Cutler Thomas Dewsnap was in one of these buildings in the 1790s, and another cutler (William Parkin) is indicated in a 1787 directory as being somewhere in Tom Lane – possibly here.

19 Up to the 1700s the trades of grinding and file-making were not as dangerous as they later became, because workers performed a wide variety of different tasks and thus spent less continuous time on the unhealthy aspects of their work. However, factory-style intensification and specialization of labour in the 19th century led to workers becoming huddled together in inadequately ventilated rooms and devoting many hours to the same harmful activities.

20 The Hangingwater Brick Company was typical of many local brick-works that were formed to meet building requirements of the city's expanding population. Opened in 1898, it operated several kilns on the site (now replaced by Hangingwater Cottages), and smoke and sulphur from its tall chimney were later reported to "injuriously affect adjacent property". Coal may have been dug from nearby pits. Its bricks (imprinted with "HBC") are to be found in many local houses of the period. The works closed during World War One (1914-1918) as a result of substantially reduced demand, although the chimney remained in place for another decade or more.

21 An 1830 map in the Fairbank Collection held by Sheffield Archives (She525L) shows the farm's owner as Hannah Elliott (1791-1857), a widow whose children later also owned nearby fields. At that time, Hannah Elliott also rented fields near Shepherd Wheel and in the Ranmoor storths (see Chapter 3). By the early 20th century several members of the Elliott family lived in recently-built terraced houses in Hangingwater Road.

22 The allotments next to Hangingwater Road and on "the roughs" on the other side of Highcliffe Road were laid out between 1906 and 1911. Sheffield Corporation had purchased the land in 1899 and subsequent years, with a view to providing council houses for rent in accordance with the 1889 Housing of the Working Classes Act. That development was opposed by nearby residents and came to lose favour with the Corporation as it became clear that the high costs and out-of-town location would make such rented property unattractive to the intended occupants.

23 These details, and accounts of other Sheffield water-wheels, are to be found in C. Ball, D. Crossley and N. Flavell (eds.), *Water Power on the Sheffield Rivers* (Sheffield: South Yorkshire Industrial History Society, second edition, 2006). Around 1800 was the peak of local water-wheel operation, before steam engines provided a more reliable source of power. For example, the Rand Moor Cutlery Works (Section 3 of this chapter) had installed its own steam-driven grinding troughs by the 1840s.

24 The River Porter was intensively used, with 20 mills operating along about 4 miles (6½ km). They were all in place by the 1780s.

25 Ceres was the Roman goddess of agricultural fertility.

26 "Stubbing" was a fairly common field description from at least the 17th century, referring to an area in which tree stumps and roots remain after felling. A nearby field was called "Well Hole", perhaps providing water for all properties in the area.

27 The soot, dust and grime created by open fires and cooking ranges in Victorian houses meant that coverings in glass or other material were often very desirable.

28 The Creswicks were active members of the Wesleyan Methodist Church in Ranmoor Road. See Chapter 6.

29 That house was presumably Snaithing Brook, now called Ranmoor Hall. See Chapter 10.

30 Creswick family members are buried in Fulwood churchyard. Those mentioned here are Nora's mother Mary (died in 1890 aged 43), Nora's sister Mary (died in 1877 aged 13 weeks), and her brothers Joseph (died in 1884 aged 3) and Hugh (died in 1884 aged 6).

31 These details are mainly drawn from *The Peace Families of Sheffield: A Story of File Makers and Steel Makers*, by L. Ralph Peace (privately published by him in 1999).

CHAPTER THREE

Lanes, Roads and Land Societies

Roads existing at the time of the 1805 Upper Hallam Enclosure Award had developed over many centuries out of ancient footways. Narrow tracks had been adequate for early pedestrian travel, but over the years additional width often became required for pack-horses, carts, horse-drawn sleds or perhaps flocks of animals. Some routes acquired parallel tracks to help travellers in muddy times, such as Sheffield's Broad Lane leading uphill to what is now Western Bank. The Enclosure Award identified most Ranmoor routes in the 1790s as "carriage or drift roads", meaning that they were suitable for "carriage" by horse or by wheeled vehicle and also for "driving" animals along them.

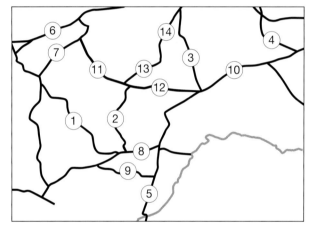

Map 3.01
The old roads of Ranmoor and district.
  1, Tom Lane.
  2, Storth Lane.
  3, Darwin Lane.
  4, Shore Lane.
  5, Hangingwater Road.
  6, Sandygate Road.
  7, Carsick Hill Road.
  8, Nethergreen Road.
  9, Carr Bank Lane.
 10, Fulwood Road.
 11, Snaithing Lane.
 12, Ranmoor Road.
 13, Ranmoor Cliffe Road.
 14, Watt Lane.

The Ancient Lanes

As shown in Map 3.01, around 1800 old roads crossed the area in several directions. Using current names and the numbers on the map, they are: from north to south: 1, Tom Lane; 2, Storth Lane; 3, Darwin Lane; 4, Shore Lane; 5, Hangingwater Road; from west to east: 6, Sandygate Road; 7, Carsick Hill Road; 8, Nethergreen Road; 9, Carr Bank Lane; 10, Fulwood Road; from north-west to south-east: 11, Snaithing Lane; 12, Ranmoor Road; from north-east to south-west: 13, Ranmoor Cliffe Road; 14, Watt Lane.

All of these were probably established as footpaths many centuries previously. Note that many of them are still called "lanes". As described by David Hey, that term "retains its original meaning of a minor way or gate[1]... The usual sense is of a track enclosed by fields or woods rather than a route across open moors... The word usually denotes a byway of some antiquity... Some lanes were so narrow that they were little more than bridleways"[2]. As suggested by that last sentence, at least some of the Ranmoor lanes (e.g., Storth and Tom) have been systematically widened in more recent times[3].

The origin of their names is not always clear, but some interpretations are possible. For example, Carr Bank Lane (9 on Map 3.01) was originally a path above (on the "bank" of) a "carr" – an area of marsh or land reclaimed from marsh[4]. Darwin Lane was in 1637 called Oxspring Lane, but its later name came from the Darwin family who farmed on adjacent fields from at least the 1790s. Shore Lane acquired its name from the Shore family who lived between the 1790s and 1853 on the site of what is now Tapton Hall (see Chapter 4). References to Snaithing Lane (with various spellings) occurred in the 16th century, and perhaps earlier. A legal document of 1497 refers to "a close in Hallom called Snathings", probably describing a curved intake (an "ing") of land[5].

Storth Lane (2 on Map 3.01) was called Water Lane up to 1886, probably because it was crossed by a stream at the bottom; it was also sometimes referred to as Watery Lane. In 1637, it had been New Ing Lane, referring to a recently-created field (an "ing"). ("Storth" is considered later in the chapter.) Tom Lane also existed before the 17th century, described variously as "ancient" and "narrow"; the meaning of "Tom" in this context is not clear[6]. Watt Lane (the extension of Ranmoor Cliffe Road) refers to the adjacent Watt Field, recorded in 1637 and probably earlier; and Nethergreen Road (still identified as Nethergreen Lane in the 1860s) is clearly the route to Nether Green.

Two other old roads shown in the 1790s Enclosure Award map are Ranmoor Road and an eastern section of Fulwood Road (12 and 10 respectively on Map 3.01). Up to the mid-1800s, these were known as Upper Rand Moor Road and Lower Rand Moor Road respectively. As shown on Maps 1.02 and 3.01, Fulwood Road around 1790 did not extend towards Fulwood beyond the current Gladstone Road, instead turning down what was then called Jenkin Hill or Lane (next to Jenkin Croft, a field on its eastern side) and then leading uphill towards Nether Green. Beyond Nether Green the road to Fulwood was known as Willow Lane.

Hangingwater Road (5 on Map 3.01) was indicated in the Enclosure Award as being an "ancient lane", and as late as 1888 it was still sometimes referred to as Hangingwater "Lane". From at least the 1700s, its extension in Highcliffe Road (towards Ecclesall) was known as "Dead Lane"[7].

Also in existence for centuries was Carsick Hill Road[8], crossing an area known similarly as Carsick. We can imagine that this originally involved two words, with "carr" as a marshy area and a "sick" being a series of ditches or streams across marshy land. A legal document of 1494 refers to "le Carre" in this area. Note that in the 1790s the eastern end of Carsick Hill Road turned north up the current Sandygate Lane before reaching Sandygate Road. The latter (6 on Map 3.01) has origins as a Roman military route (built around the year 100) between forts in Templeborough, a little to the north of Sheffield, and Brough in Derbyshire. This ran up to and beyond Stanage Edge, and subsequently served as an important pack-horse route for many centuries[9]. The reference to "gate" indicates an early Scandinavian connection (being a word for "road"), but the origin of "sandy" is no longer clear. The lower section, near to Crosspool, was described as Church Lane in a 1637 survey.

Two lesser roads that existed as short paths in the 18th century (but not with their present names) are Chapel Close and Deakins Walk. Chapel Close leads to the line of houses under Ranmoor Cliff later known as Chapel Terrace. As described in Chapters 2 and 6, some buildings were on that spot in the 1760s, linked to nearby quarrying and other work, and the "Chapel" label comes from the Wesleyan Chapel (built 1783) that was previously sited near to Ranmoor Road.

Deakins Walk, leading from Ranmoor Road to Fulwood Road, was indicated early in the 19th century as a "public footpath", and may have been that for a long time. By the 1880s it became known either as Cliff Terrace (referring to its terrace of houses) or as Deakins Walk after Isaac Deakin, who had worked as a grocer in its southernmost building (see Chapter 9). It was formally dedicated with its current name in 1922, retaining an apostrophe as "Deakin's" until at least the 1970s.

Freehold Land Societies and their Roads

The Ranmoor area at the beginning of the 19th century was thus largely open countryside crossed by a few lanes. For development as a residential suburb, new roads would be required, and several of those came to be provided by what were known as "freehold land societies".

These societies were important in many English towns for several decades from the 1830s. They were initiated by local individuals, who invested capital (often borrowed) as trustees of a society which purchased an area of land, created an estate plan, constructed roads and sewers, and sold small plots on which individuals could build a house. Loans were made available for these purchases, with regular repayment required through instalments, and the society laid down conditions about the kind of development that was permitted.

Land societies had originated in the previous century, but they received a strong boost from the Reform Act of 1832. This granted voting rights to small land-holders, so that purchasers through a land society could become entitled to vote. With that in mind, many 1830s and 1840s societies (especially in the London area) had objectives that were primarily political, aiming to increase the number of working-class voters who were thought likely to support their sponsors' political aims. Other goals were to provide more healthy living conditions for artisan families and to encourage thrift and saving[10].

The land society movement expanded particularly strongly in Sheffield after the 1832 Act, so that 38 different societies (none in Ranmoor) were listed in the *Illustrated Guide to Sheffield and Neighbourhood* published in 1862 by Pawson and Brailsford[11]. Together these had more than 3,000 plots, and were said by the *Guide*'s creators to "mark the growing intelligence and providence of the working classes" (page 98).

Most societies (for instance in Brightside, Heeley and Walkley) aimed for small terraced or semi-detached properties. Buildings were required to be of a specified size and value, and owners had to contribute to the cost of roads and help to pay for the society's outgoings or debts. All building designs had to be approved by a committee elected from among plot-holders. That centralised control aimed to create a uniform and pleasant environment and to ensure that investments maintained or increased their value, in part in order to appear attractive to new members[12].

Although intentions were benevolent and sometimes political (above), financial self-interest also played a part. Trustees establishing new societies often had an eye to personal profit, and purchasers of an individual plot may have seen it as an investment rather than as a site for a new home. Linked to that, a high proportion of purchased plots were left undeveloped or cultivated as flower or vegetable gardens[13]. Others were used to build property which could be rented as a source of continuing income, rather than as a home for oneself.

Many land societies soon faced problems. In some cases, plots remained unsold so that overall income was too low to meet interest payments on the society's initial mortgage. For individual members, the costs of roads and other obligations could become too great but plots could not be resold because no purchaser could be found. Some societies lost money through failed investments, and others were ruined by fraudulent dealings by trustees. "As a working class movement in Sheffield, the freehold land societies, misled by unscrupulous trustees [and] crippled by unexpected road charges, quickly exhausted the enthusiasm of their founders"[14].

But among the middle classes of Sheffield, land societies continued to be of interest through the 1860s and 1870s. As the town's population increased, associated with booming trade between 1845 and 1875, many relatively wealthy people sought improved accommodation of a kind to meet their aspirations. Conditions in the town were dirty, noisy, smoky and sometimes smelly, and a pleasant environment and the possibility of profit were attractive. A successful land society development of middle-class housing had been initiated in Sharrow and Nether Edge by George Wostenholm[15], and similar possibilities became apparent in Ranmoor. Broomhill was filling out with new houses, and Ranmoor – a little further out of town – became visibly desirable in the 1860s after important members of the town's establishment built for themselves mansions on its edge. (Those are described in the next chapter.)

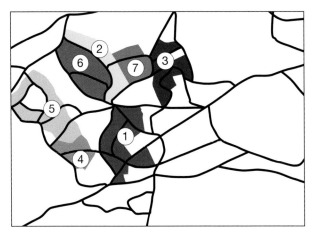

Map 3.02
The seven Freehold Land Societies of Ranmoor.
1, Storth Crescent (1864).
2, Ivy Crescent (1864).
3, Ranmoor Crescent (1874).
4, Stumperlowe Crescent (1875).
5, Carsick Hill (1876).
6, South View (1876).
7, Ranmoor Cliffe (1879).

The Ranmoor Land Societies[16]

George Wostenholm had already spotted Ranmoor's potential. In 1853, he purchased 26 acres of fields known as the storths. These fields, bounded by Upper Rand Moor Road and Water Lane (see the 1850 map at the front of the book), had for a long time been rented out as farming land[17]. George Wostenholm set about creating roads and identifying potential purchasers. In 1862, he sold much of the land to the trustees of what became the Storth Crescent Land Society; almost all of their purchase money was borrowed through a large mortgage.

That society was followed by six others in the next two decades, as described below and illustrated in Map 3.02. All seven placed restrictions on building designs, and members had to make financial contributions to the estate and its roads. Their houses were required to be of substantial size, and boundary walls were usually

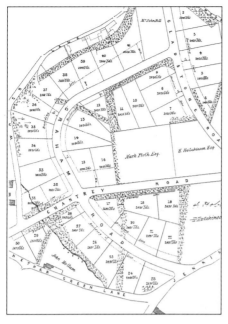

Map 3.03
Plots designated within the Storth Crescent Land Society in 1863, with separate sections sold to John Hill, Mark Firth and Henry Hutchinson.

obligatory and of a standard height and design. These seven societies were central to Ranmoor's development.

1. The Storth Crescent Estate

In preparation for his 1862 sale (above), George Wostenholm extended Fulwood Road through the lower storths directly to Nether Green[18]. He sold this new section (initially called Chantrey Road[19]) to the town in 1860.

By that time he and his colleagues had also created Gladstone and Graham Roads[20], curving through the storths. An estate of substantial properties was devised, with the area divided into 41 plots along those roads[21]. The initial layout is shown in Map 3.03. Plots were offered for sale in 1863, and the new owners and trustees together inaugurated the Storth Crescent Land Society in 1864. The 41 plots were bought by 26 individuals, with about a third of members purchasing two or three of them[22]. Less than half a dozen of the initial owners built and lived in a property in the estate, instead selling their land to others, who in turn became bound by the society's regulations.

Those regulations asserted that "no building shall be erected on the land except dwelling-houses" and that these must be built of stone. They had to be of a high value which was specified for a single house and for pairs of semi-detached houses. Owners were required to construct a stone front wall of stated size and type. In addition, "no trade or business whatever shall be exercised or carried on upon the said estate, or any building … be used as a public-house, or other house for the sale of wine, liquors, or spirits, or as a temperance hotel, or for public refreshment rooms, or tea gardens, or as a place of public resort, amusement, or entertainment, and no steam engine shall be erected upon any part of the said estate". For each plot, the owner had to pay a proportion of the cost of roads and drains and of "all other expenses and liabilities which may be incurred or sustained by the trustees or the committee". The regulations were declared to be in force for 50 years from 1864.

2. The Ivy Crescent Estate

This second local land society was inaugurated very soon after the first one – later in 1864, with 17 plots defined and sold. Another new road was soon constructed, initially called Ivy Crescent Road but renamed around 1885 as Ivy Park Road[23]. As shown in Map 3.02, the planned estate, advertised as the Ivy House Estate[24], stretched along the eastern side of this new road. Restrictions on design and use were based closely on those of the Storth Crescent Society, above.

Over the next 20 years only four houses were built on the estate[25], and unsold sections were in 1876 conveyed to a new society – the Upper and Lower Ranmoor Freehold Society[26]. Twelve plots were sold to initial members of this, but no building took place and in 1886 the society was terminated.

3. The Ranmoor Crescent Estate

Another area of open land was prepared for housing by the northward construction of Ranmoor Crescent and the eastward extension of Ranmoor Cliffe Road to the new Ranmoor Park Road. These were laid down in 1873 and 1875 respectively, associated with the Ranmoor Crescent Land Society whose prospectus was issued in 1874. Map 3.04 shows the Society's proposed use of land.

The prospectus described the site as being in "the most delightful and picturesque suburb of Sheffield", and "proposed to conduct the Estate upon the same basis as the Storth Crescent Estate". As in other cases, houses were required to be priced so that the neighbourhood would appeal only to upper middle-class purchasers. The initial layout defined 31 plots, but only about half were sold in the early years. The number of plots was increased to 36 around 1880, and (in place of the cul-de-sac towards the north of Map 3.04) Tetney Road was constructed c1885[27], anticipating houses that were not built for almost a century. On the estate as a whole, building did not start until the early 1900s.

4. The Stumperlowe Crescent Land Society

An area on the west side of the lower section of Water Lane (renamed as Storth Lane in 1886) was made accessible from Graham Road by the construction in 1875 by W. E. Laycock[28] of Stumperlowe Crescent Road and a bridge (now a listed building) over Water Lane.

Although 22 plots were established and sold, these gradually became combined into larger groups (as happened in other estates), and building was again slow; no houses were erected until 1905.

5. The Carsick Hill Land Society

The land which became this fifth estate (sec Map 3.02) was offered for sale in 1867, advertised as "well worth the attention of capitalists, gentlemen disposed to build, and others". The site changed hands several times in the next few years, with two sets of owners constructing roads[29], until the Carsick Hill Land Society was established in 1876. This set strict conditions of the kind illustrated above, including specifications of building materials and of heights of houses and walls, and the requirement that "no trade, manufacture or business of any kind shall be carried on".

Despite an initial sale of 39 plots, only two properties were constructed in the next 30 years. These were Dalebrook (c1880) on four plots on the south side of the extended Belgrave Road[30] and Carsick Grange (1882) on six plots extending towards the north of the area (see Chapter 10).

6. The South View Estate

This land, between Snaithing Lane and Ivy Park Road (see Map 3.02), was bought in 1875 by individuals who became the trustees of a sixth society. They recruited Daniel Coupe (1831-1883) (who was also on the Provisional Committee of the Ranmoor Crescent Society, above), and he arranged for the construction of Clumber Road in 1877. A second east-west road, further north in the estate, was

Map 3.04
The Ranmoor Crescent Estate as planned in 1874. Recently-built houses outside the Estate are shown to the right; those are described in Chapter 4.

Display Box Five

ROAD SURFACES AND THEIR MAINTENANCE

For several centuries up to the 1830s, most roads in England were maintained by a system of compulsory parish labour. Neighbouring owners of land were required to provide workers and equipment in proportion to their holdings, and non-owners were supposed to contribute up to six days a year; alternatively a fine could be paid. After 1691 some local rates could be raised for road repairs, and those became the only basis for the work from 1835. The system was administered by parish vestries, which annually elected a local Surveyor of Highways. The Surveyor's role became replaced in the 19th century by Highway Boards, which financed maintenance through rates collected in their own township. (This occurred in Sheffield after its 1843 incorporation as a borough.) However, not all roads were adopted by a Highway Board; some remained as "private" roads and thus the responsibility of the owners of adjacent land[42].

Many roads outside the towns were poorly managed. For example, Fulwood Road, still a track in the 1830s, was in 1852 the subject of public complaint for being "for a considerable time in a disgraceful state, through the Highway Board ... refusing to repair it"; and in 1859 a public meeting was held to seek improvements near the current Thornbury Hospital[43]. Even by the 1860s, Fulwood Road incorporated stepping stones for pedestrians across the Oak Brook at that point[44].

Solid road surfaces as we know them did not exist until relatively recently, in earlier times being merely soil and gravel. As a result, travellers often had to cope (depending on the weather) with either dust or mud, made worse by the hooves of animals or ruts created by wagons.

Improvements from about 1800 were based on better drainage and more systematic selection and layering of stones. Amongst national innovators was John Macadam (1756-1836), whose influence was substantial. Only long after his death were tar preparations used to bind together the previously loose materials, creating "tar macadam" or "tarmac"[45].

An 1889 report by Sheffield's Highways and Sewerage Committee indicated that surfaces of roads adopted by the town were one of the following: boulders alone, boulders and freestone, freestone and granite, tar macadam, or (usually) macadam[46]. Principal roads in the Ranmoor area were at that time all constructed of layered stones described as macadam[47], although for the benefit of pedestrians many pavements had been asphalted, with edge stones, from the 1860s.

In Sheffield centre, several roads were surfaced with granite setts (small stone blocks), which had the financial advantage of requiring only infrequent repair or renewal. Strong opposition to those in the 1890s was based on the potential danger to horses and carts caused by granite's slipperiness, especially on hills or after rain[48]. (It was also noisy.) Town-centre surfacing became of special concern when major roads had to be excavated to lay tracks for trams – horse-drawn from 1873 and electric-powered from 1899 in Sheffield (see Chapter 11). Opposition to granite led to the use of wooden blocks in some parts of the centre, until these in turn became replaced by macadamized surfaces and later by tarmac[49].

Resurfacing with tarmac occurred only later in the suburbs, and many roads in Hangingwater and Ranmoor remained merely gravel-covered well into the1900s. However, tramways along Fulwood Road, Oakbrook Road and Nethergreen Road from 1901 required that solid surfaces were provided for those routes at that time[50].

also built but this was later removed. It was shown on Estate plans as Welbeck Road, with a name deriving (as for Clumber) from Daniel Coupe's association with those areas of Nottinghamshire[31].

The South View Land Society was formalized in 1876, with 36 initial plots. As in other cases, building progress was slow, with no construction before the 20th century.

The South View Estate (and also the Ranmoor Cliffe Estate – see below) was split by a water conduit running from west to east. Shown on the 1850 map at the front of the book, this had been created in the 1830s by a private company to carry supplies (by gravitation) from reservoirs at Redmires to the Hadfield service reservoir in Crookes, for onward delivery to dams in Crookesmoor and then to the town. It was mainly an open construction, with occasional footbridges, but nearer Broomhill were raised sections on stone piers. The conduit and its managing company were taken over by the new Sheffield Corporation Waterworks in 1888 and it continued in use until 1909. Small sections of its route are still visible, for instance along the south of Tetney Road.

7. The Ranmoor Cliffe Estate

The final Ranmoor land society was created in 1879. Its land, shown in Map 3.02, had been sold in 1867 and again in 1874, and the later owners (Edward Weston, a wholesale and retail stationer living in Wilkinson Street, and Edward Whitworth, an accountant[32]) in 1876 received permission for a road, essential for residential development. This was initially termed Beaconsfield Road, but soon became Whitworth Road after Edward Whitworth himself.

Weston and Whitworth appear to have sold (in 1879) their land south of Whitworth Road to the new land society, but they retained responsibility for the section on the northern side of the road. However, restrictive covenants were similar in both cases. Construction of houses was rapid along the road in their northern section, but slower in the society's area to the south.

Road Construction outside the Land Societies

By 1900, Ranmoor thus had a network of roads and many of its open fields had been divided into multiple plots. House-building on local land society estates had been more limited than might have been envisaged by those societies, although its extent was apparently similar to that in Ranmoor outside a society[33]. In both cases, potential investors may have been deterred by intermittent financial recessions. Trade had been good for three decades until about 1875, but economic problems in Sheffield around 1876-1879, 1885-1886 and 1892-1893 reduced available capital and customers and presumably discouraged the taking of risks.

Despite this limited building activity, the land societies had a strong influence on the development of Ranmoor. Restrictive covenants ensured that land was used only for relatively large properties of a non-commercial kind and that construction was to a high standard; boundary walls were required even if house-building did not take place. A homogeneous and pleasant environment was thus created, with "an elegant network of curved roads which set the layout for building"[34].

Among the roads constructed by private developers was Ranmoor Park Road, financed in about 1869 by Frederick Bardwell[35] for the sale of houses within what was advertised as the Ranmoor Park Estate. (Progress by 1874 is illustrated in Map 3.04.) On the eastern side of the lower section of Darwin Lane, another "park" was envisaged. In order to attract potential purchasers, the Trustees of the Boys' Charity School (see Chapter 1) created Tapton Park Road across their land in about 1863. Up to the middle 1880s, the new road was called simply Tapton Park[36].

Riverdale Road was built in 1863-1864 by John Brown and Charles Younge, linked to the development of Endcliffe Hall (see Chapter 4); its initial name was Endcliffe Vale New Road. Oakbrook Road (built in 1867-1868) provided a route along the Porter Valley and, at the western (Sheffield) end, upwards to Riverdale Road[37]. Its eastern section later became important as a tram route from Ecclesall Road, opening up the Hangingwater area from 1901 for work-people's housing.

As in other parts of Sheffield, the availability of a cheap tram service encouraged out-of-town living, and the area around Hangingwater Road was developed at the turn of the century with terraces of small houses. Armthorpe, Bramwith and Frickley Roads were built

Photo 3.01
Frederick Bardwell, auctioneer and property developer who created Ranmoor Park Road.

between about 1895 and 1905. Their names suggest a link between the developer and the Doncaster area, since villages with those names are located there. Fulney and Westwood Roads, constructed in 1904[38], were on land purchased in 1902 by Arthur Gostelow, previously of Fulney in Lincolnshire but then a fruiterer and florist in Sheffield[39]. And Pendeen Road (c1896), a cul-de-sac at the top of Nethergreen Road, was developed by local builders Samuel and Joseph Hancock, who had bought the land in 1894[40].

Marr Terrace (next to the Bull's Head pub) was an earlier commercial venture (in 1876) by Frederick Leggoe, who also purchased and developed other land in the area. (See the account of Ranmoor Grange in Chapter 10.) Houses in that short cul-de-sac were built to meet the demand for rented accommodation by domestic servants, gardeners, coachmen and similar workers, who had moved into the expanding area. It was initially known as Market Place, linked to the retail shops nearby on Fulwood Road. Those were collectively called Ranmoor Market, similar to the names of Fulwood Road Market in Broomhill, Glossop Road Market and others at the time. The road was renamed in 1904 to avoid confusion with another Market Place in the city[41].

Also constructed later were several roads (often cul-de-sacs) fitted in where space was available: Carsick View Road (c1902), Cruise Road (1899) (within land sold from the Riverdale estate, and named after local builder Martin Cruise), Darwin Close (c1968), Hangingwater Close (c1969), Meadow House Drive (c1980) (next to Meadow House, 72 Carsick Hill Road), Ranmoor Rise (1992) (on land previously part of the grounds of Cliffe Cottage), Snaithing Park Close (c1958), and Storth Avenue (c1923).

These three sets of Ranmoor roads – ancient lanes, land society developments, and more recent ventures – provided additional housing space for the increasing population of the city as a whole. The new residents in Ranmoor, Hangingwater and Nether Green and the buildings they created are the subject-matter of chapters which follow.

Notes to Chapter Three

1 "Gate" is an early Scandinavian word for road or small track.

2 See David Hey, *Packmen, Carriers and Packhorse Roads* (Ashbourne: Landmark Publishing, 2001), pages 17-18.

3 For example, Tom Lane was only 11 feet (c3.3 metres) wide near to where it met the standard 40-feet (c12 metres) Fulwood Road prior to its widening in 1911-1912.

4 In the 19th century and perhaps earlier these fields – next to a stream flowing towards the River Porter behind the current Rising Sun car-park – were known as Little Carr, Rough Carr and Nether Carr. See Map 2.03.

5 The "curved" suggestion is plausible because "snaith" also described the curved handle of a scythe. Alternatively, the English Place-Name Society suggests the name comes from "sneiding", which means "a detached or small piece of land".

6 An earlier name was "Webster Lane", running alongside Webster Field with Webster's Farm at the top (now remodelled as Carsick Cottage; see the end of Chapter 2).

7 The name "Dead Lane" occurred in documents as late as 1889 and had been used from at least 1715. It may have originated because the route was used to transport coffins from Fulwood and Ranmoor to Ecclesall Church cemetery. That Church presumably arranged burials prior to the consecration of its present burial ground in 1789.

8 In the 1790s Enclosure Award map, this was identified as Carsick "Hall" Road, either by mistake or because that was the road's earlier name.

9 The large stones along parts of the Long Causeway, on an extension of Sandygate Road up to Stanage, are not of Roman origin, but were placed there to assist transportation of grindstones and other material in the 18th or 19th century.

10 A general account of objectives and achievements has been provided by S. M. Gaskell: Yorkshire estate development and the freehold land societies, *Yorkshire Archaeological Journal*, 1971, 43, 158-165.

11 Incidentally, both Joseph Brailsford and Henry Pawson were initial members of the Storth Crescent Land Society, purchasing plots in Graham Road.

12 Several Sheffield societies are described in pages 180-197 of J. H. Stainton's *The Making of Sheffield 1865-1914* (Sheffield: E. Weston and Sons, 1924).

13 Many Sheffield work-people were at the time keenly interested in the cultivation of their own garden allotment, sometimes renting a small plot at the edge of the town. This widespread enthusiasm was described by R. E. Leader in pages 145-152 of *Reminiscences of Old Sheffield* (Sheffield: Leader and Sons, 1876). He quotes a Member of Parliament's view that "the multitude of small, nicely-kept gardens in the suburbs was a characteristic of Sheffield, in which it was way in advance of any other large town" (p. 146). However, land became increasingly taken for building, and private allotment-holding gradually declined. From the 1890s, the Council and the Duke of Norfolk made available allotments for public rent. For example, see Note 22 at the end of Chapter 2 about the Hangingwater "roughs".

14 See page 165 in the article by S. M. Gaskell cited in Note 10.

15 George Wostenholm (1800-1876) was chairman and managing director of George Wostenholm and Son (his father was also George), based in Washington Works in Wellington Street. This was one of the town's major cutlery manufacturers, with substantial sales in America. (Washington Works was named with that link in mind, and it figured prominently in advertisements and other documents.) He is said to have sailed to and from America around 30 times in the course of his business life. His own principal residence, Kenwood in Nether Edge, was built in 1844-1845.

16 A comprehensive account of land society activity in Ranmoor is provided by M. C. Ling in *The Contribution of the Freehold Land Societies to the Development of Western Sheffield 1850-1905*, MA Thesis, University of Sheffield, 1974.

17 "Storth" (a word with Scandinavian origins) refers to a wooded section of land, often managed through coppicing. The local field names, for instance Upper Storth, Little Storth, Great Storth, Far Lane Storth, Middle Storth, and Long Storth, thus indicate an earlier use as coppiced wood-lands. They had largely been cleared well before the 19th century, but trees (mainly oaks) remained in certain sections. The

Ranmoor storths had long been the property of the Dukes of Norfolk (see Chapter 1) but were sold by the 11th Duke in 1812.

Other local woods and their many uses have been described by Melvyn Jones in *Sheffield's Woodland Heritage* (Rotherham: Green Tree Publication, third edition, 2003). Wood from managed coppices was used for charcoal, building, fences, ladders, broom handles, baskets and many other purposes. Bark was important for leather-making, and sap could be used for sugar or as an ingredient of wine.

18 Previously, one had to travel down what is now Hangingwater Road and then turn right along Nethergreen Road; see for example the 1850 map at the front of the book. The new road also required a small extension to the bottom of Water (now Storth) Lane; this previously had a 90-degree turn towards Nether Green before turning into Fulwood Road.

19 Named after Sir Francis Chantrey (1781-1841), the sculptor born and buried in Norton.

20 These were given names that might attract respectable society members. W. E. Gladstone (1809-1898) was Chancellor of the Exchequer at the time and later four times Prime Minister. J. R. Graham (1792-1861) held many prominent political positions, including First Lord of the Admiralty and Home Secretary. Both supported Liberal policies, suggesting that the Estate's trustees may have held similar views.

21 George Wostenholm had previously sold three segments to purchasers likely to enhance the area. In 1856, Henry Hutchinson (1815-c1896, a surgical instrument manufacturer who would become one of the new society's trustees) acquired land on which (c1861) he built Storthwood, on the corner of the new Gladstone and Chantrey Roads (now 408 Fulwood Road); he also contributed to the cost of the roads. In 1862, Mark Firth bought land on the north side of the new Chantrey Road in order to build Ranmoor College (see Chapter 5), and in that year John Hill (chemist and druggist) purchased a site on the left at the top of Gladstone Road, where he built Storthholme. Those transactions placed the same restrictions on the use of land as were included in the Storth Crescent Society's regulations; see the text.

22 Their occupations were varied: architect, boot-maker, builder, chemist and druggist, confectioner, contractor, cutlery manufacturer (two), draper, grocer, hair-seating manufacturer, iron founder, merchant's clerk, music seller, pawnbroker (four), plumber, polishing paste manufacturer, printer and bookseller (two), plumber, share broker, and slater.

23 "Park" was a fashionable name for middle-class housing developments in this period. See Note 36.

24 At the top end of the road (near where Carsick Hill Road previously turned sharply left up what is now Sandygate Lane) stood Ivy House Farm and outbuildings. These were demolished as part of the land society's extension of Carsick Hill Road eastward into Sandygate Road.

25 In addition, the bottom section (edged by Ranmoor Cliffe Road as well as Ivy Crescent Road) was sold in 1883. Arthur Davy, provision merchant, built Hill Crest on this site around 1885, living there until 1902; see Display Box 12 in Chapter 9.

26 In 1870, the Ivy Crescent Society bought additional land from the Storth Crescent Society, at the top end of Nethergreen Road. This dual set of plots led to the new society's name – in both upper and lower Ranmoor.

27 Tetney is a village in Lincolnshire, near to Grimsby, suggesting some link to that part of the country.

28 W. E. Laycock (1816-1895) already owned the two plots on the Storth Crescent Estate which had to be crossed by the new road, perhaps having planned this development since the early 1860s. He is routinely described as a manufacturer of hair seating for domestic and public furniture, railway carriages, etc., and his company also made brushes, matting and similar products. He had lived in Stumperlowe Grange since 1855, was Mayor of Sheffield in 1865, and by the 1871 census was a magistrate and alderman and an employer of "392 hands". He was also involved in other local developments, for example being an initial trustee of the Storth Crescent Land Society and a signatory on the initial deed of the Ivy Crescent Land Society.

29 First were Snaithing Park Road in 1876 and a westward extension of Belgrave Road in 1877; Stratford Road and Carsick Hill Crescent were laid down in 1878.

30 Dalebrook was the house of Edward Porter (1826-c1882), grocer and wine merchant. After his death (then a widower), it was occupied until 1919 by his brother and business partner Charles G. Porter (1832-1919). The house was demolished around 1960 and replaced by the present blocks of apartments known as Dalebrook Court.

31 Although born in Woolwich, Daniel Coupe (1831-1883) came to Sheffield from Worksop around the age of 20. He started work as a self-employed carter, expanding to operate more than 80 horses around the town. He also became a coal merchant, had an interest in Albion Brewery in Ecclesall, and set about building properties which he could rent out. He became a substantial landlord, allegedly paying more rates than anyone else in the town, and by 1871 had moved to Storth House in Fulwood (south of Fulwood Road). He gradually fell on harder times, in part

linked to recessions in trade, and died at the age of 52. He was a councillor for Brightside and then for Upper Hallam. An obituary article in the *Sheffield and Rotherham Independent* (08/11/1883) indicated that he "occupied a somewhat unusual position in the Council, and often relieved the otherwise dull discussions by his quaint and humorous remarks".

32 An 1879 street directory describes Edward Whitworth as a "public accountant, auditor and estate agent, finance agent, and agent for the County Fire and Provident Life Insurance Company, 6 Vicar Lane, home 29 Westbourne Road".

33 This comparison is presented in Part 4 of M. C. Ling, *The Contribution of the Freehold Land Societies to the Development of Western Sheffield 1850-1905*, MA Thesis, University of Sheffield, 1974.

34 Nyrah Wilson, *The Development of Middle-Class Housing in Western Sheffield during the 19th Century* (PhD Thesis, University of Sheffield, 1999) (page 214).

35 Frederick Bardwell was born in Sheffield in 1819. At the time of the 1861 census he was with his parents and own family near York – a "landowner and farmer". His father was then also described as a landowner, and the family had been established as auctioneers in Sheffield from at least the 1820s, trading in 1845 as T. N. Bardwell and Sons of High Street. In 1871 and 1881, Frederick was living in Ecclesall with his wife and several servants – a "landowner" in 1871 and a "magistrate" in the later year. He was a director of the Sheffield Banking Company, of Joseph Rodgers and Sons (then the largest cutlery company in the world) and of the Sheffield Water Company. He died in 1890.

36 Describing the two estates as a "Park" (and also "Ivy Park", see Section 2) followed a national fashion at the time, illustrated also in the successful "Broomhall Park" near to the new Ecclesall Road. The first part of the name (also in the established Taptonville area of Broomhill) probably derives from the Tapton family, substantial Ecclesall land-owners in the 14th century.

37 The eastern section, initially known as Lower Oakbrook Road, was created by local land-owners Mark Firth and Robert Younge in 1867-8, and the western section (Upper Oakbrook Road) was financed by Mark Firth alone in 1868.

38 The short section of Westwood Road from Oakbrook Road to near what became Fulney Road came earlier, after Elias Middleton purchased the Oakbrook Road frontage in 1887.

39 A joint purchaser was unmarried Helen Welburn, also described as a fruiterer. She sold her share to Arthur Gostelow in 1903.

40 Other houses built by the Hancock family include several in Nethergreen and Fulney Roads and at the bottom of Tom Lane.

41 It was described as Marr Place in some street directories between 1905 and 1925.

42 For example, the Upper Hallam Enclosure Award of 1805 designated Fulwood Road as "public", but identified Ranmoor Road, Tom Lane and others as "private" roads.

43 See the *Sheffield and Rotherham Independent* of 18 December 1852 and 25 June 1859 respectively. Despite later improvements, the section of the road near the current Thornbury Hospital became known as "Mappin's Dip". (F. T. Mappin built the house; see Chapter 4.)

44 See James Dixon's recollections in the *Sheffield Daily Telegraph* of 18 August 1933, page 6.

45 In fact, tar was used only briefly, as it was soon replaced by asphalt – a quite different substance. Asphalt is a by-product of petroleum production, and it became increasingly available with the spread of car ownership and increased refining activity to produce fuel.

46 See the *Alphabetical List of the Streets, Roads, and Lanes in the Borough*; classified as 352.7SQ in Sheffield Local Studies Library. In 1868, the Town Council purchased its first steam-roller to prepare the foundations for macadamizing roads within 2½ miles (c4 kilometres) of the parish church; see page 148 of the book cited in Note 49.

47 A pre-construction specification for Belgrave and Snaithing Park Roads (built in the 1870s) indicated that they were to be made of rubble with a three-inch coating of ganister (fire-clay from refractory furnaces); their footways were to be covered with ashes and gravel, with side-stones and side-channels.

48 A leading objector in this campaign was Councillor John Bingham, a resident of West Lea in Ranmoor Park Road. See Chapter 10 and Note 5 in Chapter 11.

49 A report by the Surveyor of Highways in 1909 indicated that 27% of city-centre roads were then surfaced with free stone or boulders, 18% with granite, 3% with wood, 46% with dry macadam, and 4% with tarmacadam. See page 164 of H. Keeble Hawson, *The Growth of a City* (Sheffield: J. W. Northend, 1968).

50 Details are limited, but the Minutes of the town's Highway Committee of 3 April 1868 indicate that "two-coat asphalting" has been done on Fulwood Road between Ranmoor and Stumperlowe. That probably refers to foot-paths rather than the carriageway; the Minutes are ambiguous in that respect. Asphalt was used on new foot-paths in Snaithing Lane in 1907, as it presumably was elsewhere.

CHAPTER FOUR

Mansions, Manufacturers and Merchants

There are very few buildings on the 1850 map at the front of the book, and the 1851 census indicates that there were then only 97 households in Ranmoor, Hangingwater and Nether Green. Those contained 440 people on the census day. By census day in 1891, the area had 309 households with 1,397 occupants – more than three times as many. The suburb's rate of increase was slightly greater than for Sheffield as a whole.

The New Arrivals

The difference through the second half of the 19th century was not simply one of numbers; the nature of the population also changed. In 1851, more than half the local people had been born nearby, in Upper Hallam, Nether Hallam or Ecclesall, but by 1891 that percentage had dropped to only nine – most people came from further afield. Jobs also changed, with a shift away from the ancient trades of cutlery and file-making, and a growth in either domestic service in the area or white-collar and managerial jobs in the town[1].

This separation into two groups was accompanied by another shift – many later companies were very large. In the 1851 census, the eight manufacturers with employees in the Ranmoor area had on average six workers. By 1891, there were more than 30 manufacturers living in the area, often with companies employing several hundred people in recently-built "works" in the town. Most of those large employers were in the recently-developed "heavy trades", manufacturing steel and engineering products in substantial establishments often with the use of costly equipment. Sheffield's traditional "light trades" (cutlery and associated businesses) were also flourishing in much of this period, but those continued to operate mainly through small units requiring only modest investment[2].

The 1891 census also identified locally about a dozen "merchants", a category not present in 1851. Such people were engaged in commercial activities, selling and perhaps buying for resale goods on a wholesale basis. In other documents, Sheffield employers increasingly described themselves as both "manufacturers and merchants" – selling products made by their own company, perhaps overseas as well as in this country[3].

Sheffield's trade (both "heavy" and "light") was generally prosperous between about 1845 and 1875, with the following few decades having periods of economic depression as well as boom. The town became a manufacturing powerhouse. Many companies expanded, technical innovation was strong, and owners became wealthy in a way that was not possible for small cutlery or file-making employers earlier in the century[4].

Wealthy people of that kind are the focus of the present chapter. Ranmoor was initially shaped by a small group of successful manufacturers and merchants (three of whom were brothers) who built their homes in the area. In the 1850s and 1860s nine large houses, often described at the time as "mansions", were constructed in quick succession along the eastern edge of Ranmoor. Their locations are shown in Map 4.01.

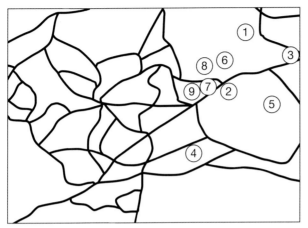

Map 4.01
The first large houses of Ranmoor.
1, Tapton Hall (1855).
2, Oakbrook (1860).
3, Tapton Edge (1864).
4, Riverdale (1865).
5, Endcliffe Hall (1865).
6, Thornbury (1865).
7, Moordale (1865).
8, Tapton Park (1866).
9, Tapton Grange (1867).

First came Tapton Hall (1855) at the top of Shore Lane (number 1 on the map), and then in 1860 Oakbrook House (number 2) on the south side of Fulwood Road. Tapton Edge (3) was built in 1864 at the bottom of Shore Lane, and Riverdale House was built in 1865 near the junction of Riverdale and Graham Roads (4 on the map). Also constructed in 1865, on opposite sides of Fulwood Road, were a new Endcliffe Hall (5), Thornbury (6) and Moordale (7) (now the Fulwood Inn). Very soon in Tapton Park Road were built Tapton Park (8) (1866) and Tapton Grange (9) (1867). All of these mansions and their landscaped grounds communicated the status and respectability of their occupants, and some were as grand as any in the town. Three are now listed as being of special architectural or historical interest: Endcliffe Hall (grade 2*), Oakbrook (grade 2) and Tapton Hall (grade 2).

1. Tapton Hall

In 1855, a fine house (number 1 on Map 4.01) was constructed on the Broomhill edge of Ranmoor by Edward Vickers (1804-1897) of Naylor, Vickers and Company based at Millsands. His company, described in directories as "merchants, steel converters and refiners, importers of iron, manufacturers, cast steel founders, forgers and rollers", was a world leader in producing steel for railway equipment and other engineering needs[5]. At a time when "respectability" was much prized, Edward Vickers was clearly a person of much distinction. In addition to his business reputation (described in directories as a "merchant and manufacturer"), he had been mayor of Sheffield in 1847, as well as serving as a magistrate and town trustee.

In 1854, he bought an eight-acre site to the west of Shore Lane, extending all the way between Fulwood Road and Manchester Road. Near the top of this site stood Tapton Grove[6], a house that had been built about 1788 by Joseph Badger[7]. (See Drawing 4.03 on page 52). William Shore (1755-1822), a Sheffield banker, had bought this in 1790, and after his death it was occupied for three decades by his widow Mary (1757-1853)[8].

Immediately after his purchase in 1854, Edward Vickers demolished the earlier house[9] and in its place constructed a larger building, renamed as Tapton Hall[10], with parkland and an ornamental pond. Since the days of Tapton Grove, entrance to the site had been up a long path from a lodge near the bottom of Shore Lane. This path was retained, and a large area of woodland also remained in place along the western side of the estate. The owner lived there in some style. In the 1861 census, he was accompanied by his wife and seven other family members as well as eight servants – a cook, two housemaids, a kitchen maid, two lady's maids, a butler and a footman.

Photo 4.01
Tapton Hall before its recent extensions, with the path which previously led from the estate's entrance near the bottom of Shore Lane.

Retiring from work in his 60s, Edward Vickers left Tapton Hall in 1867[11], and it was bought by another wealthy manufacturer, George Wilson (1802-1878). The Wilson family had made snuff at Sharrow Mills since the 1740s, and had acquired substantial land-holdings around Sheffield, including several farms in the Ranmoor area[12].

George Wilson had married Emily Kingsford (1827-1904) in 1852, living in one of the eight houses in The Mount in Broomhill before moving to Tapton Hall in 1867. His continuing income was very considerable, and he invested widely in

Advert 4.01
This 1879 advertisement for Thomas Firth and Sons (page 46) shows its wide range of products, including "gun work in general".

railway, mining and other shares. He was a substantial stock-owner and from 1845 director of the North Midland Railway Company. He purchased large areas of moor-land around Moscar to indulge his passion for grouse shooting[13].

After George Wilson's death in 1878, Tapton Hall was occupied by his widow until she died in 1904, then by their eldest son, George Kingsford Wilson (1853-1933), and after the latter's death by his son George Ronald Wilson (1888-1958). In 1959, Sheffield freemasons purchased the property for use as a masonic hall, extending it in 1968 and replacing the ornamental pond with a car park. They sold sections of land above and below the Hall, to the City Education Department and to Sheffield University (1964) respectively. The University opened a newly-built student hall of residence (Ranmoor House[14]) on the lower section in 1968, and this was replaced by new student accommodation in 2009.

2. Oakbrook House

A second "mansion" in the open countryside of Ranmoor (number 2 on Map 4.01) was constructed in 1860 by Mark Firth (1819-1880)[15]. He had acquired considerable wealth through the family firm, established in 1842 by himself, his brother Thomas (1821-1860) and (from the following year) their father Thomas (1789-1850), an experienced steel-melter. (Hence the name Thomas Firth and Sons – see Advert 4.01 on page 45.) While the two Thomases developed the products and manufacturing processes, Mark built up commercial networks, establishing agencies in America, Australia, Belgium, Canada, Denmark, Germany and Russia within the company's first decade[16].

In 1859 Mark Firth bought 26 acres of farm-land to the south of Fulwood Road, including Oakbrook Farm named after the brook that flowed down the site's eastern boundary. The farm was refurbished and continued working within the

Photo 4.02
Oakbrook House and the ornamental fountain in its garden lake. The House, supplemented by more recent buildings, is now Notre Dame School.

Photo 4.03
The front of Oakbrook House, showing the entrance porch constructed in 1874-1875 for a royal visit.

estate, and a spacious family home[17], named as Oakbrook House, was designed in Italianate[18] style by William Flockton and Son. The grounds were landscaped to include "pleasure grounds" (the conventional term at the time), and a lake with a water fountain was created within the Oak Brook (see Photo 4.02); additional land was bought in the early 1870s. In 1874-1875, the house was extended, with additional rooms and a substantial front porch (Photo 4.03), linked to the visit to Oakbrook of the Prince and Princess of Wales, later King Edward the Seventh and Queen Alexandra. That visit to Sheffield was the occasion for much pomp and public excitement, with specially-composed pieces of music – the "Oak Brook Galop" (shown in Print 4.01) and the "Firth Park March".

In addition to lodges, conservatories, heated greenhouses, vineries, coal houses and the farm buildings, the grounds contained dog kennels[19], pigsties and accommodation for cows. On the ground floor was the entrance hall, a dining room,

Print 4.01
Music specially written for the Ball held during the 1875 visit to Sheffield of the Prince and Princess of Wales, when they stayed with Mark Firth and family at Oakbrook House.

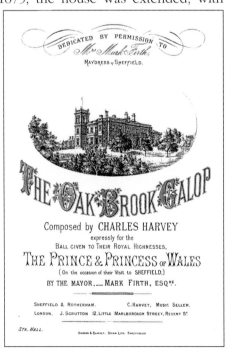

Photo 4.04
Mark Firth, the builder of Oakbrook, also funded alms houses in Nethergreen Road and contributed to the Methodist New Connexion College in Fulwood Road.

drawing room, billiard room, morning room, library, kitchens, lavatories and other rooms, and the first floor contained 11 dressing and bedrooms and four bathrooms, with several servants' rooms on the floor above.

The 1875 royal visit was linked to the Prince's opening of a new public space donated to the town by Mark Firth (named as Firth Park). Mark had been prominent in Sheffield life for many years, having been a town councillor, alderman and mayor, as well as serving as master cutler for three consecutive years. He contributed financially to many charitable causes, and constructed the Alms Houses in Nethergreen Road (see Chapter 5). He was a strong supporter of New Connexion Methodism[20], and was prominent in the creation of Ranmoor College financed by his brother Thomas (also described in Chapter 5).

Mark Firth was concerned to develop education in the town, both through the School Board (of which he was the initial vice-chairman from 1870 to 1879; see Chapter 7) and by inaugurating programmes of "extension lectures" (i.e., extending beyond basic education). The success of these lectures (started in 1875) led him to contribute more than £25,000 for the creation in 1879 of what became Firth College in Leopold Street[21]; in turn, this became one basis of Sheffield University College in 1897 and then the University of Sheffield in 1905. In recognition of Mark's extended help and guidance, the new University in 1905 named its principal chamber as "Firth Hall", and the entire principal building on that site is now called "Firth Court".

Mark Firth died in 1880 at the age of 61. His brothers Charles Henry and Edward had been partners in the company since 1870, and in 1881 Charles Henry Firth took over as managing director[22]. Subsequent changes and amalgamations gave rise in 1930 to the firm of Thomas Firth and John Brown Ltd., often referred to simply as Firth-Brown.

Oakbrook House was occupied by Mark's widow (his second wife Caroline, born 1833) until her death in 1893. The next owner, up to his death, was William Samuel Laycock (1842-

Photo 4.05
A 1910 photograph of William S. Laycock, who moved into Oakbrook House in the 1890s.

1916; see Photo 4.05), who had previously lived in 404 Fulwood Road. He developed his father's business (see W. E. Laycock in Note 28 of Chapter 3) with special reference to railway transport. According to Sheffield's *Who's Who* of 1905, William S. Laycock did "more than any individual in England to promote the comfort and secure the safety of the railway passenger by his many inventions for the perfecting of equipment and conveniences of railway rolling stock". Those included carriage heating from the locomotive boiler and the vertical sliding windows operated by a leather strap which remained in use for many decades[23].

After a period in World War One as a convalescent hospital, Oakbrook was bought in 1919 for use as a convent by the Sisters of Notre Dame of Namur, a Catholic teaching group that had been in Sheffield since 1855. The nuns already ran a private school for girls (Notre Dame High School) in Cavendish Street, and in 1935 they opened a second school in Oakbrook House. Additional buildings were constructed there, and the two schools were amalgamated in 1948. Since 1976, the intake has been comprehensive for both boys and girls. Further details are provided in Chapter 7.

3. Tapton Edge

In 1864, Edward Firth, brother of Mark (above), built a fine villa at the corner of Fulwood Road and Shore Lane (number 3 on Map 4.01). This land had been fenced off from the adjacent Tapton Hall estate for at least two decades.

Named as Tapton Edge and designed by local architects Flockton and Abbott, the Italianate-style villa (Drawing 4.01) contained seven principal bedrooms and four servants' rooms. On the ground floor were dining, drawing, breakfast, smoke and billiard rooms. Outside were stables for four horses, as well as additional loose boxes, two carriage houses (with space for nine carriages), three heated greenhouses, and several gardeners' sheds. The landscaped gardens were laid out by Robert Marnock, one of the outstanding horticulturalists of the 19th century[24].

Edward Firth (1831-1907) also worked for the family firm, describing himself in the 1881 census as a "steel and iron merchant, manufacturer of cast steel, files, saws and edge tools, employing 700 men and 70 boys". In that census he was accompanied at Tapton Edge by his wife, five children and six servants (a cook and five maids, labelled as house-, kitchen-, parlour-, pantry- and serving-maids). He was a "retired steel manufacturer" in the 1891 census, and was there as a widower in 1901 and until his death in late-1907[25].

Tapton Edge was then occupied by William Tozer[26] (from c1910) and later by his widow (between 1923 and c1942). It became a nurses' home for the Royal Hospital in Division Street up to that hospital's closure in 1978, after which it has served as a privately-run home for elderly people.

Drawing 4.01
Tapton Edge was built at the bottom of Shore Lane in 1864 by Edward Firth, one of three brothers to move into the Ranmoor area at the time.

4. Riverdale House

Four more "mansions" were built in the open spaces of Ranmoor in the following year – 1865. One of those was in the south of the area below Graham Road, near its junction with the new Riverdale Road[27]. Riverdale House (number 4 on Map 4.01) was constructed by Charles Henry Firth (1837-1892), the younger brother of Mark and Edward, who also worked in the family business (see the previous two sections).

The new building was set in an attractive open position, with pleasant views over the Porter Valley below. Its grounds extended east-to-west all the way from Riverdale Road to Hangingwater Road, and north-to-south from newly-extended Graham Road to what became Lower Oakbrook Road (laid down in 1867-8). The scale and style of the building and its setting demonstrated the status of its owner, with ornamental stone carvings and the inscription "CHF" in a prominent external position. The house provided ample space for a large family; for instance, in the 1881 census Charles and his (second) wife were accompanied by six children, a nephew and nine servants.

Charles Henry Firth was less active in public affairs than his brother Mark, being described in a newspaper obituary as "of an exceedingly retiring disposition"[28]. He also differed from Mark in his preference for the Church of England over New Connexion Methodism. In 1879, he donated an organ to the newly-constructed St John's Church (see Chapter 5), in 1891 he and his wife provided a lectern, and they were regular contributors to church funds[29]. He was only 55 when he died in 1892, after several years as an invalid.

Photo 4.06
Riverdale House was built in 1865 by Charles H. Firth. Here, behind the building in the early 1900s, is later owner J. George Graves (bottom right) with some of his company's staff.

Photo 4.07
J. George Graves at work in his office. He owned Riverdale House for four decades, and has been described as Sheffield's greatest benefactor.

Marianne Firth (Charles's second wife, born 1853) remained in Riverdale with the family (and a second husband) for several years, before the house was bought in 1902 by John George Graves (1866-1945). Known by his family and friends as George, he was born in the Lincolnshire village of Horncastle, moving with his family to Heckmondwike in West Yorkshire in 1874. After becoming an apprentice watch-maker in Sheffield in 1880, he started business on his own in 1886. By 1903, he had more than 2,000 staff in a mail-order business, selling watches, jewellery, cutlery, electro-plated items, clothing, furniture and other goods[30].

George Graves and his family lived at Riverdale up to his death in 1945, apart from a period (1908-1915) in a smaller property in Beauchief when he rented out Riverdale to cope with temporary business difficulties. He was an active Methodist and a supporter of the Young Men's Christian Association, the Salvation Army and similar bodies; he became a magistrate, a city councillor, an alderman, the city's lord mayor (in 1926), a freeman of the city (1929) and a town trustee (1933). Sometimes described as Sheffield's greatest benefactor, he was generous in transferring his wealth to others, in part through the J. G. Graves Charitable Trust established in 1930 (and still active) whose income came originally from profits of his company. For example, he purchased and donated the 206-acre Graves Park (from 1926), financed part of the cost of Ecclesall Woods (1927), and provided the Graves Art Gallery in Surrey Street (1934)[31].

After J. G. Graves's death in 1945, Riverdale was occupied by his daughter, Ruth, and her husband, Stanley Drummond-Jackson, before being taken over for offices by Brown Bayley Steels Ltd. around 1955. The present apartment complex in the grounds, known as Riverdale Park, was built in the mid-1970s.

5. Endcliffe Hall

1865 also saw the opening of Sheffield's grandest residence of the period. Endcliffe Hall (5 on Map 4.01) was the new home of John Brown and his wife, providing opulent splendour in a landscaped estate of some 35 acres.

Like many other wealthy Sheffielders of the time, John Brown (1816-1896) came from quite modest surroundings; his father was a slater living in Favell's Yard off Fargate. However, he achieved much more than most. An obituary in 1896 (*Sheffield and Rotherham Independent*, 27 December) noted that his career was "practically the career of Sheffield for the past half century, and it is not too much to say that in the making of that history he played a larger and more distinguished

Drawing 4.02
This sketch of John Brown was published in the Illustrated London News *of July 1867, soon after he had been knighted by Queen Victoria.*

part than any other man of his time". The obituary described "how by his energy and enterprise he brought new industries to the town which found employment for thousands; how, when most actively engaged as an inventor and manufacturer in building up a colossal business, he found time to serve the town of his birth as a councillor and alderman, as mayor and master cutler[32], as magistrate and town trustee, and later on as chairman of the School Board, and in other ways; and how at the same time he took the keenest and most generous interest in all movements having for their object the improvement – socially, morally, and religiously – of the people".

After a six-year apprenticeship, having left school at 14, John Brown set up on his own at the age of 21 in 1837, making and selling cutlery, tools and similar items; he is also recorded as a "steel converter and refiner" in that year. By 1844 he had moved into the production of steel files and railway springs. A first major commercial success came after his invention (1848) and active promotion of coiled spring buffers for railway coaches and vans, to replace the very uncomfortable chain links used until then.

Drawing 4.03
An 1808 sketch by surveyor William Fairbank of an earlier Endcliffe Hall viewed from the south. The Hall is the large building in the centre-left of the picture, with Fulwood Road running from left to right behind it. An earlier Tapton Hall is in the background at the top of Shore Lane.

Peter WARR

Contacts @ nanmoor society . org .

ATLAS STEEL & IRON WORKS, SHEFFIELD.

JOHN BROWN & CO.

(LIMITED),

MANUFACTURERS OF

ARMOUR PLATES, BOLTS, &c.

IRON AND STEEL PLATES, for the

BRITISH AND FOREIGN GOVERNMENTS,

FOR BOILER, AGRICULTURAL IMPLEMENT MAKERS, &c.

ATLAS MILD STEEL PLATES, BEAMS, ANGLES, &C.

(To Stand the Admiralty and Lloyd's Tests.)

WELDLESS IRON AND STEEL TYRES, RINGS (TO 14 FEET DIAMETER),
ATLAS STEEL RAILS, STRAIGHT AND CRANK AXLES, PISTON RODS,
BESSEMER STEEL FORGINGS AND CASTINGS OF EVERY DESCRIPTION.

PATENT PAPER-CENTRE RAILWAY WHEELS,

EAVES' PATENT DEAD-WEIGHT SAFETY VALVES,
RAILWAY SPRINGS, BUFFERS, POINTS, CROSSINGS, SWITCHES, WHEELS & AXLES,
FILES, TOOLS, SPIEGELEISEN, FOUNDRY, AND FORGE PIG IRON.

BESSEMER, CRUCIBLE & ALL KINDS OF STEEL.

PATENTEES AND MAKERS OF

SPECIAL CHROME STEEL,

FOR TOOLS, BRIDGE-WORK, &c.

LONDON OFFICES, 10, John Street, Adelphi, W.C.

Advert 4.02
Armour plate is prominently offered in this 1879 Sheffield directory advertisement, although the number of its potential purchasers in the town was presumably not large.

Photo 4.08
Endcliffe Hall was created by steel-maker John Brown on the south side of Fulwood Road in 1864-1865. It is now occupied by the Territorial Army.

With a wide range of other products and through the development of innovative equipment and processes, John Brown and Company expanded through the 1850s, opening the Atlas Steel and Spring Works in Savile Street, Brightside in 1856. Originally on a site of less than three acres, the works expanded more than tenfold in subsequent decades. Armour plating designed and made by the company proved to be more effective against the impact of shells than any made by the navy's own dockyards, and warship plate sales in the 1860s were very substantial. That was also the case with the company's newly developed steel railway lines. By the mid-1860s, the firm had more than 3,000 employees[33].

As illustrated in the obituary above, John Brown was also active in public affairs[34]. He was knighted in 1867. His business and public activities brought him into contact with influential people both in Sheffield and in national and government circles, and early in the 1860s he set about creating a new house that reflected his position in society and his enjoyment of fine things.

In 1863, living in Nether Edge[35], he bought an estate of open fields from

Photo 4.09
Endcliffe Hall's Grand Conservatory was more than 50 yards long. It was demolished in the 20th century.

54

Henry Wilkinson on the south side of Fulwood Road, next to the newly constructed Oakbrook House (above)[36]. On the estate was an earlier Endcliffe Hall which appears from Drawing 4.03 (1808) to have been quite substantial, facing towards the south-east[37]. The old Hall was immediately demolished, and architects Flockton[38] and Abbott designed a new property (Photo 4.08) that would be suitable for large-scale entertaining as well as for everyday living. With 36 rooms, the style was described as "French in the Italian manner", and it was built, decorated and furnished largely by local craftsmen[39]. The Hall's scale and flamboyance were unusual in a town where visible extravagance was usually treated with some suspicion.

The ground floor contained an entrance vestibule, a conservatory, a ballroom/saloon (also serving as a gallery for the family's pictures, and the site for an organ powered by water from a reservoir in the grounds), a library, dining, drawing and morning rooms, kitchen facilities, and (at mezzanine level) servants' rooms. On the first floor, reached by a wide staircase and gallery, were nine bedrooms and additional servants' quarters. A tower provided space for a billiard room and observatory.

The estate itself, with entrance lodges and cottages, stretched from Fulwood Road in the north to Riverdale Road in the south (constructed largely by John Brown in 1863-1864). As well as two glass summer houses and a "boarded cattle shed", it included the Grand Conservatory, which was more than 50 yards long and topped by a central dome (Photo 4.09). This faced a raised Italian garden next to an ornamental lake and more gardens. Behind the Hall (towards Fulwood Road) was a walled kitchen garden, vinery, greenhouses and laundry rooms, as well as a coach-house for 10 carriages, stables and a "farmery". This contained a cow-house for four cows, stalls for horses, a piggery, a blacksmith's shop, and buildings for corn-crushing and other tasks. The lower section of the grounds was landscaped and richly wooded[40].

This was a fine setting for John Brown and his wife to entertain guests and to enjoy on their own. Since they had no children, most occupants of the house were servants. In the 1881 census, those included a housekeeper, two housemaids, a ladies' maid, a kitchen maid, a cook and a footman. Within the grounds were also housed, with their families, a head gardener, two other gardeners, an undergardener and a coachman. Near the end of that census year Mary Brown

Print 4.02
Illustrated post-cards were immensely popular early in the 20th century. Here the war-wounded patients in Endcliffe Hall Hospital around 1917 could encourage recipients to dispatch letters and parcels to be delivered by their postman "mascot".

died, and Sir John came to spend increasingly long periods in the south of England. At the time of the 1891 census he was in a lodging-house in Torquay, and soon after that he left Sheffield completely, dying in 1896[41].

By 1892, it had been decided to sell Endcliffe Hall and its contents. It was offered to the Town Council for about half its original cost, suggested to be suitable for "a hospital, infirmary, convalescent home, asylum, orphanage, technical college, or public park, with museum and library". However, the Council were already over-burdened with demands on their funds, and the offer was declined.

The contents of the Hall, stables and other buildings were put up for sale in 1893, ranging in a five-day auction across more than 1,500 items but yielding only a modest return. Two years later, the buildings and land were bought for property development by local businessmen forming the Endcliffe Estates Company[42]. New roads were constructed in the south of the estate (Endcliffe Grove, Hall and Park Avenues), and about 20 houses had been built on those by 1905. The Hall itself was made available for renting for social events and exhibitions, but interest was limited. By 1913, it was proposed to demolish the Hall and outbuildings in order to make space for more new homes.

At this point, the West Riding Territorial Force Association offered to buy it as headquarters of the Fourth (Hallamshire) Volunteers. That purchase (with the recently-reduced area of land) was completed in 1914. The Hall was used as a hospital for military casualties later in World War One (Print 4.02), and has since then been occupied by different elements of the Territorial Army Reserve. The structure remains largely as it was, but modifications have included conversion of the stables and coach-house into a general-purpose hall and demolition of the Grand Conservatory; the Hall was completely surveyed and refurbished in 1997-1998.

6. Thornbury

In the same period as Endcliffe Hall was being planned, another leading merchant-manufacturer was arranging for his new house to be built on the other side of Fulwood Road (6 on Map 4.01). Frederick Thorpe Mappin[43] (1821-1910) had since 1859 been the senior partner of steelmakers Thomas Turton and Sons. Before then he had worked for some 20 years in the family cutlery firm (founded by his father Joseph in 1810 and from 1851 called Mappin Brothers), creating one of the largest in Sheffield. Travelling widely on behalf of the company, he had built up international as well as national trade[44].

Photo 4.10
Seen here around 1885, Frederick Thorpe Mappin, creator of Thornbury, was very influential in Sheffield and as a Member of Parliament.

Frederick Thorpe Mappin (Photo 4.10) was very successful in his business affairs. He had been master cutler in 1855, and by 1863 he was also a director of the Sheffield Gas Company, being appointed its chairman ten years later. He later became president of the File Manufacturers' Association, and from 1869 director of the Midland Railway Company. In public affairs, he had been a town councillor

Photo 4.11
Thornbury was built in 1865 in an imposing position at the top of landscaped gardens extending southwards to Fulwood Road.

for a period in the 1850s, and he re-entered the council in 1876, becoming mayor in 1877. He was a magistrate (from 1870) and a town trustee (from 1871), becoming the town collector (chairman of the trustees) in 1893. He was elected to parliament in 1880 (representing East Retford) and for 20 years from 1885 was Liberal MP for the Hallamshire Division of the West Riding of Yorkshire. The latter role involved him in many local events and activities over a long period. He was knighted in 1886, was appointed a Deputy Lieutenant of the West Riding, and became one of the first freemen of the city in 1900[45].

Most of these distinctions were ahead of Frederick Mappin when he moved to Ranmoor in 1865, but he and his impressive new mansion clearly added to the growing importance of the area. Thornbury (designed by M. E. Hadfield and Son) was built on farmland sold by the trustees of the Boys' Charity School (see Chapter 1), and the six acres of grounds were extensively landscaped by Robert Marnock (see Note 24).

As was customary, the house (Photo 4.11) provided accommodation for servants as well as the family. At the time of the 1871 census, it was also occupied by a butler, a cook, a lady's maid and two housemaids. In the lodge at the entrance to the drive were a groom and his family. However, after becoming a member of parliament Frederick and his wife spent much of their time in London. In the censuses of 1881 and 1901, they were accompanied there by six and eight servants respectively.

Frederick Mappin made many gifts to religious and other causes, including pictures to the Mappin Art Gallery (see Note 46) and bequests to several local hospitals. He is also credited with financing Sheffield's first coffee house, in Highfields in 1877, and was active in the Town Trust's rescue in 1898 of the financially-struggling botanical gardens. He is particularly known for his contributions (in actions as well as money) to the development of technical education in Sheffield. Throughout the 1880s he financed and promoted lecture courses and was influential in the establishment and funding of the Sheffield Technical School in 1886. That was one foundation on which was built the University of Sheffield (established in 1905), to which Sir Frederick devoted much time and money. He became one of the University's first pro-chancellors and was chairman of its Applied Science Department. The University's Faculty of Engineering is now housed in the Sir Frederick Mappin Building on the road named in his honour (Mappin Street, previously Charlotte Street), and within that building is Mappin Hall itself.

Frederick's eldest son Frank (1846-1920) also lived in Thornbury until Frederick's uncle, John Newton Mappin, died in 1884[46]. Frank then moved into the latter's house, Birchlands on Fulwood Road (later the site of the Hallam Tower Hotel). Lady Mappin died in 1908, and after Sir Frederick's death in 1910 (allegedly leaving a fortune of nearly £1 million) Thornbury was occupied by his second son, Wilson Mappin (1848-1925) and then by the latter's widow until about 1940. After World War Two the house became an annexe to Sheffield Children's Hospital, and in 1991 it opened as a private hospital.

7. Moordale

To the west of Thornbury, Tapton Park Road had been created in 1863 by the trustees of the Boys' Charity School (see Chapter 1). Land at the junction of that road and Fulwood Road became the site for another large house (7 on Map 4.01), when it was bought in 1865 by James Nicholson (born 1825). He worked with his brother William and (in the 1861 census) "20 men and 5 boys" in John Nicholson and Sons, cutlery and steel manufacturers of Mowbray Street. In the 1861 census, he lived with his wife, five children and two servants in Burngreave Road, describing himself as a "steel manufacturer and merchant".

Moordale, identified in the planning application of 18 April 1865 as a "villa residence", had five bedrooms, a billiard room and other rooms on the first floor, and a morning room, dining room, drawing room, library, two kitchens and other rooms on the ground floor. It was decorated with ornate stone-work, and elaborate gargoyles protruded from the gutters. Outside were two carriage houses, a three-stall stable and harness room, a servants' house, a laundry and several greenhouses. The owner's respectability was conveyed by a Latin inscription over the entrance porch: Malum Bono Vince (conquer evil with good)[47]. At the time of the 1871 census, James Nicholson lived in the house with his wife, three children and three servants.

Between 1874 and 1881 the house was occupied by Francis Ebenezer Smith (1825-1908), a stock and share broker who was active in the Sheffield Baptist community. Later owners included William Dransfield (1829-1898), a civil engineer and railway contractor, his widow (there from 1898 to 1922), R. V. Wheeler,

Professor of Fuel Technology at Sheffield University (from 1922 to c1932), and Norman Neill of James Neill and Company.

During World War Two (1939-1945), Moordale was used as offices by Midland Amalgamated Coal Mines, after their city centre offices

Photo 4.12
This 1865 "villa residence" is now the Fulwood Inn. Originally built by cutlery and steel manufacturer James Nicholson, it was being used for offices when this photograph was taken in 1943.

had been destroyed by bombing. The coal industry was nationalized in 1946, and these offices became the property of the National Coal Board. After subsequent use by insurance and computer-system companies, in 1999 Moordale was converted to become the Fulwood Inn.

8. Tapton Park

Land on both sides of the new Tapton Park Road was sold in 1865 to two partners in the cutlery firm of Harrison Brothers and Howson of Norfolk Street[48]. One of these, William Howson (1824-1884), constructed a substantial house on the northern side, opposite Moordale and next to Thornbury. As with similar mansions, the large grounds (more than two acres, again designed by Robert Marnock) were elaborately laid out and generously provided with trees and plants.

Called Tapton Park (8 on Map 4.01), the house (Photo 4.13) had (and has) a stone inscription above the front door – "H" (for Howson) in front of "W" (for William) and the year "1866". It contained seven principal bedrooms and two bathrooms, with three servants' rooms on the second floor. Outside were heated glass-houses, vineries, and store-rooms for peaches, nectarines and tomatoes. Attached

Photo 4.13
Tapton Park was built for cutler William Howson in 1865-1866. In 1936, when this photograph was taken, it was converted to be the Head Office of the General Refractories Company.

to the house was a conservatory and orchid house, and at the end of the drive was an "ornamental lodge".

After William Howson's death in 1884 (he had retired in 1875, being replaced in the firm by his son George), Tapton Park continued to be occupied by his wife Jessie. She died in 1902, and their son George (1851-1928) moved in with his wife and family (from Ranfall in Ranmoor Park Road). Whereas his father had devoted himself to his company (and to Totley Orphanage, of which he was treasurer), George (Drawing 4.04) was also active more widely. He was master cutler in 1893, president of the Cutlery Manufacturers' Association, on the board of management of the Royal Hospital, a magistrate, a trustee of the Hallamshire Savings Bank, and a director of Truswell's Brewery.

George died in 1928, and Tapton Park was then occupied by other members of the Howson family[49], before being converted in 1936 to become the head office of General Refractories, later Hepworth Refractories Ltd. The company extended the building, which was renamed as Tapton House when new properties were built (1999-2000) in what became Tapton Park Gardens.

9. Tapton Grange

William Howson's business partner, James William Harrison (1816-1897), also moved to Ranmoor at this time. In 1867, he built Tapton Grange (9 on Map 4.01) on the south side of Tapton Park Road, between Moordale and what became St John's Church. In that period, Darwin Lane continued southwards as far as Fulwood Road, and that Lane was initially the western boundary of James Harrison's new site; the site itself (more than three acres) extended down to Fulwood Road.

Shown in Photo 4.14 on page 62, Tapton Grange was a substantial house for the unmarried owner. The ground floor contained a drawing room, a dining room, a morning room and a billiard room, as well as the kitchen and associated rooms. On the first floor were eight bedrooms and two bathrooms; and three servants' and other rooms were on the second floor, all topped with a tower room. The gardens (designed by Robert Marnock) included greenhouses, conservatories, a vinery and other buildings, as well as two carriage houses and a stable. An entrance lodge was located in Tapton Park Road, with its own accommodation including two bedrooms.

At the time of the 1871 census J. W. Harrison was accompanied there by his sister and three servants, but in 1881 (having retired from his job in 1875, as did William Howson, above) he was alone with three servants. He served as a church burgess in the town (from 1878), a guardian for the Ecclesall poor, a trustee of Sheffield Savings Bank, and a director of the Sheffield Water Company, the Sheffield Gas Company, and Thomas Jessop and Sons steelmakers. Both in his lifetime and through his will he made substantial gifts to local hospitals and charity schools, and he provided the (adjacent) land on which is built St John's Church (see Chapter 5).

Tapton Grange was bought in 1897 by John Brocksopp Wilkinson (1849-1919), who was James's nephew and by then a partner in the family firm. In the 1901 census, he was there with his wife[50], daughter and four servants, and a coachman/groom and family lived in the lodge. He was a church-warden of St John's Church for nearly 20 years (1895-1913). After his death in 1919, Tapton Grange was occupied by other members of the Wilkinson family, before being purchased in 1928 by the National Union of Teachers' Benevolent Fund to serve as a home for teachers' orphans. Around 1970 it was demolished and the site was divided into two. In the southern part was constructed Oakbrook View, including a hostel for clients of the city's Social Services Department. The northern section was joined with land to the west to create space for the construction of Ballard Hall,

Drawing 4.04
A 1900 caricature of George Howson, the occupant of Tapton Park (page 59) at the beginning of the 20th century.

Display Box Six

SHEFFIELD IN THE 19th CENTURY

In 1801, the population of Sheffield was around 45,000. This increased by more than eight times in the next century.

Some notable dates:

1819: Sheffield canal and canal basin opened, improving the transportation of raw materials and manufactured products to and from the town.

1821: Sheffield to Glossop turnpike opened via Crosspool, now the A57. (Other turnpike roads had been constructed in the area since 1756.)

1832: Cholera epidemic in Sheffield kills 402 people.

1836: Botanical Gardens and General Cemetery opened by private companies.

1837-1843: Severe slump in Sheffield trade, with widespread distress.

1838: Sheffield's first railway station opens at the Wicker. (Later stations include Victoria, opened in 1851 and closed in 1970, and Midland, opened in 1870.)

1843: Sheffield incorporated as a municipal borough, managing its own affairs (police, highways, sanitation, etc.), financed by rates paid by residents.

1850s to c1875: Golden age for Sheffield trade.

1850s onwards: Large factories constructed on the eastern side of the town, linked to the development of steel manufacture and expanding American and other markets. (In this period Sheffield is reputed to produce each year more than half the world's steel.)

1855: Bramall Lane cricket ground opens.

1856: Sheffield's first free public library opens.

1857: Sheffield Football Club inaugurated – the world's earliest continuous soccer club. (Hallam Football Club, on Sandygate Road, is the second oldest – since 1860[51].)

1860: Cutlers' Company adopts a new statute to include steel, saw and edge-tool manufacturers, reflecting the expansion of Sheffield's manufacturing base.

1864: The "Great Sheffield Flood" from a collapse of the Dale Dyke Dam devastates large areas and kills 270 people.

1860s: A time of workers' agitation for better pay and acceptance of trade unions, with some destruction of employers' equipment, known as "rattening".

1867: A Royal Commission held in Sheffield concludes that 12 of 60 local unions had been responsible for rattening "outrages", and identifies the main culprits.

1867: Sheffield Wednesday Football Club founded. (Sheffield United commenced in 1889.)

1870-1903: Following the 1870 Education Act, the Sheffield School Board constructs or redevelops more than 50 schools.

1873: First Sheffield trams, drawn by horses; electric trams start in 1899.

1876-1894: Difficult economic and trade conditions, with intermittent improvements.

1884: Hunter's toll bar removed from Ecclesall Road.

1885: Sheffield Corporation purchases Endcliffe Woods for "public walks and pleasure grounds".

1893: Sheffield granted the title of "city".

1897: New Town Hall and Lyceum Theatre built.

1897: University College opens, deriving from Firth College, the Technical School and other institutions. This became the University of Sheffield in 1905.

Photo 4.14
Tapton Grange, here seen in 1897, was demolished around 1970, approximately a century after it was built.

accommodation for students of Sheffield Polytechnic (later Hallam University) based in Pond Street in the city centre. Ballard Hall was vacated around 2002, and houses are currently planned for the site.

Notes to Chapter Four

1 In 1851, 49% of Ranmoor heads-of-household worked in either cutlery or file-making, but by 1891 only 11% were in those trades. At the later time, most common in the area were either domestic employment, as a gardener, coachman, servant, etc. (none in 1851 but 17% in 1891) or non-manual jobs such as clerks, managers, professional workers, manufacturers or merchants (31% in 1891).

2 Implications of the co-existence in Sheffield of the two kinds of operation have been examined by Sidney Pollard in *A History of Labour in Sheffield* (Liverpool: Liverpool University Press, 1959).

3 A flourishing community of merchants is often considered essential to the development of an area. They provide jobs, incomes, and products to purchase; they attract people in search of work or to transact business; they have contacts with other areas and import new ideas and equipment;

they spend their money not only on personal projects but also for civic and charitable gain.

4 Sheffield's success, and potential for wealth, was summarized by Geoffrey Tweedale in *Steel City* (Oxford: Clarendon Press, 2004): "In its late nineteenth-century heyday, Sheffield had the world's largest cutlery industry and was the leading centre for saw, scythe, and file manufacture. It also had a major toolmaking sector, characterized by the immense variety of its products" (page 15). In addition, Sheffield "was the world's chief centre for steel armaments manufacture in the late nineteenth century" (page 72). The development of these industries and many local companies up to the 1990s is comprehensively reviewed in that book.

5 Naylor, Vickers and Company was formed in 1828, bringing together the expertise of Edward Vickers and his father-in-law George Naylor. The

company expanded to become one of the country's major steel producers, for instance exhibiting at the Great Exhibition in London (1851) the largest steel ingot ever made. From the 1850s, Edward Vickers passed control to his two sons, Thomas and Albert, and in 1863 the company built a large works in Brightside (the River Don Works), becoming Vickers, Sons and Company and before long employing more than 1,000 people in the manufacture of marine shafts and propellors, armour plate, artillery pieces and other items. It later incorporated several other businesses in a range of sectors, for example in the 20th century moving into ship-building, motor-car production and electrical equipment. It eventually became merged with other companies as part of Sheffield Forgemasters.

6 The house was sometimes referred to as Tapton Hill (as in Drawing 4.03). It is possible that this was the original name of the path that became Shore Lane, named after the next owner of the house and his family. An 1801 map describes an area to the west of the lane as "Tapton Hill Field", with the house indicated as "Tapton Grove", and the 1850 map inside the front cover identifies the northward extension of Shore Lane as Tapton Hill.

7 The land was just inside an area covered by the Ecclesall Enclosure Act of 1779. That Award was made in 1788, probably being followed by some sales including this one.

8 One of William and Mary Shore's grand-children was Florence Nightingale (1820-1910), noted for her contributions to nursing care during and after the Crimean War (1854-1856). Her surname derives from the fact that her father William Edward Shore (1794-1874) had changed his name to Nightingale in 1815, following the will of his mother's uncle, Peter Nightingale of Lea near Matlock. Florence Nightingale has left several written records of her visits to Tapton Hall.

9 Edward Vickers had bought the property from Robert Brightmore Mitchell, who had purchased it after the death of Mary Shore, apparently with a view to developing an estate of houses on the site. (This reference to "Robert" is from Hunter's *Hallamshire*. Only a William Brightmore Mitchell has been located in other local documents, identified as a land surveyor. It is possible that William was the intermediary, with "Robert" cited in error.)

10 The principal architect was William Flockton (1804-1864), who designed the Mount in Broomhill, Wesley College (later King Edward VII School) in Glossop Road, and other important buildings in the town. See also Note 38.

11 Edward Vickers apparently had aspirations to be a country gentleman. By the 1881 census (aged 77) he was living in a large estate in Worcestershire with his wife, several family members and visitors, and no less than eleven servants. Nearby cottages housed the estate's gamekeeper, coachman and labourers. He also had eleven servants at the time of the 1891 census (then in Northamptonshire), when he was 87.

12 An account of the family and its activities has been provided by M. H. F. Chaytor in *The Wilsons of Sharrow* (Sheffield: J. W. Northend, 1962).

13 Newspapers in the 1870s and 1880s regularly published the numbers of grouse shot by principal individuals ("sportsmen"), often described as having "capital sport". Members of the Wilson family repeatedly had large "bags".

14 This name derived from the student hostel it replaced in Fulwood Road nearer to Nether Green, which had previously been Ranmoor College for training ministers in a branch of the Methodist Church; see Chapter 5.

15 Around this time private companies started to supply gas and water to the area, contributing to its attractiveness for residential development.

16 The company, initially on the corner of Charlotte (now Mappin) Street and West Street, expanded steadily, and in 1852 built larger premises – the Norfolk Works in Savile Street. They produced many types of steel goods, but developed particular expertise in forging artillery barrels. The Crimean War (1854-1856) and other threats to the nation created a demand for military equipment, and Thomas Firth and Sons installed larger and more modern equipment to produce guns of unequalled size. By the 1870s, they also had another works near Chesterfield and forging and rolling capacity at Wadsley, altogether employing more than 1,000 people; see Advert 4.01.

17 Mark Firth's first wife, daughter of a local scissor manufacturer, had died in 1855, and in 1857 he married Caroline Bradley, the daughter of a Nottingham alderman. He had at least nine children, with some dying in their early years.

18 Italianate style was very popular in the period, partly because of its use in Osborne House completed by Queen Victoria and Prince Albert in 1851. The style was based on some features of Italian villas, with low-pitched roofs, overhanging eaves, tall and narrow windows, and sometimes small towers and balustrading at roof level.

19 In common with other wealthy Sheffield men, Mark Firth was active in Derbyshire grouse-shooting. In 1872 he constructed Moscar Lodge near Strines, with kennels for dogs and accommodation for staff and participants. The surrounding area was for some years known as "Firth's Moors".

20 His father and first wife had also supported this movement. Details are provided in Chapters 5 and 6.

21 The opening of Firth College gave rise to another royal visit to Oakbrook, by Prince Leopold the youngest son of Queen Victoria. (Leopold Street was named in his honour.)

22 Sons of the three brothers also worked in the company, including Mark's son Bernard (1866-1929) who was chairman from 1903 until his death.

23 His company later became Laycock Engineering Ltd., which continued operating in Millhouses up to the middle of the 20th century.

24 Robert Marnock (1800-1889) was the designer and first curator (1834-1840) of Sheffield's botanical gardens. He was subsequently curator for the Royal Botanic Society in Regent's Park, London, for nearly 30 years. In Ranmoor, he designed the gardens of Tapton Edge (number 3 in this chapter), Thornbury (6 below), Tapton Park (8 below), Tapton Grange (9 below) and Storth Oaks (described in Chapter 10). His other Sheffield designs included those of Weston Park, High Hazels and the Kenwood Park Estate.

25 Edward Firth also owned a large estate to the north and east of Hope in Derbyshire, purchased in 1875, where he built Birchfield Hall. He financed some of the repairs made to Hope Church in the 1880s, and with other members of the family he is buried there.

26 William Tozer (1858-1923) joined the family firm of Steel, Tozer and Hampton in 1875. This became Steel, Peech and Tozer in 1883 and later (1918) part of United Steel Companies Ltd., of which William was a director.

27 Riverdale Road had just been built by John Brown and neighbour Charles Younge, around the edge of John Brown's new estate; see house number 5 later in the chapter.

28 He shared his brothers' liking for Derbyshire moorland, also owning Sugworth Hall near Low Bradfield. (Mark Firth built Moscar Lodge and brother Edward constructed Birchfield Hall near Hope.)

29 After a fire in 1887, the foundation stone of the new St John's was laid by Mrs C. H. Firth.

30 J. G. Graves was among the earliest people to exploit the potential of postal selling, apparently being one of the first to offer mail-order purchases though a small deposit and monthly payments. In 1903, with support from national newspapers he won a long battle with the Post Office about their pick-up of his registered letters, and the firm expanded to send out more than a quarter of a million orders each month. Its 27 different buildings were brought together in 1903 into Westville, opposite what became the University of Sheffield (on the site occupied since 1983 by the Octagon Centre). The firm was later sold to the Sheffield company Wigfalls, and

subsequently became part of the Great Universal Stores Group.

31 His charitable gifts also included Concord Park (1929), Blacka Moor (1933), Dronfield's Cliffe Park (1934), land for Tapton Court Nurses' Home (1934), Beauchief Garden and what became the Abbeydale Industrial Hamlet (1935), extensions to the Children's Hospital (1935) and to the Mappin Art Gallery (in Weston Park, 1937), sections of the Sheffield Round Walk (1938), Forge Dam (1939), a large number of playgrounds for children, sports-grounds and public areas, 230 homes for elderly people, several hospital facilities, and hundreds of donations to smaller projects. A detailed account has been provided by Keith Farnsworth in *The Graves Inheritance*, published by the J. G. Graves Charitable Trust in 1990.

32 In fact he had twice served as mayor (in 1861 and 1862) and as master cutler (in 1865 and 1866).

33 Important in these developments were John Brown's partners in the company, taken on in 1859 – William Bragge and John Devonshire Ellis. They became joint managing directors, with John Brown as chairman, when the private undertaking was converted into a limited liability company in 1864. After John Brown's retirement in 1871, J. D. Ellis became Chairman and Managing Director until his death in 1906. The history of this and many other Sheffield companies has been charted by Geoffrey Tweedale in *Steel City* (Oxford: Oxford University Press, 2004).

34 In addition to the activities listed in the obituary, he was also a Poor Law Guardian for Ecclesall, a Church Burgess, the Town Collector (principal Town Trustee), and a Deputy-Lieutenant of the West Riding. He made frequent donations to charitable causes, and was a strong adherent of the Church of England, financing All Saints Church in Brightside (1867) (in part for his workers and their families) as well as that church's school buildings (1871).

35 John Brown and his wife lived previously in Shirle Hill, a house in Cherry Tree Road.

36 In addition, he bought some adjacent land in separate transactions.

37 This drawing is by surveyor William Fairbank; see his Fieldbook 61, page 102, in Sheffield City Archives.

38 The member of the Flockton family in "Flockton and Abbott" was Thomas G. Flockton, son of the William in Note 10. The firm of Flockton and Son (i.e., William and Thomas) had previously designed Oakbrook. Thomas Flockton and colleagues' other buildings included Tapton Edge, the Cutlers' Hall, offices for the Sheffield Water Company, Firth College, and the Central Schools in Leopold Street.

39 Many of the items were specially designed and made to John Brown's own specification, intended to match the Hall's overall style. The house was opened for public viewing over a three-day period soon after its completion.

40 Details have been provided by Douglas Hindmarch and Anthony Podmore in *Endcliffe Hall in the Manor of Hallamshire*, prepared in 1999 for the 4th Battalion of the Yorkshire Volunteers. Furniture and fittings were emphasized in an account by Julie Goddard (Endcliffe Hall: The residence of a gentleman industrialist, in M. Jones (ed.), *Aspects of Sheffield 1*, Barnsley: Wharncliffe Publishing, 1997).

41 In 1895, lawyers in the role of "Masters in Lunacy" declared John Brown to be "a person of unsound mind". The nature of his mental illness is not known, nor whether it was the basis of his health problems in earlier years. For instance, he was unable to fulfil some of his duties as Master Cutler, and his 1871 retirement from John Brown and Company followed failures to attend board meetings because of ill-health; his retirement in 1879 from the chair of the Sheffield School Board was also publicly attributed to "the state of his health".

42 Advertising catalogues for both sales, with extensive photographs and plans, are held in Sheffield Local Studies Library, dated April 1893 and 30 July 1895.

43 Following a convention of the time, Frederick's second name was the surname of his mother before her marriage. She was Mary Thorpe, the daughter of a Bedfordshire land agent and surveyor.

44 Frederick's younger brother, Joseph Newton Mappin (1835-1913), also moved from Mappin Brothers, leaving it in the hands of their other two brothers. Joseph Newton instead set up his own plating and cutlery business, which later became well-known as Mappin and Webb, acquiring a royal warrant and producing silverware until the 1950s. The company is still active as a retailer.

45 Like several other wealthy Ranmoor residents Frederick Mappin enjoyed grouse-shooting. His performance (the number of birds shot) was regularly summarized in newspapers of the 1870s and 1880s.

46 John Newton Mappin (1800-1884) was proprietor of the Masborough Brewery in Rotherham. He funded St John's Church in Ranmoor (1879) (see Chapter 5), left money to finance the Mappin Art Gallery in Weston Park (opened in 1887), bequeathed to the Gallery more than 150 pictures, and made many other charitable gifts.

47 This motto remains in place to greet customers on their way into the present public house.

48 The company had been run as John Sanson and Sons between 1796 and 1847, when it was taken over by James William Harrison (1816-1897) and William Howson (1824-1884); they were shortly joined by James's brother Henry (1825-1893). The firm manufactured cutlery and tableware of all kinds as well as other items, and it expanded to employ more than 600 workers in the 1890s. In 1900 it moved to new works between Division Street and West Street, facing Carver Street, which now provides office accommodation. The company was later (1959) bought by Viners.

49 The property was advertised for auction in June 1928. Perhaps it remained unsold, since it was next occupied by other members of the family. The auction also offered the kitchen garden, an acre of land extending west to Darwin Lane, which appears to have been brought within the estate in 1873.

50 In 1882 J. B. Wilkinson had married Jessie, the daughter of William Howson, who was James Harrison's business partner and owner of Tapton Park.

51 The Hallam Cricket Club had played on the Sandygate Road site since at least 1804. A football club in the same location was largely initiated by John Shaw (1831-1918), who lived in Water (later Storth) Lane and who became influential in shaping national rules for the game. In its early days football was unknown to most people and it lacked regulation and clear rules.

An early newspaper account of a match between a Hallam team (18 players) and a 15-strong Sheffield team reported how "after about an hour of remarkably good play [the ball] was safely landed by the Hallam men [also described as "the countrymen"] through the goal of their opponents ... Night at last put a stop to the game." See *The Countrymen* by John A. Steele (Sheffield: Henry Boot, 1986).

Building on Success:
Three Community Gifts

The new residents of Ranmoor from the 1860s contributed more than merely fine houses and an attractive environment. Many of them gave money, time and their status in society to what they saw as deserving causes. Thousands of charitable gifts remain unknown, but three substantial buildings financed by local people were particularly important. St John's Church was made possible by John Newton Mappin and James William Harrison, and Ranmoor College and Firth's Alms Houses were initiatives of Thomas and Mark Firth respectively. Those buildings are indicated as numbers 1, 2 and 3 respectively on outline Map 5.01.

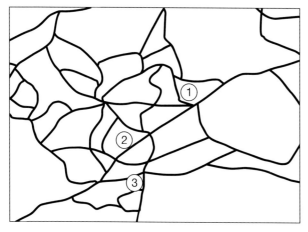

Map 5.01
The location of three buildings created and financed by local residents.
1, The Church of St John the Evangelist.
2, Ranmoor College.
3, Firth's Alms Houses.

1. The Church of St John the Evangelist

The imposing St John's is located at the meeting point of Ranmoor Road, Ranmoor Park Road and Fulwood Road. It has been described as "the finest of Sheffield's 19th-century churches"[1] and is listed by the Department for Culture, Media and Sport as grade 2* – "of outstanding regional importance". But it is not the church that was built in 1879.

For the growing number of local residents at that time, church attendance was an important part of life and essential for a respected position in society. Without a local place of worship, Ranmoor members of the Church of England had to travel elsewhere, perhaps to Ecclesall (All Saints Church, rebuilt 1788), Fulwood (Christ Church, opened in 1839) or Broomhill (St Mark's, consecrated in 1871). Ranmoor Wesleyan Methodists had in 1870 rebuilt their own church in Ranmoor Road (see Chapter 6), and a local Anglican parish church increasingly appeared desirable.

That required land, money and of course a parish. Ranmoor was then within the parish of Fulwood, but its own parish was created in 1877 from parts of Fulwood and Crookes parishes. Land for a new church was provided by James William Harrison, the occupant of adjacent Tapton Grange (see Chapter 4)[2], and the

Photo 5.01
This original St John's Church was built in 1879, but it was destroyed by fire in January 1887.

building was financed almost entirely by John Newton Mappin (1800-1884), who lived on Fulwood Road where more recently has stood the Hallam Tower Hotel[3]. St John's was designed by the Sheffield architect E. M. Gibbs to accommodate some 560 people[4]. The original building (Photo 5.01) differed from the present church in having an open-timbered roof which spanned its whole width. Many internal features were paid for by local people. For instance, J. Y. Cowlishaw (see below) donated the pulpit, the organ came from C. H. Firth (see Chapter 4) and the font from W. H. Brittain (see Chapter 10).

Foundations were laid in 1877, and St John's was consecrated on 24 April 1879. Its initial trustees were the Bishop of Fodor and Man (in the Isle of Man), John Newton Mappin (the donor, above), Frederick Thorpe Mappin (J. N. Mappin's nephew and owner of Thornbury; see Chapter 4), and another of J. N. Mappin's nephews, John Yeomans Cowlishaw, who lived in Tapton Cliffe (also on Fulwood Road, on the Broomhill side of the Shore Lane junction)[5].

This was a period of national religious expansion, with many new churches coming into use. How could their operation be financed? St John's followed a common procedure of the time, renting out seats in the church. Regular members of the congregation were asked to pay a yearly rent for a specified sitting in a particular pew. For St John's that was initially set at £1.10.0 (£1.50), and some 400 rented sittings were created. That left approximately 160 "free pews" for other people, perhaps those who could not afford to pay, were infrequent attenders, or were visiting from outside the area. In addition, a "voluntary rate" was also contributed by some of the seat-holders, and donations were made by people attending each service[6].

These "pew rents" provided the vicar's stipend and met other expenses for more than 60 years, not being abolished until 1945. That became possible only after a long period of money-raising to increase the church's endowment fund. Other subscriptions from parishioners had made possible many other projects, including construction of a Parish Room (later called the Parochial or Parish Hall) at the bottom of Ranmoor Road (opened in 1886) and after World War One (1914-1918) a memorial to the 59 local soldiers who lost their lives in the war (erected in the grounds in 1921).

A nationwide religious census taken on 20 November 1881 indicated that Ranmoor's parish church was about half full in both its morning and evening services (267 and 245 people respectively)[7]. Although many wealthy residents of

Photo 5.02
St John's Church after the 1887 fire. The steeple was saved and included in the new design.

Ranmoor were regular in their attendance, it is not clear how often their servants, gardeners, coachmen and others joined the congregation of St John's. In Sheffield as a whole, middle-class people were more active church-goers than those who were less wealthy[8], and this general pattern is reflected in the names of Ranmoor's pew renters. However, servants and others may have taken advantage of the free pews, or perhaps attended other services in Ranmoor or elsewhere.

In terms of required attendance for ceremonies of marriage, the artisan class was the more numerous. Between 1879 and the end of 1899, approximately 10 weddings took place each year in St John's. In those, only around 15% of bridegrooms' occupations suggested a wealthy background – merchants, manufacturers, gentlemen, stock-brokers and so on. White-collar employees made up about 25% of the bridegrooms – shop-keepers, clerks, policemen, publicans etc., but in the majority of cases local bridegrooms were domestic servants, cutlery, building or farm workers, or in other manual jobs.

Disaster struck in 1887. The church's Anniversary Booklet of 1929 describes it like this:

> The year 1887, the year of Queen Victoria's Jubilee, came in with the country in the grip of a severe frost. It was the evening of New Year's Day; and, as the following day was a Sunday, the caretaker of the church, Thomas Leighton, anxious that the church should be kept warm, kept a big fire burning in the stove all night. He was in the church very early in the morning, and at 8.30 went home for breakfast. Returning at 9.20 he at once detected a smell of smoke, and, hurrying into the church, he found the organ on fire. It transpired later that the cause of this was a beam of wood, too near the boiler flue. Leighton hastened to the Ranmoor Inn, and a messenger was despatched on horse-back to Broomhill Police Station, whence a telephone message was sent to the Sheffield Fire Station; but, before the fire-engine could be on the spot, the flames had got the mastery, and running up the organ screen quickly set fire to the roof. Soon the roof fell in, and the nave was a vast furnace, the flames and smoke from which were seen from the hills of Ecclesall, Sharrow, Crookes, and Fulwood. The tower and spire, which were somewhat detached from the main block of the building, were saved by the courageous action of Superintendent Pound, who made his way up the spiral staircase to the belfry, taking a hose-pipe with him. He found that the fire was already creeping through to the belfry; but from this

point of vantage he was able to pour a great quantity of water upon the flames, and thus hold them in check. But, with the exception of the tower and spire, in a very short time the church was burnt to the ground; and the bare walls alone remained standing.

The Alliance Assurance Company paid out £9,400 on the following Monday, and an additional £3,650 was donated by local people. A new building (Photo 5.03) was designed by E. M. Gibbs (the original architect), this time with space to accommodate 750 people, almost 200 more than previously. The foundation stone was laid in July 1887 by Mrs C. H. Firth (see Chapter 4), and services were held in the newly-built Parish Hall in Ranmoor Road until the new church was opened on 9 September 1888[9]. The tower is 190 feet (58 metres) high, and on either side of the nave is a gallery of arches.

As previously, many items were provided by local people, including the pulpit from J. Y. Cowlishaw (1888), the lectern from Mr and Mrs C. H. Firth (1892), and the chancel screen and altar from Sir Frank and Lady Mappin (1911)[10]. The donation in 1924 of West Lea (5 Ranmoor Park Road) as a vicarage, serving from the early 1980s as the Parish Centre[11], is described in Chapter 10.

Ranmoor's parish church has been central to local life in many ways. It has been responsible for a large number of social and community activities, for example supporting boy scouts, girl guides and many, many meetings. Groups with names unlikely to be used today have included the Men's Club, the Girls' Friendly Society, the Young Wives' Club, the Mothers' Union, and the Ranmoor Mutual Improvement Society; in the 1950s and 1960s summertime "Gay Garden Gatherings" were held in order to raise funds. Over the decades, many thousands of parishioners have contributed to local activities and made financial donations to projects all over the world[12]. The interior of the church was re-ordered between 1990 and 1993, removing some pews and modifying the chancel and altar, and the Parish Hall in Ranmoor Road was sold in 2005.

Photo 5.03
The second St John's church (here photographed in 2009) is now a listed building with many outstanding features.

2. Ranmoor College

Chapter 3 described how in 1860 Fulwood Road was extended to Nether Green from the bottom of what became Gladstone Road. On the northern side of that extension, where now are the apartments of Ranmoor View, a substantial building

Display Box Seven

SOME 1890s EXCERPTS FROM RANMOOR PARISH MAGAZINE

September 1891: Bell-ringers' Outing

"On Monday July 27th the Ranmoor Bell-ringers had their Annual Outing, the place selected being Southport, where they arrived at 10 a.m. Owing to unavoidable circumstances, the bells of Christ Church, Southport, could not be rung until 5 p.m., and . . . . very little ringing was done. An attempt was made on the next day for Holt's ten part, which unfortunately collapsed after ringing 1 hour 10 minutes. The ringers, however, had a very enjoyable time."

September 1891: Mothers' Meeting Outing

"On Friday August 14th, 35 members of the Mothers' Meeting, accompanied by the Vicar and several ladies and friends, left Ranmoor Parish Room at 10 a.m. in waggonettes for Castleton . . . . Castleton was reached about 2 o'clock. Having put up at the Nag's Head, a walking party was formed and a start was made for the Blue John Mine – a climb not easily forgotten . . . . At 5 o'clock all returned to the Inn, where a substantial meat tea had been provided . . . . A brighter or more successful outing could not well have been."

October 1891: The Choir Outing

"On Monday September 14th . . . . the members of our choir were enabled to spend a very pleasant day at the seaside. Leaving Sheffield by the early train, Blackpool was reached at 10.30. The early part of the day was unfortunately wet, but towards noon the weather cleared . . . . After an excellent dinner, the afternoon was spent in visiting the various places of amusement and interest . . . . We are sure that it is not a matter of indifference to the congregation to know that they all thoroughly enjoyed the holiday and outing, which they so well deserved."

November 1891: St John's, Ranmoor, Mutual Improvement Society

"We have during the last month established a Mutual Improvement Society for men over 21 years of age. A paper followed by a discussion will be read on the first and third Wednesdays in each month at 8 p.m. in the Parish Room, and lectures will occasionally be given."

April 1895: Annual Social Tea and Entertainment

This "took place on Shrove Tuesday, February 26th. At 6 p.m., when tea commenced, a large and representative gathering of the parishioners and seat-holders filled the Parish Room to overflowing. After an excellent tea, the following programme was rendered." This included a "piano solo by Miss Hartley"; songs, such as "There is a green hill far away" by Mr Garland, "The morning of life" by Mrs Arthur Laycock, and "The baby on the shore" by Mr Fox; recitations, such as "The women of Mumbles Head" by Miss A. Oldaker; and a duet "In the dusk of twilight" by Miss Helen and Miss Margaret Peace.

July 1895: Whit Monday Sunday School Treat

"On Whit-Monday June 3rd the children who attend the Ranmoor Sunday School met at the Parish Room at 10 a.m. Headed by the fife and drum band, they proceeded to Crosspool, where they were joined by the Crosspool Sunday School children. At 11 a.m. a short service was held in the church, during which the children sang very sweetly and accurately the special Whitsuntide hymns . . . . At 2.30 p.m. the children again assembled, and proceeded to the grounds of Riverdale. Tea was provided in the Parish Room at 5 p.m.

Photo 5.04
*Ranmoor College provided
training for ministers of religion
for half a century after 1864.
It was demolished in 1965.*

was erected in 1864 (2 on Map 5.01). This was a theological college to train ministers within the New Connexion branch of Methodism.

That branch no longer exists as a separate entity, but in the middle of the 19th century it had about 25,000 members and was important to many people in Sheffield. For example, in a religious census taken in 1851 more than 2,000 attended the five New Connexion churches in the town[13]. By 1881, Sheffield New Connexion attendance (in 12 locations) was approaching 3,000. The movement had split from other Methodists in 1797, seeking greater lay participation in ministry and church government. Its egalitarian emphasis was attractive to many work-people, including Thomas Firth, the father of Mark Firth who had built Oakbrook House in 1860[14] (see Chapter 4).

After an upbringing within the New Connexion, Mark had become an enthusiastic member. So too had his brother Thomas[15], who had developed a particular interest in the training of its ministers. The New Connexion had originally preferred its ministers to learn by attachment to senior colleagues, avoiding the creation of what might be viewed as an elite class. However, by the 1830s members were coming to favour more systematic theological education, and from 1846 funds had been sought for a training establishment.

With many other calls on limited finance, progress was slow until Thomas Firth the younger died in 1860. In his will he offered £5,000 for the construction and operation of a new college, provided that this was in or near Sheffield and that building work started within four years of his death. As pointed out in an 1862 newspaper article, "these stipulations had a beneficial effect in stimulating exertion and preventing any jealous contention as to the location of the college"[16]. Thomas Firth had in his lifetime made many contributions to religious causes in this country and overseas, apparently aiming to give away ten per cent of his income in that way.

Subsequent fund-raising almost doubled the sum available (including £1,000 from Thomas's brother Mark), and land was purchased within George Wostenholm's development of the Ranmoor storths (see Chapter 3)[17]. Mark Firth was central to these activities, and he also served as treasurer of the new institution until 1878. It was he who laid the corner-stone in September 1862, behind which was placed a bottle containing current coins, the day's Sheffield newspapers and appropriate documents about the Methodist New Connexion and the College.

Ranmoor College opened in April 1864, containing 16 studies and bedrooms, a library, two lecture rooms, a dining hall, and separate accommodation for the Principal; it also housed three domestic servants. Its style was described as "English

Drawing 5.01
This 1873 picture gives a more cheerful impression of Ranmoor College than does Photo 5.04.

collegiate gothic of the 14th century", with gables, buttresses, gargoyles, pointed arches, elaborate windows, a central tower, and much ornamentation. A lodge was provided on Fulwood Road at the western edge of the site, housing a gardener and his family.

The first Principal (until 1876) was James Stacey (1818-1891), already a leading member of the New Connexion[18]. Students attended classes in theology, moral philosophy, church history, literature, logic, apologetics (arguments in support of Christian doctrine), and homiletics (principles and skills of preaching), in later years also learning Latin and Greek at Firth College in the town. They were also active as local preachers, and themselves attended the Methodist New Connexion chapel in Glossop Road, Broomhill, which had opened in 1863[19].

Although the course of training was envisaged as two years, students often attended for only a single year. The college was rarely full, with an average of 12 trainees[20], and appears to have retained its early routine and curriculum for several decades, based on a certain austere formality.

In 1907, the Methodist New Connexion joined with other groups to form the United Methodist Church[21]. One consequence of this was that the combined group had two theological colleges – at Ranmoor but also in Manchester. Both continued in operation, but World War One (1914-1918) drew away potential trainees, and in 1917 Ranmoor College was rented, and subsequently sold, to Sheffield City Council.

The Council first used the building as a hostel for the city's Teacher Training College (housing about 50 women), and then it was rented to the Royal Hospital as a home for nurses. During World War Two (1939-1945) it served as a Civil

Defence ("Air Raid Precaution") Station, staffed 24 hours a day. In 1947, it was leased by the University of Sheffield, becoming Ranmoor House for the accommodation of 50 male students. The building was demolished in 1965 and replaced by the current apartments (Ranmoor View). The University instead built a larger hall of residence in 1968 at the bottom of Shore Lane, retaining for that the name "Ranmoor House" in memory of its predecessor (see the account of Tapton Hall in Chapter 4).

3. Firth's Alms Houses

Another significant product of the Firth family's wealth and generosity took shape in 1869-1870. Mark Firth provided the inspiration, and also money for land, building and charitable investment, so that a set of alms houses for impoverished elderly people could be built in Nethergreen Road at the corner with Hangingwater Road (3 on Map 5.01).

Shown in Drawing 5.02, Firth's Alms Houses shared with Ranmoor College a design that was described as "early Gothic". The building contained 36 self-contained apartments on three levels, each with a bedroom, a living room and a cellar/pantry. Of these, 24 were for single persons who received seven shillings (£0.35) a week, and 12 were for married couples or siblings receiving ten shillings (£0.50) a week[22]. As was common at the time, toilet facilities were in a separate block in the grounds. A chapel was set in the middle of the building, and a minister was paid £50 a year to "watch over the spiritual interests of the almspeople", to offer brief daily prayers, and to conduct a full service on Sundays. The minister lived in a house next to the chapel[23]. Above that was a tower and spire, described as being in "early decorated style", containing a single bell[24].

To be accepted as a resident, a person had to be at least 60 years old, born in Sheffield, and "a recognised attendant of some Protestant place or places of worship". Written applications had to be supported by four written statements[25]. The trustees of the alms houses, initially mainly members of the Firth family, managed the charity's funds (originally donated by Mark Firth) as well as making decisions about residents and overall management.

Firth's Alms Houses continued as a notable feature of the area for almost a century. Photo 5.05

Drawing 5.02
In 1870, Mark Firth created these alms houses for 36 elderly people in Nethergreen Road. This 1873 drawing also illustrates clothing and transport at the time.

Photo 5.05
*Firth's Alms Houses around 1920.
This original building was
replaced by the current Firth's
Homes in 1969.*

shows how it extended along Hangingwater Road as well as facing Nethergreen Road. The 1870 buildings were demolished in 1968, and new accommodation (Firth's Homes) opened in 1969. This has 28 apartments, four bungalows and a warden's house. There is now a central meeting room which also serves as a chapel, but regular services are no longer held. The chaplain's role is filled by the minister of Nether Green Methodist Church (see Chapter 6).

Notes to Chapter Five

1 See page 267 of the *Pevsner Architectural Guide to Sheffield* by Ruth Harman and John Minnis (New Haven and London: Yale University Press, 2004).

2 This land had been offered for sale in August 1868, and it is likely that J. W. Harrison bought it then – next to his own residence, Tapton Grange. An 1874 plan (see Map 3.04) indicates that he owned the site in that year. He also paid for the boundary walls and for setting out the church grounds, designed by eminent horticulturalist Robert Marnock. Other professional activities of Robert Marnock are summarized in Note 24 at the end of Chapter 4.

3 In addition, John Newton Mappin paid for the closure in 1878 of Darwin Lane below Tapton Park Road. See also Note 46 in Chapter 4.

4 Comparable numbers of places were 750 in All Saints Ecclesall, 368 in Christ Church Fulwood, and 900 in St Mark's Broomhill.

5 J. Y. Cowlishaw (1830-1895) was also one of the two initial church-wardens, between 1879 and 1881. He had developed a successful business making knives (particularly silver fruit knives) and pearl handles for knives. He was also a director of the Masborough Brewery (owned by his uncle, J. N. Mappin), Newton Chambers and Company, and the Sheffield and Hallamshire Bank. After his uncle's donations to what became the Mappin Art Gallery, he was an active committee member for the gallery. In 1895, apparently depressed after his wife's death some months earlier, he committed suicide at home by shooting himself with one of his own sporting guns.

6 Some pews contained eight sittings, and a few individuals paid for more than one pew. For instance, in 1899 Frederick Thorpe Mappin rented 14 seats in two separated pews; he also paid almost as much again through a voluntary contribution. In that year, three members of the Firth family rented 21 sittings in three different pews. During the 1880s, the initial rent of £1.10.0 was reduced to £1.5.0 (£1.25). It was not unusual in the 1890s to refer to seat-holders and parishioners as separate groups.

7 That was also the case in Ecclesall and Fulwood Churches, but Ranmoor's Wesleyan Methodist Church had only about one-third occupancy and St Mark's at Broomhill was about two-thirds full.

8 See E. R. Wickham, *Church and People in an Industrial City* (London: Lutterworth Press, 1957).

9 The second St John's was built by William Bissett and Sons. This firm had constructed many significant buildings in the town, including the Central Schools, Firth College and the Mappin Art Gallery. They were also active in other parts of the country, with offices in Birmingham. William Bissett (c1827-1888) had started as a plumber and glazier, expanding to undertake major projects. He lived in Rock Mount, 402 Fulwood Road, from about 1878, but suffered a stroke in 1887. The firm was continued by his three sons, but it collapsed in bankruptcy in December 1889. At that point two of the sons fled the country.

10 Many other gifts are listed in the church's Anniversary Booklet of 1929, including several elaborate stained glass windows.

11 That building was purchased around 1980 by St John's from the Church Commissioners, with funds from several sources: the Sheffield Church Burgesses, sale of its own property in the area, and through donations and fund-raising activities by many parishioners. Its renovation included the creation of two apartments on the first floor.

12 For example, in the 1890s donations were made to bodies such as the British and Foreign Bible Society, the Church Aid Pastoral Society, the Colonial and Continental Church Society, the Irish Church Mission, the Indian and Crimean Veterans' Fund, and Missions to Seamen. In the 1960s and 1970s regular grants were made to the Church Missionary Society, Christian Aid, Mothers' Union Overseas, the Leprosy Mission and to many others, as well as frequent donations to charities in the Sheffield area.

13 On that Sunday, nearly 15,000 attended the 23 Anglican churches and 10,500 the 16 Wesleyan Methodist churches in Sheffield. In addition to Roman Catholics (about 4,000) and Independents (about 4,500), there were also many smaller groups – General Baptists, Particular Baptists, the Society of Friends, Unitarians, Primitive Methodists, the Wesleyan Association, the Catholic Apostolic Church, and others. See page 108 of E. R. Wickham, *Church and People in an Industrial City* (London: Lutterworth Press, 1957).

14 The Methodist New Connexion had close links with Sheffield. Its movement out of Wesleyan Methodism in 1797 was led by Alexander Kilham, a minister in the town, and its constitution was drawn up at a 1798 Sheffield conference. In that year, the New Connexion established Sheffield's first Sunday school (in Pea Croft), and the movement was active locally throughout the next century.

15 As noted in Chapter 4, another brother, Charles Henry, preferred to attend the parish church of St John's. After Mark Firth's death in 1880, so too did his widow (his second wife).

16 See page 2 of the *Sheffield and Rotherham Independent* of 26/09/1862. For example, New Connexion members in Manchester also had aspirations for a new college there.

17 The cost of the 1.75-acre site was about £900 including part of the new road. Vendor George Wostenholm donated £125 to the College fund.

18 James Stacey was the son of a Sheffield cutler who had been ordained in 1839. He is said to have been "slight in build, of delicate health, fastidious and reserved"; see E. Alan Rose's chapter "Ranmoor College 1864-1919" in *Preachers All*, edited by C. Dews (Leeds:

Yorkshire Branch of the Wesleyan Historical Society, 1987). On his retirement, aged 58, he moved to a house he had constructed at the bottom of Ranmoor Crescent (now number 7) on land purchased from Mark Firth. He then served (presumably part-time) as a classical tutor in Ranmoor College.

19 Broomhill Methodist New Connexion Chapel was located between Ashdell and Westbourne Roads, at their junction with Glossop Road. Mark Firth also contributed generously to its construction and he paid for its high-quality organ. The chapel was closed in 1942 and later demolished; an office block (Pegasus House) was subsequently built on the site.

20 In the census records between 1871 and 1901, resident student numbers were always less than 10.

21 At that time the New Connexion had about 45,000 members and about 250 ministers in the country as a whole.

22 The design of the central spine was for back-to-back homes, each with only a single external wall. That layout had been prohibited in Sheffield from 1864, but an application for planning permission was submitted, presumably successfully, on 21 May 1868. (The 1864 Minutes of the Highway Committee allow variations to the prescribed layout "at the discretion of the Council".) The architects were Hill and Swann of Leeds and Sheffield; William Hill had previously designed Ranmoor College for the Methodist New Connexion (see earlier in the chapter).

23 Consistent with Mark Firth's beliefs, initial ministers were from the Methodist New Connexion, but the rules permitted them to be "of some other Methodist or Nonconformist denomination professing the doctrine of the Trinity". Sheffield street directories as late as the 1950s indicate that services were then still held daily in summer in addition to regular Sunday services.

24 In addition to other uses, this was rung to mark the funeral of a resident – indicating his or her age by the number of peals. That procedure continued into the middle of the 20th century.

25 These were required to be (1) from a church minister and "three respectable members of the congregation" of a person's church "testifying to the fact of his or her attendance", (2) from three respectable members of another Protestant church "testifying to the candidate's good character", (3) from two respectable householders testifying that the candidate had insufficient means of support, and (4) from two "duly qualified medical men" testifying to a person's incapacity to earn his or her own living. See page 273 of Sheffield's *Return to the Charity Commission* (London: Her Majesty's Stationery Office, 1897).

CHAPTER SIX

Methodism in Ranmoor and Nether Green

The 19th century saw a national upsurge in religious interest and participation. Religious groups in Sheffield and elsewhere had considerable impact advocating moral ideals and assisting less fortunate members of society. For example, more than 100 day schools and Sunday schools were initiated by Sheffield's churches, providing basic education (not only religious) to children who would otherwise have received almost none (see Chapter 7). The beliefs and practices of religious groups played a major part in fostering the Victorian notion of respectability among the middle class and those of the working class who chose to become involved in church life.

By 1881, Sheffield had 178 places of worship, but less than a quarter of those belonged to the established Church of England. Instead, nonconformist groups (those which are Protestant Christian but do not conform to all the Anglican doctrines) had a greater number of chapels and meeting-houses and were increasingly influential in the town[1].

Primary among Sheffield's nonconformist denominations were several forms of Methodism. Of Sheffield's places of worship in 1881, 29 belonged to Wesleyan Methodists, 25 to Primitive Methodists, 15 each to United Methodist Free Churches and to Wesleyan Reform groups, and 12 to the Methodist New Connexion[2]. In David Hey's words, "Sheffield had long been a stronghold of Nonconformism; now it had become a Methodist borough"[3]. Some Ranmoor activities of the New Connexion have been considered in Chapter 5, and this chapter will look at Wesleyan Methodists and their successors (see Display Box 8).

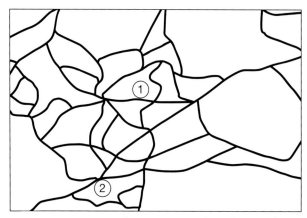

Map 6.01
Methodist churches in Ranmoor and Nether Green.
1, Wesleyan Methodist Chapel.
2, United Methodist Church.

Ranmoor Wesleyan Methodist Church

John Wesley set out on his years of Methodist preaching in 1738, and already in that year a convert to his cause had moved to Upper Hallam. David Taylor became employed as a domestic servant in Fulwood, and in addition preached for several years in the Sheffield area. John Wesley also occasionally conducted services locally, perhaps including Upper Hallam, and the foundations for a neighbourhood society gradually became established.

Display Box Eight

JOHN WESLEY AND METHODISM

"Methodist" is the term used to describe Protestant Christian denominations whose origins can be traced to the evangelical work of John Wesley (1703-1791)[14]. Himself a minister of the Church of England, John Wesley emphasized the need to study and practise religion through experience, reason and tradition in addition to a reliance on the Bible.

After a profound spiritual experience in 1738, John Wesley felt the need to promote his Christian faith widely, and he became an active preacher throughout the country. As a movement developed around him and his followers, missionary activities were extended into other countries, and Methodism became a world-wide form of religion. Local societies were formed, often meeting in homes or other non-church buildings, and outdoor preaching was encouraged where a larger audience could be expected.

Within his unceasing travels, John Wesley preached in Sheffield as early as 1742 and again on several later occasions. Methodism was initially the target of insult and even riot, facing criticisms for allegedly unsound doctrine and possible disloyalty to the established order – including the monarchy[15]. Several meeting-houses in Sheffield were destroyed by mobs of protesters during the 1740s. However, after a troubled start gradual progress saw its members and acceptability grow. Many Sheffielders appreciated the fervour and clarity of the Methodist message, its emphasis on equality of worth and personal responsibility, and its explicit concern to help those in need. John Wesley himself became well-known and was viewed rather like a "celebrity" of our own times. He reported that his visit to Sheffield in 1779 (preaching in Paradise Square) attracted "the largest congregation I ever saw on a weekday". Although it started as an evangelical contribution within the Church of England, Methodism gradually evolved into a separate denomination.

The earlier small meeting-houses were complemented in Sheffield from 1780 by the construction of larger places of worship[16]. Ranmoor Chapel was one of the earliest (in 1783), and by 1841 Sheffield supported at least 15 Wesleyan chapels in addition to approximately ten others for related Methodist denominations. By 1881, the Wesleyan Methodists had 29 chapels in Sheffield. Linked to the growth in numbers was a greater public acceptance, and by the middle of the 19th century Wesleyan and other forms of Methodism were established in society at all levels.

The several branches continued separately for several decades, with some combination in 1907. In 1932, almost all branches of Methodism came together into the Methodist Union, and Wesleyanism ceased to have a separate existence.

Drawing 6.01
The farm and beerhouse in Goole Green, Fulwood, in which Wesleyan services were held from about 1760.

That was inaugurated in 1756, with an initial 12 members. Around this time, services were sometimes held in the house or garden of Nathan Clayton, who lived on the northern side of Ranmoor Road. Another location was the farm and beerhouse of William Woodhouse (1726-1821) in Goole Green, Fulwood (Drawing 6.01); in 1764 he obtained a licence for preaching there, in addition to his licence for beer-selling[4].

Wesleyan Methodist supporters in the area continued without their own chapel for another two decades. (Meeting in houses or available rooms or in the open air was usual for the movement at this time.) Locally there were only about 20 committed individuals and funds were limited[5]. However, by 1776 plans had been made for a purpose-built place of worship on land occupied by Nathan Clayton (above) and owned by the Duke of Norfolk. Building was not undertaken until 1783, when a new chapel was opened in Ranmoor Road (location 1 in Map 6.01)[6]. It is shown in Photo 6.01 (probably in the 1860s), and its setting at the time was described in Chapter 2.

Ranmoor Chapel was the Methodists' first such building outside the town centre, and its initial trustees were almost all local people. In 1788, they included a file

Photo 6.01
Ranmoor had one of Sheffield's first Wesleyan chapels. Erected in 1783, here it is in the 1860s.

Photo 6.02
A 1908 gathering of Ranmoor Wesleyan Sunday school. Its banner refers to 1810 – the year of the School's foundation.

cutter, a saw plater and a clock maker, as well as William Woodhouse, the Fulwood farmer introduced above. Attendance increased slowly into the next century, drawing worshippers from other parts of the town as well as from nearby. A Sunday school was formed in 1810, for which a separate building was constructed in the grounds in 1815.

Subsequent decades saw the number of Sunday school pupils exceed 100, and attendance in the small chapel also increased, reflecting steady growth in the local population and consolidation of Methodism within the community. By the 1860s, the chapel was described as "dilapidated and uncomfortable" and "small, inconvenient and time-worn"[7]. Together with the school it was replaced in 1870[8].

The new buildings, designed by Sheffield architect John Dodsley Webster, were more substantial (260 sittings in the church) and in keeping with Victorian stylistic preferences. The design was described as "early geometrical", with a tower and spire rising to 85 feet (26 metres) and a gallery over the entrance porch (Photo 6.03).

A contemporary newspaper account indicated that the church does "not have any great pretensions to architectural beauty" since funds were scarce. Money had to be raised from well-wishers and by selling a section of land[9]. The school building (accommodating 150 children) was used as both a day school and a Sunday school[10]. Soon, however, both buildings proved too small, and extensions were built during the 1880s.

The day school was closed in 1901, and the building was then used for three years by the City Education Committee as a temporary location for pupils of the new Ranmoor Council School (later Nether Green School) until that was completed in 1904 (see Chapter 7). It also housed infants from that school during World War

Photo 6.03
The original Wesleyan chapel in Ranmoor Road was replaced by this more substantial building in 1870 (seen here around 1930). It was demolished in the mid-1960s.

One (1914-1918), when their building was taken over as a military hospital. Throughout the period, Sunday school activities were maintained, and the need for space was such that in 1907 the school-room was enlarged to twice its original size.

The church itself continued to attract worshippers, and it contributed actively to the local community. In 1932, several groups of Methodists (including the Wesleyans) joined together to become the Methodist Union, and as part of that national development the Ranmoor church's "Wesleyan Methodist" designation became simply "Methodist". For part of World War Two (1939-1945) it was occupied by civil defence members of the Home Guard.

However, by the late 1950s attendance at evening services had dwindled and financial demands were great. Within the Methodist church nationally pressures were growing to amalgamate neighbouring groups, and in 1962 the local Methodist circuit urged the creation of "one centre for the Fulwood/Nether Green/Ranmoor area with a minister".

There were attractions in combining Ranmoor activities with those of St George's in Nether Green (see below), and in 1963, after some years of deliberation, the two churches were joined as one. The final service in the Ranmoor Road church was held on 25 August 1963, and the site was sold for residential building in the following year. The church was demolished and replaced by the houses and apartments now on Chapel Close. St George's in Nether Green was at that time renamed as Hallam Methodist Church, serving both the previous societies.

Hallam Methodist Church

This church has stood since 1912 at the junction of Nethergreen and Fulwood Roads (2 in Map 6.01). It was initially known as Nether Green Church (between 1912 and 1942) and then St George's (1942-1963), before becoming Hallam Methodist Church in 1963.

Its origins lay in the work of the Methodist New Connexion introduced in Chapter 5. Staff and students of Ranmoor College (for training New Connexion ministers) contributed in many ways to local life, assisting with services in the small chapel of Firth's Alms Houses (also described in Chapter 5) and sometimes preaching in Broomhill New Connexion Chapel in Glossop Road. But they lacked a purpose-built home for worship in their own area.

In 1900, local New Connexion supporters purchased a site on Fulwood Road[11]. They quickly sold the rear section (on which was built Wood View Terrace), and a small building was erected in 1901 close to the back of the remaining site. This was intended as a Sunday school and a temporary chapel while funds were gathered for a more substantial place of worship, to be erected at the front of the site.

This second phase was carried out ten years later, with a United Methodist church opening in 1912[12]. The building (designed by W. H. Higginbottom of Nottingham) was said to be of Gothic design, and the space below its main hall (as the ground sloped downward) was left unfinished because of insufficient funds[13].

The church's financial position continued to be difficult for the next three decades, and in 1942 it was decided to amalgamate with Broomhill Chapel in Glossop Road. The latter was closed in that year (see Note 19 in Chapter 5), and Nether Green Methodist Church was renamed as St George's. The substantial organ in Broomhill Chapel was transferred to St George's in 1946 and was fully restored in 1994. With its larger combined membership, St George's gained in strength, and enhancements to the building and church activities continued to be made. As described in the previous section, in 1963 the two societies of St George's and Ranmoor together became Hallam Methodist Church.

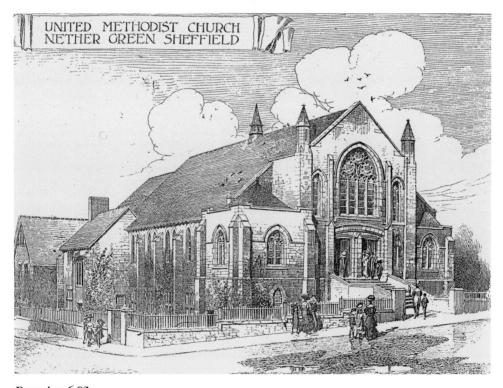

Drawing 6.02
An architect's 1911 drawing of what was originally known as Nether Green Church. Located at the junction of Fulwood and Nethergreen Roads, this was called St George's between 1942 and 1963, becoming Hallam Methodist Church from that year.

Notes to Chapter Six

1 Details of Sheffield's religious history are provided by E. R. Wickham in *Church and People in an Industrial City* (London: Lutterworth Press, 1957).

2 As well as several Independent groups, the Roman Catholic Church in that year had six Sheffield places of worship, the Society of Friends (Quakers) had a meeting house, and there were two Jewish synagogues.

3 See page 209 of *A History of Sheffield* (Lancaster: Carnegie Publishing Ltd., 1998).

4 Preachers usually walked from place to place and their schedule was uncertain. In order to announce that a Wesleyan service was imminent, Sarah, the wife of William Woodhouse, is said to have hung a white sheet on a tree which could be seen from afar.

5 Details of these and later developments have been presented by Neville Flavell in *From Goole Green to Nether Green: The Roots and History of Hallam Methodist Church*, published by that church in 2005.

6 In the list drawn up for the Upper Hallam Enclosure Award in the 1790s (see Chapter 1), the site (plot 173, still occupied by Nathan Clayton) was described as a "meeting house and garden". Nathan Clayton also occupied two adjacent plots, one probably containing his house. All were owned by the Duke of Norfolk.

7 See the *Sheffield and Rotherham Independent* of 09/11/1869.

8 The planning application of October 1869 was made by three trustees of the church: Joseph Pell (born 1823), a town councillor and leather merchant living at Hallam Head; Joseph Bramhall Ellison, a steel manufacturer and merchant who then lived in Ashcliffe adjacent to the church; and William Kirkby Peace (1821-1898), a steel and file manufacturer who lived in Brook Hill, Sheffield. (For the last of these see L. R. Peace, *The Peace Families of Sheffield*. Windsor: Thameslink, 1999.) The church's foundation stone was laid in November 1869 by Samuel Osborn (1826-1891), a steel refiner and merchant who came from an established Wesleyan family and was himself also a trustee of the church. A second foundation stone, for the school building, was laid by Councillor Pell.

9 After the 1805 Enclosure Award the land had thus passed from the Duke of Norfolk to the chapel trustees. An indenture of 06/10/1814 indicates that the trustees had "some time since" made an "absolute purchase" of "the cottage,

meeting house, buildings and hereditaments" from the Duke of Norfolk, freehold for £15.

10 The new school was placed behind the church, and behind the school itself was the customary separate building for "privies" (two) and a place to deposit ashes. The earlier school had been a short distance down Ranmoor Road, in a section to the east of the church that was sold in 1871 to Charles Nodder and then to Jabez Shipman; Cleveland House (68 Ranmoor Road) was built on that plot.

11 This was bought from Mrs Catherine Biggin, the widow of a farmer who had bought it in 1885 from the family of the late John Warbleton (1784-1852). He had obtained the leasehold rights in 1815 from William Murray of Banner Cross Hall, who had received it through his wife's links to the Dalton and Bright families (see Chapter 1). The land's freehold was purchased from the Duke of Norfolk in 1884.

12 As described in Chapter 5, the Methodist New Connexion had combined with other groups to take the United Methodist name in 1907.

13 Additional details and a wider account have been provided in Neville Flavell's book cited in Note 5. The lower space was rented as an additional class-room by the adjacent Nether Green School between 1926 and 1961, and finally completed as a New Hall in 1980.

14 The term was used in the early 1730s by students in Oxford University to criticise the "Holy Club" formed by John Wesley and his brother Charles (1707-1788). This group followed a rigorous daily schedule which included specific hours of the day for visiting the poor, administering to the sick, and attending religious services. They also prayed out loud three times a day, stopped for silent prayer every hour, and abstained from most forms of entertainment and luxury. These practices were not required of later "Methodists", but a systematic approach was retained.

15 It has been said that disturbances were sometimes encouraged by local Anglican church-men, in part because they resented intrusion into their area of religious responsibility.

16 Norfolk Street Chapel, opened in 1780, had 1,300 sittings of which 300 were free of rental charges. It cost more than £3,000, all of which had to be raised by public subscription. Carver Street Chapel was opened in 1804, with 1,150 sittings (350 free); it was said to be the finest Methodist chapel in the country at the time, and is now a pub (on the corner with West Street).

Church, Private and Council Schooling

For centuries past, most young people received very little formal education. Although children of wealthy parents might attend schools with an academic curriculum, poorer boys were mainly restricted to learning practical skills needed for a job (often the same as their father's) and most girls concentrated on sowing, cooking and other domestic activities.

By the middle of the 19th century many churches and voluntary organizations had become concerned to improve the education of working-class children. Initially, from about the 1780s, church schools provided lessons on Sundays. These had an explicitly religious and moral emphasis, but their content was in many cases gradually expanded also to cover reading and writing. Encouraged by societies such as the Church of England National Society (formed in 1811) and the British and Foreign Schools Society (a Nonconformist development from 1798 and renamed in 1814), churches started to provide week-day as well as Sunday education[1]. From 1833, government funding (later subject to satisfactory inspection) became available to help this process.

Although church day-schools were likely to have a qualified staff member, instruction was often given by teenage children who were themselves also pupils. Those were first identified as "monitors", but from the 1840s gradually became treated as "pupil-teachers"[2].

Attendance at church and other (so-called "voluntary") schools was sometimes free of charge but usually required payment of one or two pennies a week. Church schools were explicitly linked to a particular denomination and they emphasized religious thinking within that denomination[3], often through procedures that were strict and formal. Also available were private "academies" which usually emphasized classical themes. Instead of those two kinds of school, many parents took advantage of the more casual teaching which was offered by local people, mainly women, in their own homes. The number of such "dame schools" increased rapidly in the first part of the 19th century, providing basic instruction for children and also convenient child-care for their parents. Attendance was again at a cost of one or two pence a week, but intermittent absence to assist with family or other activities was considered acceptable.

Dame-school quality varied widely, and was often extremely poor by modern standards. Conditions, facilities and teaching materials were very basic, with lessons being held in the kitchen or another room. "Dames" usually lacked any qualifications, and they sometimes attended simultaneously to their domestic chores[4].

For most working-class children, education (sometimes part-time) lasted two or three years at the most. Their parents had themselves received little schooling, and in many cases needed their children to earn money for the family or to help with domestic activities. A Royal Commission of Enquiry into the Employment of Children reported in 1840 that "scarcely one-third" of working-class children in Sheffield "are even able to read fairly, and not one-half attend day-schools at all"[5].

Writing in 1846 about the situation in Sheffield, the Reverend Robert Bayley bemoaned the "shoals of ragged, dirty children, who are educating themselves in all sorts of mischievous indolence; preparing, by too rapid tuition, to become the pests of society in a few years . . . . Scarcely one in a hundred of their parents can read his bible fluently, or write his own name. How can it be expected that they should value Education? . . . . Their apathy and objections have to be overcome, and these can only be overcome by opening schools"[6].

An 1849 directory of Sheffield lists more than 150 "academies" in the town. A few of these were substantial, such as the Anglican Collegiate School near Ecclesall Road (founded in 1835) and the Wesleyan Proprietary School (later called Wesley College) in Glossop Road (1838)[7], and several others also had several hundred pupils. However, many schools were very much smaller, and those were rarely recorded in currently-available documents. They often remained in a particular house for only a brief period, as the "dame" moved into another rented property, and detailed information about their activities is lacking. Only one "academy" is identified in 1849 for Ranmoor, but other directories of 1833 and 1843 cite (without location) a single "day school" in Ranmoor. (The named teacher differs between the years.)[8]

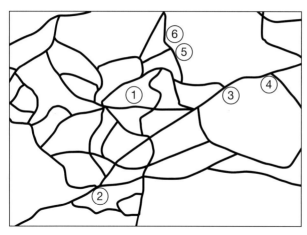

Map 7.01
Principal schools in Ranmoor and Nether Green.
1, Ranmoor Wesleyan School
(1870-1901).
2, Ranmoor Council School
(1904+).
3, Notre Dame School (1935+).
4, St Marie's Primary School
(1973+).
5, Tapton School (1960+).
6, King Edward VII Lower School
(1969+).

Sheffield School Board 1870-1903

With an expanding middle-class and a growing concern for education to cope with new technological complexity, national pressure for more systematic schooling increased through the 19th century. The 1870 Elementary Education Act introduced major changes and expanded provision considerably. Existing church and other schools were allowed to continue, receiving increased financial help, and in addition local "school boards" were to be elected with powers to build, maintain and manage their own schools for children between five and 13 years. School boards' activities were to be financed jointly by central government and local rates, and pupils' payment for attendance was to be up to three pence a week. Attendance was not initially compulsory, partly because of a shortage of schools[9]. However, schooling became free in 1891, and by then all children of elementary age were required to attend each day.

Sheffield's first School Board was elected by ratepayers in November 1870, with 15 members chosen from 52 candidates. Many of the candidates emphasized their

Drawing 7.01
*John F. Moss was Clerk to the
Sheffield School Board between
1870 and 1903. He built Cliffe
End at the top of Ranmoor Road
in 1879.*

religious affiliation. That influenced voting decisions since there was widespread concern about schools' possible bias in favour of particular denominations to the detriment of others. From among their members, the Board chose two prominent residents of Ranmoor as their chairman and vice-chairman – Sir John Brown and Mark Firth respectively. Those two played a major part in creating Sheffield's educational framework; their careers have been described in Chapter 4.

Another Ranmoor citizen was also at the heart of School Board activities. John Francis Moss (1844-1907) was appointed as its Clerk (in effect chief officer), and he served the Board throughout its existence (to 1903) and also (until his death in 1907) its successor, the city's Education Committee. He moved to Ranmoor in 1871, subsequently (1879) building Cliffe End at the top of Ranmoor Road (see Chapter 10), where he lived until 1890. J. F. Moss (Drawing 7.01) was extremely successful in co-ordinating and driving forward the Board's work, and Sheffield's education system gained a high national reputation under his guidance.

In March 1871, John Moss summarized for the new Board the local situation. He emphasized the inadequacy of many of the dame schools: "for the most part [the teachers] are females – many of them widows or aged people – who earn by this means a scanty livelihood instead of being dependent altogether on the Parish. The education of a large majority of them is only very limited – some of them seem unable to spell correctly simple words of two syllables". The report described one teacher who "teaches reading only, and appears to attend to household work at the same time", and another who indicated that "the parents of some children are in the habit of getting too much beer every week or two, so that they cannot pay the 'school money' and the children don't come"[10].

The Sheffield School Board immediately set about creating the requisite accommodation for all local children aged between five and 13. In total, 22 new schools were constructed, no less than 12 of them within the Board's first three years. A related task was to identify and count the town's children, setting in place procedures to monitor and increase their attendance; school attendance officers were appointed from 1872. Already by 1874, attendance in elementary schools had increased by 100% (the largest increase in the country), and by 1902 the Board claimed nearly 90% of full attendance[11]. Over that period, the population of Sheffield had approximately doubled, but school attendance increased more than fivefold.

Board schools were erected in Crookesmoor, Fulwood, Hunter's Bar, Walkley and Whiteley Wood, and some Ranmoor children no doubt attended those,

Drawing 7.02
Ranmoor Council School on its opening in 1904. It was described at the time as "the latest type of elementary school".

walking there and back each day. In addition, church and privately-run schools continued outside the Board system, educating a substantial proportion of young people. In Ranmoor, Misses S. A. and E. Blenkhorn ran a "ladies school" in Graham Road (with some boarders) in the late 1870s[12], and a larger establishment was that of the Wesleyan Church in Ranmoor Road (number 1 in Map 7.01). As described in Chapter 6, that church had been rebuilt in 1870 with a school-house at its rear. Its Sunday school had been active since 1810, and a day-school for boys, girls and infants was opened after the church's 1870 reconstruction.

Known as Ranmoor Wesleyan School or Ranmoor Day School, this catered for up to about 150 pupils. It was recognized as efficient by the School Board, thus being eligible for grant support, but over the years it came to have increasing difficulty meeting official requirements for accommodation and facilities. The school closed in 1901, but pupils remained in a temporary Board school on the same site, before moving in 1904 to their new school. This was Ranmoor Council School, which is described below. (That started as a project by the School Board, but construction was taken over by the new Sheffield Education Committee when all school boards were abolished in 1903[13].)

Photo 7.01
Ranmoor Council School around 1920. The caretaker's house is to the right of the picture.

Among the private schools in Sheffield were several which offered more substantial and advanced education, perhaps appealing to middle-class residents of Ranmoor. In addition to the Collegiate School and Wesley College (founded in the 1830s; see above), the Girls' High School was opened in 1878, and preparatory schools included Westbourne (from 1885) and Birkdale (1905). Although supposedly restricted to the elementary level, the town's School Board took steps to develop advanced instruction by opening in 1880 the Central Schools in Leopold Street. Those included infant and junior schools, but also a higher grade school with a technical emphasis[14].

The wealthy merchants and manufacturers who moved into Ranmoor had typically been educated in the city's more academic schools[15]. In addition, it was not unusual for some part of their education to have been in boarding schools elsewhere in this country or abroad. Several Victorian Ranmoor residents thus had a perspective that extended well beyond Sheffield, and many were prosperous enough to ensure that their own children also received part of their education outside the town.

Local Schools in the 20th Century

For younger children, an elementary school was opened in 1904 by the Education Committee. This was Ranmoor Council School, built on land in Fulwood Road purchased in 1901 from Sheffield Town Trustees (number 2 in Map 7.01). During the two-year building period, approximately 150 children were taught in what was called Ranmoor Temporary Board School, in premises rented from the Wesleyan Church in Ranmoor Road (see above). From 1904, these children were also in the new building on Fulwood Road.

Photo 7.02
A lesson in Ranmoor Council School around 1910.

Photo 7.03
Units of area: an outdoor lesson in Ranmoor Council School around 1908.
Headmaster J. Eaton Feasey ensured that the grounds were regularly used for teaching.

Faced with stone from the nearby Bole Hill quarries, Ranmoor Council School (Drawing 7.02 and Photo 7.01) was built for 600 pupils. It had eight classrooms (three more were added in 1910) and a large central hall from which all classrooms could be supervised. Separate playgrounds and playsheds were provided for boys and girls (each with drinking fountains and pencil sharpeners), and entrances to the school were similarly segregated.

The school's first head teacher (until 1921) was Jesse Eaton Feasey (1869-c1950). He was an enthusiastic and progressive educator (indicated in the 1901 census as a "science master"), who was also active as a Sunday school teacher and as an author of books for children[16]. One of his early initiatives was to establish gardens in the school grounds, which were tended by pupils and used extensively for teaching a variety of subjects. Some of the school's lessons are illustrated in Photos 7.02 and 7.03, and another view is Photo 9.07 in Chapter 9.

J. Eaton Feasey was soon appointed an Honorary Lecturer in Education at the University of Sheffield (opened in 1905), and he encouraged the use of Ranmoor Council School for teaching practice and for trying out new procedures; it thus became known as a "University Demonstration School"[17]. Many trainee teachers spent time in the school, and these attachments continued into subsequent decades.

In the early years, a school's income was strongly determined by the number of children in attendance[18]. The Ranmoor School log-book (a daily diary required to be kept by each head teacher until 1974) frequently indicated that lessons (and thus the school's income) had been hampered by poor attendance caused by bad weather or periods of illness. In addition to coughs and colds, early log-book entries recorded epidemics of diphtheria, ringworm, scarlet fever, whooping cough, measles, mumps and chicken-pox. For several decades the school included a special section for children with different forms of handicap, sometimes referred to as the "cripples section". Staff were frequently moved at short notice between schools to cover needs elsewhere, and problems from enforced sudden regrouping of pupils were frequently noted. Most entries in the head teachers' log books are of that kind, but some more unusual excerpts are included in Display Box 9.

During World War One (1914-1918), the school buildings were taken over as a military hospital, with Royal Army Medical Corps staff from the Territorial Army

Display Box Nine

ENTRIES IN NETHER GREEN SCHOOL LOG BOOKS

7 November 1904: Councillor Nowill called this morning to make enquiries about underfed children. There are no children who come breakfastless, but there are a few who could be recommended for free breakfasts if such were provided.

29 June 1905: Criticism lessons have been given . . . . on a typical seed (the broad bean) and on the magnet and mariner's compass.

11 July 1905: In honour of the visit of their Majesties the King and Queen of England to Sheffield to open the University, July 12 1905, medals were presented to the children this afternoon. . . . . The children were assembled in the hall and after distribution they sang the National Anthem.

3 November 1905: Sir Frederick Thorpe Mappin Bart. M.P. called to protest against the "abominable waste of ratepayers' money" involved in the use of fish-tail burners instead of incandescent gas-lights.

19 May 1907: During the past fortnight work has proceeded vigorously in the gardens. Girls' plots were laid out, 25 each to plant a plant. A plantation of 27 forest trees has been made, being all different.

15 February 1912: There are a few children in every class who need special attention in Singing – the training of the ear and voice. These children are receiving a special lesson each week.

7 March 1915 (*i.e., during World War One*): Three Belgian refugees admitted. Two girls speak Flemish and some English and some French, but the boy speaks only Flemish.

30 April 1915: Work stopped at 11.00 a.m., all children employed in helping to make respirators for the army. 320 were made.

21 June 1916: This afternoon the Programmes, Medals and chocolates, presented to the children by the City of Sheffield, in honour of the coronation of their Majesties King George V and Queen Mary, were distributed... The children gave a short programme of singing, including "The Coronation Ode" and the National Anthem ... Hearty cheers for the King and Queen, our Visitors, and our Empire concluded the ceremony.

11 November 1918: This day at 11.00 a.m. the war ended. The school assembled outside the Parish Church, sang, saluted the Flag, cheered, and then entered the Church for a short Thanksgiving service conducted by the Vicar[21].

3 December 1923: The school has been successful in winning the Shield presented by Sir William Clegg for the best cultivated school garden under the Education Committee.

30 September 1938: Miss Elliott and Mr Thraves attended a special A.R.P.[22] lecture this afternoon, and for the next two days will be employed fitting and distributing gas masks from this school.

1 September 1939: The school is closed today, the entire staff attending Salmon Pastures School to assist in the evacuation of children.

13 December 1940: This morning all the staff reported for duty but very few children. The severe air-raid which lasted from 7.00 p.m. on the 12th until 4.30 a.m. on the 13th accounted for the small attendance. Neither teachers nor scholars were in a fit condition to remain, so I dismissed them all.

4 June 1943: The War Savings effort on behalf of the "Wings for Victory" campaign ended today with the school having subscribed the magnificent total of £2,522.

20-21 May 1947: The first May Day celebrations in the history of the school took place, with maypole dancing, crowning ceremonies, installation of the School Captain, and singing of hymns and "Jerusalem".

21 January 1960: Superintendent Marshall (Western Division Police) visited the school to enquire about policemen using the premises for mashing tea.

27 September 1965: School closed to celebrate Magna Carta.

24 April 1969: The police horse visited the school this morning.

caring for wounded soldiers in 110 beds (see Photos 7.04, 7.05 and 7.06). For that period, the pupils were moved to classrooms nearby – in the adjacent Methodist Chapel (infants), St John's Parish Hall in Ranmoor Road (boys) and the Wesleyan Chapel also in Ranmoor Road (girls).

Ranmoor Council School was renamed as Nether Green Council School in 1928, and has since been restructured in several ways[19]. Since 1992 it has been known as Nether Green Junior School, and it currently caters for approximately 370 pupils aged between 7 and 11.

Another school opened in Ranmoor in 1935 (number 3 in Map 7.01), when the Sisters of Notre Dame of Namur built premises in the grounds of Oakbrook, a house they had occupied as a convent since 1919 (see Chapter 4). The nuns' order had been in Sheffield since 1855, and they already had a school in Cavendish Street – Notre

Photos 7.04 to 7.06
Patients and staff of Nether Green Military Hospital in Ranmoor Council School during World War One.

90

Dame High School. Their two Sheffield schools operated separately until 1948, when they were amalgamated, with Oakbrook primarily serving the older pupils. In 1976, the school joined the country's comprehensive system, providing for boys and girls between 11 and 18, and the Cavendish Street school was closed in 1988.

The Sisters transferred the school and its grounds to the Catholic Diocese of Hallam in 1989, and they left Sheffield in 1991. Notre Dame High School has since expanded its buildings and its activities, now also operating as a specialist technology college[20]. Recent additions include a sports hall, a technology block, a music centre, and an open learning centre. With a total of approximately 1,300 pupils, its sixth form contains around 250 students.

As shown on Map 7.01, three other schools were opened in Ranmoor in the 1960s and 1970s. St Marie's Catholic Primary School (number 4) was built in the north-east corner of Oakbrook's grounds in 1973, currently having about 270 pupils aged between 4 and 11. Tapton and King Edward VII Schools were constructed in the previous decade on land to the east of Darwin Lane. The former (number 5 on the map) opened in 1960 and was rebuilt in 2001. It has been awarded specialist status in both science and arts, and has around 1,600 pupils between 11 and 18, of whom about 450 are in the sixth form.

King Edward VII School has long been in Glossop Road, originally as Wesley College (see above). Wesley College amalgamated with Sheffield Grammar School (located in Collegiate Crescent) to form King Edward VII School in 1905. In 1969, that school opened a second campus in Darwin Lane (6 in Map 7.01), through amalgamation with Crosspool Secondary Modern School already on the site. Those buildings (accommodating the Lower School) were replaced by new ones in 2001, and the King Edward VII Lower School now caters for around 690 boys and girls aged between 11 and 14. As a whole (with the Upper School in Glossop Road) it has about 2,200 pupils between 11 and 18, including around 500 in the sixth form. It has been designated as a specialist language college and training school.

Notes to Chapter Seven

1 For example, the Church of England National Society erected by subscription a substantial school in Sheffield's Carver Street in 1812, and by 1850 the Society operated almost 20 day schools and 25 Sunday schools in the neighbourhood. An 1870 report to the Sheffield School Board identified 50 local schools aided by a parliamentary grant, of which all but two were explicitly linked to a religious denomination.

2 Children who were pupil-teachers also received some training as instructors. That was traditionally provided only by their headteacher, but from the 1870s external courses became available. Pupil-teachers (at least 14 years of age by that decade) were then able to take examinations after three years, perhaps moving on to more advanced teacher training.

3 For instance, the stated purpose of the Church of England National Society was that "the national religion ... should be the first and chief thing taught to the poor".

4 Although many dame schools were undoubtedly inadequate, some privately-run institutions had high educational standards. In middle-class districts, the quality of education provided was often substantial, creating a firm base for the careers of many successful merchants, manufacturers and professional people. See D. P. Leinster-Mackay, Dame schools: A need for review, *British Journal of Educational Studies*, 1976, 24, 33-48.

5 See the Introduction to *The Sheffield School Board 1870-1903* by J. H. Bingham (Sheffield: Northend, 1949).

6 Excerpted from page 9 of the *People's College Journal*, 1846. R. S. Bayley opened the People's College in 1842, providing lessons between 6.30 and 7.30 in the mornings and between 7.30 and 9.30 in the evenings. Initially located in George Street, it continued in various forms (including also a day school and a Sunday school) until 1878. See G. C. Moore Smith, *The Story of the People's College, Sheffield* (Sheffield: Northend, 1912).

7 As was common, those two schools had explicitly religious as well as educational intentions. Sheffield Collegiate School aimed "to provide for the children of the upper classes of the town a course of instruction in classical learning, mathematics, science and literature in conformity with the religious principles of the Church of England". The Wesleyan Proprietary School set out to combine "the advantages of a sound classical and literary education with a religious and Wesleyan training"; see R. Millington, *A History of the Sheffield Training College* (Sheffield: Sheffield Training College, 1955). A Wesley College advertisement in 1856 indicated that "the utmost importance is attached to Moral and Religious Culture, and ample time is devoted to it". In addition to religious instruction during week-day classes, evening and weekend sessions for boarders included "expository and theological lectures" and scripture reading "under the superintendence of the Governor, the Reverend Samuel Waddy".

8 Some aspects of education in Sheffield from 1843 are reviewed in pages 298 to 363 of *The History of the City of Sheffield 1843-1993* (volume 2: Society), edited by C. Binfield, R. Childs, D. Hey, D. Martin and G. Tweedale (Sheffield: Sheffield Academic Press, 1993). See also sections in *A History of Labour in Sheffield*, by S. Pollard (Liverpool: Liverpool University Press, 1959).

9 A Sheffield bye-law of 1871 permitted non-attendance by children who lacked a school within two miles of their home.

10 See page 7 of *The Sheffield School Board 1870-1903* by J. H. Bingham (Sheffield: Northend, 1949).

11 To cope with the expanding number of pupils, schools also became larger. By 1892, Sheffield had 23 schools with over 1,000 pupils, including four with more than 1,500.

12 The Blenkhorn family (with father George, born in 1794) had previously operated a boarding school in Lincolnshire. By the 1881 census, Sarah Ann was running a similar school on her own near Selby in Yorkshire. Other private schools in the Ranmoor area at different times included 91 Endcliffe Vale Road (c1915-c1925), 405 Fulwood Road (c1930-c1935), 411 Fulwood Road (c1929-c1970), 69 Nethergreen Road (c1902-c1935), 157 Oakbrook Road (c1902-c1907) and 23 (also in some years 25) Ranmoor Crescent (c1910-c1925).

13 The 1902 Education Act created 330 local education authorities across the country, and a greater emphasis was placed on secondary and technical education. "Board schools" became "Council schools".

14 The last of those moved to High Storrs in 1933. It retained the name "Central School" until it became High Storrs Grammar School in 1940 and High Storrs School in 1969.

15 For example, several incomers to Ranmoor had attended the National School in Carver Street or the Collegiate School in Ecclesall. Others had been to well-regarded private "academies" such as that of Samuel Eadon in Eldon Street or Edward Hebblethwaite in Paradise Square.

16 Publications by J. Eaton Feasey included *Religion, Morals and Manners: A Course of Bible Teaching; Poems and Prose for Comparative Study; In the Open Air: A Series of Out-of-Door Lessons in Arithmetic, Mensuration, Geometry, etc., for Primary and Secondary Schools; In the Garden: A Series of Lessons in Nature Study; Robin Hood and Other Tales of Yorkshire*; as well as many *Notes on Scripture Lessons*.

17 At that time, the University's Department of Education provided professional training for students of the University Training College and also Saturday morning courses for teachers already in post.

18 School registers were regularly checked by visiting Council officials to ensure that financial claims were legitimate.

19 Developments have been illustrated by Marie Taylor in her book, *Nether Green School* (Sheffield: ALD Design and Print, 2004). For several decades two schools worked separately on the site (the "infants' school" and the "mixed school") and street directories referred in the plural to "Ranmoor Council Schools".

20 The school and its background have been described by Gabrielle Wilkinson in *A History of Notre Dame School* (Sheffield: Notre Dame High School, 2004).

21 This event was later described by the vicar of St John's in these terms: "November 11 1918: Germany signed the terms of the Armistice. Hostilities ceased at 11.00 a.m. Flag was raised in the Church grounds by Lady Bingham. The National Anthem was sung, and a service of thanksgiving was immediately held in St John's Church. The Church bells were rung. The Church was decorated with flags for the next Sunday and the following weeks."

22 These initials stand for "Air Raid Precaution", and were widely used in World War Two (1939-1945). The Air Raid Precaution Act of 1937 had required local authorities to draw up plans to protect their population, including setting up a voluntary service of Air Raid Wardens. (A local base was in Ranmoor College: see Chapter 5.) During the war, more than a million volunteers were trained as observers, ambulance drivers and providers of first aid. Wardens also monitored the "black-out", ensuring that external lights were extinguished at night to reduce information available to enemy aircraft. They issued gas-masks to protect against gas attacks from the air, and also air-raid shelters, for example made of curved corrugated iron sheets.

Beerhouses and Inns

B y the late 1700s alcoholic drink was firmly established at the heart of English life. Beer (fermented and thus cleared of bacteria) was commonly drunk as the usual way to quench thirst, since alternatives were often harmful or unpleasant. In town, water could be polluted and milk might contain chemicals to extend its shelf-life. Coffee was highly taxed until 1808, and tea was too expensive for working people until the 1830s. Other non-alcoholic drinks such as lemonade or ginger-beer were not widely produced until late in the century. It was usual for families and large estates to brew their own beer for personal consumption[1].

How did the Ranmoor-area pubs fit into that general picture? Let's look first at the national scene in Victorian England, within which local lives were led.

Alcohol and Temperance

Intoxicants were widely thought to be nutritious and to impart physical stamina. Beer was considered the normal accompaniment to hard physical labour, and a desirable male physique had what we might now describe as a "beer belly", considered to indicate strength. The medical profession was dependent on alcohol in many of its suggested remedies, and beer was widely supplied in hospitals to avoid illness from infected water. The perceived benefits of alcohol were reinforced by early insurance companies, which preferred to cover alcohol drinkers and sometimes refused to insure abstainers[2].

The drinking of beer was sometimes claimed to be desirable because its consumption of malt and barley gave support to some of the nation's farmers. Beer was also considered to be preferable to the currently-popular gin, with associated public drunkenness. An uncontrolled beer-supply was advocated by some believers in "free trade", a political and economic doctrine that sought to open markets of all kinds to competition in the expectation of lower prices.

Arguments of that kind came together to create the Beer Act of 1830. Duty on beer was removed, and beer-selling licenses were taken out of magistrates' control and made available to any householder who paid a two-guinea annual fee; beerhouses registered in that way were also permitted to brew their own beer to sell. Magistrates retained their licensing control of inns and taverns; these differed from beerhouses in that they were allowed to sell spirits such as gin, brandy and whisky as well as claret, port, sherry and other wines.

After 1830 the number of beerhouses increased rapidly in Sheffield as well as elsewhere, although part of that increase may have been due to some previously unlicensed establishments now becoming legal[3]. The public houses of Ranmoor may have started around this time, but in the absence of central control and record-keeping early beerhouse information is limited[4].

Beerhouses remained free of magistrates' control until 1869. Prior to that year, all the Ranmoor establishments had acquired licenses as full public houses, and thus were permitted also to sell wines and spirits[5]. They probably served simple meals, and may have provided limited lodging accommodation. Pubs also sought to attract customers by offering rooms for group meetings and entertainment facilities such as billiard tables and bowling greens. (An 1889 advertisement for the Bull's Head refers to a "cricket ground attached"[6].) Some pubs were also informal employment exchanges, where information could be gained about labouring and other jobs. Credit was sometimes provided to established customers.

Large undivided customer spaces were not introduced into pubs until later, and separate rooms (originally sometimes deriving from a building's residential use[7]) gradually became differentiated in terms of furnishing, prices and titles – public bar, tap room, private bar, parlour, lounge, saloon, and (in the 20th century) cocktail bar. Bars in the sense of counters onto which glasses were placed did not come into general use until later in the 1800s, and drinks were carried to the customer by waiters, potboys or barmaids[8].

During the Victorian period an anti-alcohol movement was active throughout the country, seeking to reduce drinking and drunkenness. The national picture is summarized in Display Box 10[9]. Within Sheffield and elsewhere the temperance movement organized public exhibitions, distributed pamphlets, and held meetings in praise of abstinence. Several temperance groups arranged processions through the town. For example, the Sheffield Band of Hope Union's annual Gala Day saw large numbers of children and adults converge on the Botanical Gardens in Clarkehouse Road. The procession was made up of bands and horse-drawn wagons, with prizes given for the best designs.

An 1884 programme for the Gala Day describes how "great public meetings" and a "grand display of banners" would be held. There was "music in various parts of the gardens", and ginger beer could be bought. Children were "supplied with a mug of tea and a piece of plum loaf for 3 pence", and "Montgolfier balloons" and a "rotary stereoscopic exhibition" were available[10]. A choir of several thousand Sheffield children offered encouraging songs such as "Onward, still onward!", "Take back the bowl" and "Temperance and liberty for ever"[11].

Other local anti-alcohol groups included the Sheffield branch of the Independent Order of Rechabites, which was instituted in 1837. Taking their name from a biblical tribe which drank no alcohol, the Rechabites provided insurance cover for members' sickness, funeral and accident expenses. Members were required to take and keep the pledge of total abstinence and to report others who broke that pledge. For the local movement as a whole, a substantial Temperance Hall was built through public subscription near the top of Townhead Street in 1856[12], and smaller Temperance Halls were sited in Barker's Pool and elsewhere[13]. Temperance members were prominent in the advancement of choral and other music in the town, organizing many concerts and providing instruction and practice for children and adults.

The temperance movement also sought to have impact through local political and administrative decisions. For example, most members of the 1880s Sheffield School Board (see Chapter 7) were temperance supporters, and the Board made several recommendations in favour of temperance activities in schools. Pupils were advised to read books such as the *Manual of Health and Temperance* and the *Temperance Lesson Book*; the local Band of Hope was allowed to give lectures in schools on the physiological effects of alcohol and the scientific basis of temperance; and schools were urged to appoint "teachers in temperance science" analogous to their demonstrators in cookery and traditional aspects of science.

Display Box Ten

THE NATIONAL TEMPERANCE MOVEMENT

Opposition to alcoholic drink among many sections of Victorian society came together in what became known as the temperance movement. Preceded in America, Ireland and Scotland, this developed in England from 1830.

National societies included the British and Foreign Temperance Society (founded in 1831), the British Association for the Promotion of Temperance (from 1835), and the National Temperance Society (1842). The Salvation Army (established in 1865 and named in 1878), the British Women's Temperance Association (from 1876) and Quaker religious groups were also active and influential. The Band of Hope, a Christian temperance society for working-class children, was founded in 1847 and soon had a widespread presence throughout the country.

Temperance workers initially agitated against alcohol in the form of spirits rather than supposedly healthy British beer, being concerned to reduce people's intake rather than to stop that altogether. However, many members of the movement soon came to promote total abstinence ("teetotalism"), with a central activity of "signing the pledge" that one would never again drink alcohol. Local meetings often had a religious fervour within what was sometimes seen as a "holy cause"; for example, pledge-signing sometimes echoed the practice of baptism.

Temperance efforts included the publication and distribution of literature about the evils of drunkenness and harmful effects on health, families and society. Sympathisers wrote doom-laden books with titles like *The Bottle* and *The Drunkard's Children*, a huge number of pamphlets were produced, and rallies, marches, demonstrations and leisure excursions were organized. Pressure was exerted on local councillors, magistrates and publicans, as well as nationally through newspapers and contact with members of parliament. Coffee houses were established in many areas, aiming to draw people away from beerhouses and inns[26]. These often contained facilities similar to pubs, and they served non-alcoholic drinks of all kinds (not merely coffee) as well as providing food. They sometimes sought to improve their customers through anti-alcohol notices and slogans and by organizing temperance or religious meetings.

During the 1850s, following legislation in some American states, attention shifted from the persuasion of individuals to legal prohibition on a national scale: if no alcohol was sold to anyone in the country, drunkenness was expected to disappear. The United Kingdom Alliance was formed in 1853 to promote legislation preventing the sale of any alcohol; the Alliance and other groups also sought to restrict supply in the meantime by pressing local magistrates to refuse license applications.

Despite decades of temperance effort, alcohol consumption remained high. By the end of the 19th century it was becoming accepted that the drink problem could not helpfully be separated from other socio-economic issues; instead, a range of factors harming the welfare of working class communities came to receive attention. That more general perspective gained support in the next century through groups like the Labour Party (originating in 1900), which advocated collective action to change many aspects of working people's living conditions.

Photo 8.01
William J. Clegg (1826-1895), shown here as mayor of Sheffield, built Cliffe Tower in Whitworth Road and was a prominent anti-alcohol campaigner.

Some temperance supporters may have been active in Ranmoor, but attention was directed mainly at working-class districts in the town, where drunkenness had repeatedly been shown to be particularly high. For a brief period one Ranmoor resident was at the heart of national as well as local temperance activity, when William Johnson Clegg (1826-1895) moved into the newly-built Cliffe Tower (10 Whitworth Road) from 1887. A solicitor, he became Sheffield's first Official Receiver in Bankruptcy from 1883, was elected to the town council in 1872, was mayor three times, became an alderman in 1880, and for many years was the leader of the local Liberal party[14].

The Clegg family were strongly committed to the temperance cause, and William J. Clegg rose to become "one of the giants of northern teetotalism"[15]. He regularly addressed open-air and other meetings, and he led the Sheffield Sunday Closing Association and the Sheffield branch of the United Kingdom Alliance. He became chairman of the British Temperance League and made substantial contributions to temperance thinking at the national level. Soon after his death in 1895, Cliffe Tower in Ranmoor was sold.

The impact of the temperance movement on national drinking patterns is difficult to isolate from other possible influences – improved water and milk for drinking, greater access to other non-alcoholic drinks such as lemonade, ginger-beer and fruit cordials (even in pubs), increased availability and popularity of tea and coffee, better public facilities for recreation and entertainment, more effective medical treatments without alcohol, and many changes in life-style, education and social attitudes. However, the temperance movement undoubtedly contributed to a widespread Victorian middle-class belief that drinking in public houses was not appropriate for people who aspired to be respectable.

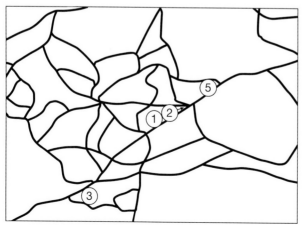

Map 8.01
Public houses in Ranmoor and district.
1, Bull's Head (previously Highland Laddie).
2, Ranmoor Inn.
3, Rising Sun.
5, Fulwood Inn (from 1999).
(Number 4, the Ball Inn, is outside the top-left corner.)

Three of the four pubs currently in Ranmoor and Nether Green became established in the early 1800s. A fifth, previously on the north-western edge of the area, closed more than 100 years ago. Their locations are shown on Map 8.01[16].

1. The Bull's Head, previously the Highland Laddie

A survey of Upper Hallam carried out in 1830 described the site of the current Bull's Head (number 1 on Map 8.01) as a "house, shop and garden", occupied by Jonathan Swann. (As generally in the period, a "shop" was a "workshop".)[17]. He also used his property as a beerhouse, being cited as both a pen and pocket-knife manufacturer and a beerhouse proprietor. In 1841 he purchased the site from Isaac Deakin (see Chapter 9).

The establishment's increasing success can be seen through its description in the ten-yearly national census. In 1851 Jonathan Swann was entered as a "cutler and beerhouse keeper", but "beerhouse" was crossed through and replaced with "inn". By 1861, the occupier Jonathan Dungworth was simply an "innkeeper" (and also a saw-handle maker at the rear of the pub), and Charles Slowe was described as a "publican" in 1871 and a "licensed victualler" in 1881.

At some point before 1850 (see the map at the front of the book) the name "Highland Laddie" was chosen[18], but this was changed around 1866 to the "Bull's Head Inn". Photo 8.02 shows that the inn originally occupied only a part of the building, with a separate residence to the left of the picture[19]. By the time of the photograph (c1885) "wines" and "spirits" are also advertised; that had not been permitted in its days as a beerhouse.

The photograph also draws attention (in the top-right corner of the building) to the presence of "Collis's Cab Stand". Horse-drawn cabs were available here and outside the Ranmoor Inn, and the Bull's Head forecourt also served as the terminus

Photo 8.02
The Bull's Head, here in the 1880s, originally occupied only part of its building, with a separate residence to the left.

Photo 8.03
The last horse-bus between Ranmoor and Nether Green in July 1901. Chapter 11 describes how most buses were more substantial than this very local service.

Photo 8.04
By the early 20th century the Bull's Head had expanded into the adjacent house and acquired larger bay windows. The telegraph pole in the background served a telegram office in a nearby shop (see Chapter 9).

for horse-drawn omnibuses making the mile-long journey (1.6 kilometres) from the York Hotel in Broomhill. Details are in Chapter 11.

Space at the front of the Bull's Head was also used by others. Photo 8.03 shows the last horse-bus from Ranmoor to Nether Green in 1901. Its owner and driver, Robert Middleton, ran this to the Kensington Bus Station and Tea Garden in

Oakbrook Road in Hangingwater (less than a mile away). Robert Middleton owned and operated both the bus (meaning "horse-bus") station and the tea garden, which will be described more fully in Chapter 9.

A planning application in 1877 to build "conveniences" in the Bull's Head was granted "subject to the pig-stye being omitted". A "stable and shed" (presumably at the rear) were permitted in 1893, and in 1899 "stabling and additions" were allowed but subject to "the manure pit being roofed over". Animals still were a central part of life.

In its early days as a beerhouse, brewing was no doubt carried out by the proprietor and his wife. However, as in many similar establishments, it soon became sensible to obtain supplies from one of the increasing number of "public brewers". The Bull's Head became part of the network of pubs operated by Richdale and Tomlinson of Bramall Lane, presumably also receiving from them funds for refurbishment. This company started around 1860 and kept that name until 1898, when it was registered as Richdale's Britannia Brewery Company. It continued, with 25 tied public houses, until being taken over by Hammonds of Bradford in 1956. The Bull's Head stayed within that group, which itself became absorbed in the 1970s by Bass Charrington.

2. The Ranmoor Inn

At the end of the 1700s a small area of land on the corner of Ranmoor and Fulwood Roads (now the site of the Ranmoor Inn; number 2 on Map 8.01) was owned by Jonathan Worrall, who also had three other plots nearby. By 1830, the site was described as a "house, garden &c" owned and occupied by George Worrall, perhaps the son of Jonathan. In street directories as early as 1825 and in the 1841 census George (born about 1802) was identified as a boot and shoe maker.

However, an 1841 street directory tells us that George Worrall also kept a beerhouse. By the 1851 census, James Worrall (born in Upper Hallam c1812 – perhaps George's brother) is described as a "shoe maker and beerhouse keeper". His household then included an apprentice shoe maker, his wife Sarah and two children; Sarah probably helped as brewer and by serving customers in one or more of their house's rooms. Early in the 1850s the name Ranmoor Inn appears in documents, and by the 1860s a bowling green was established on the adjacent land. (This was replaced by a terrace of houses in the late 1870s.)

The Worrall family continued in the Ranmoor Inn until the early 1870s. In 1867, James Worrall received planning permission for "room and chamber [i.e., bedroom]

Photo 8.05
As a beerhouse in earlier times the Ranmoor Inn possibly contained only the rear section shown in this 1870s or 1880s photograph.

Photo 8.06
By about 1900 the Ranmoor Inn had been expanded to include stables and retail space at the rear (in the extreme left of this photograph).

additions". These prob-ably added a new block to the front of the building; the pattern of stonework makes it clear that the two sections were built at different times. Photo 8.05 shows the pub in the 1870s or 1880s, before construction of stables and other buildings at the rear. Those probably followed an 1891 planning application for "additions and alterations". Additional buildings can be seen at the left of Photo 8.06, which is likely to date from the 1890s and advertises above the pub's name "Cab Stand in the Yard".

A later view (Photo 8.07) from early in the 20th century shows a modified frontage and offers "Good Stabling" – presumably for short-term use by local people and visitors. At that time the Ranmoor Inn was a meeting-place for the Royal Antediluvian (or Ancient) Order of Buffaloes ("RAOB" in Photo 8.07). This was a philanthropic and social organization for men which also provided support for members and their families in times of need. By the 1930s (Photo 8.08) the inscription above the door simply refers to the landlord – Henry Stokes.

Photo 8.07
Early in the 1900s the front of the Ranmoor Inn (now with ground-floor bay windows) still offered "Good Stabling".

Photo 8.08
The Ranmoor Inn landlord in the 1920s and 1930s signed his pub's photograph, presumably to encourage custom.

From the middle of the 1890s, the landlord was George Walker, who for some 20 years had been a grocer and beer retailer in Broomhall Street. In 1902, he built a substantial home in the village of Findhorn in Morayshire on the north-east coast of Scotland, presumably for his retirement (Photo 8.09). (He was then approaching 60.) He inscribed the name "Ranmoor" over the front door of this Scottish house, together with the initials "GW" and the year "1902". Findhorn was the village in which Elspet Falconer (who became Mrs Walker) had spent her childhood[20].

George Walker died almost immediately after his new house had been completed, and the Ranmoor Inn and the Scottish investment became the responsibility of his widow and 23-year-old son, George Falconer Walker. Sadly, Elspet Walker died a few months later, the house in Findhorn had to be sold, and their son, previously a joiner and carpenter, ran the Ranmoor Inn on his own for the next five years.

Photo 8.09
Ranmoor on the north-east coast of Scotland, here seen in 2008. Ranmoor Inn landlord George Walker built this house in 1902, naming it "Ranmoor" in stone over the front door.

From the late 1890s, James Whitaker Collis operated part of his cab business from the back of the Ranmoor Inn (see also the Bull's Head section), and those buildings were used for cabs and taxis until about 1917. Other occupants of the attached buildings from the 1870s were butchers and bootmakers/repairers. From c1913 to 1942 a bank branch was established there, becoming part of the Midland Bank around 1922. (It moved along the road in 1942; see Chapter 9.) Occupants in the 1940s and 1950s included builders, a watchmaker/repairer and a confectioner.

In its initial days as a beerhouse the Ranmoor Inn no doubt brewed its own beer, and it followed the fashion of having several small rooms for customers. It later became part of Tennant Brothers' chain of pubs and received supplies from them (as indicated in Photos 8.07 and 8.08). This company was founded (with a different name) around 1820 and expanded to become one of Yorkshire's largest beer producers. Based around its Exchange Brewery near Lady's Bridge in the centre of town, it grew through acquisitions, mergers and other developments to control some 700 public houses by the 1950s. The company was absorbed into the national Whitbread Company in 1962, and Exchange Brewery was closed in 1993.

3. The Rising Sun

Another local beerhouse was that of Alethea Biggin, variously described from the 1830s to the 1850s as being either in Hangingwater or Nether Green. Alethea (born 1780) was the wife (later widow) of Joseph Biggin, a grinder who in 1817 bought the cottage which became (after extensions around 1900) either 231 or 237 Oakbrook Road. By 1830 she occupied premises (since demolished) a little higher up the road towards Rand Moor. Alethea ran her beerhouse until the early 1850s either in one of those Hangingwater houses or perhaps near the Nether Green site of the current Rising Sun (number 3 on Map 8.01)[21].

The 1790s Enclosure Award map (Map 1.02) shows two sets of buildings on that site. At the rear (away from Fulwood Road) were cottages, at some point extended to include file-makers' workshops (see Chapter 2), and in front were buildings which later included a beerhouse. Photo 8.10 (taken late in the 19th century) shows the pub at a right angle to the road with a substantial house next to it. An 1846 document describes that as a dwelling-house with a "stable, gighouse, shops, mangle room, privy and appurtenances".

At the time of the 1805 Enclosure Award the plot and others around it were owned by William Murray of Banner Cross Hall (see Chapter 1). They were purchased by filesmith John Warbleton in 1815,

Photo 8.10
The original Rising Sun in Nether Green (here in the 1880s or 1890s) was a small building at right angles to the road.

Photo 8.11
John Taylor was landlord of the Rising Sun from the 1870s.

and inherited by his second son (also John) in 1852. Their family had been tenants here since at least the 1750s.

The elder John Warbleton's first son Philip lived on the Nether Green site in the 1850s. Aged 39 at the 1851 census, he was then described as a file manufacturer employing 10 men, and by 1854 he was also a shop-keeper perhaps within the same building as the beerhouse. In an 1856 directory he appears under both "file makers" and "inns and taverns". The fact that his establishment was not in the separate section on "beerhouses" suggests that he had by then acquired a license also for wines and spirits. The position of landlord was soon afterwards taken by William Marsden (born c1833), and Philip Warbleton moved elsewhere in Sheffield. John Warbleton (the owner – see above) moved from Slayleigh into the adjacent house. He was a file forger born about 1824.

By 1859 the name "Rising Sun" had come into use[22]. It has been described as the site for occasional sessions of bull- and bear-baiting[23], although those were banned by the 1835 Cruelty to Animals Act. The publican at the time of the census in 1861, William Marsden, died aged 35 in 1868, leaving his widow Ann in charge of the pub and their four children. Ann Marsden (born c1833) married again during the 1870s. Her second husband, John Guest Taylor (born c1840), pictured in Photo 8.11, bought the building from its previous owner John Warbleton in 1876.

From the 1890s several areas of land south of this section of Fulwood Road were acquired by the Town Trustees[24], including the Rising Sun site which they bought around 1900. The opening years of the 20th century saw considerable development in the area, including construction of the Methodist Sunday School in 1901 (see Chapter 6) and of Nether Green School in 1904 (see Chapter 7). The Town Trustees arranged for the Rising Sun's rebuilding in its present form. That change was in part required by Sheffield Corporation's intention to widen this section of Fulwood Road, as a terminus was being established for the new electric tram lines (see Chapter 11). In 1902, the Trust agreed to provide land for the road-widening free of charge in return for the Council's demolition and reconstruction of the Rising Sun.

The widened Fulwood Road was built through the site of the old pub. Photo 8.12, shows the new layout as construction was underway. The modern building is set some way back from the original road, which is close to the right of the old pub. That was very much smaller than the new Rising Sun.

The Town Trustees had resolved in the previous year that the rebuilt Rising Sun should operate according to principles then being promoted by the current Earl

Photo 8.12
The old Rising Sun and adjacent house were demolished in 1903-1904 to make way for a wider Fulwood Road and to create a larger replacement pub.

Grey, which had become known as "the Earl Grey system". In 1900 he had formed the Public House Trust Company, setting up local trust associations around the country.

A Sheffield association was set up in 1902, with the enthusiastic backing of the Bishop of Sheffield and other prominent citizens. In that year the Town Trustees agreed to let the reconstructed Rising Sun to the new group. The national company described itself as "an organization formed for the purposes of promoting temperance by the elimination of private profit from the retail sale of liquor, and securing to the public the monopoly value of licences". It was financed by shareholders whose financial gain was limited to a 5% annual return on their investment; additional profits were spent on "objects of public utility which are not properly chargeable to the rates". The Company's pubs were not tied to a particular brewery, and managers received no commission on sales of liquor but did so for their sales of meals and non-alcoholic drinks. Customers were never granted credit for their purchases.

The new Rising Sun opened in July 1904, with J. Rowbotham as its first manager (see Photo 8.13). By 1917 the Sheffield Public House Trust Company had five public houses in Sheffield, and the Company continued leasing the Rising Sun for several decades before the license was taken over by the Courage group. From 1992 the pub was operated by Sheffield University Students' Union before being leased at the end of 2005 by Abbeydale Brewery. Changes over the years have included the addition of a front porch and side entrance, and the removal of internal walls which previously created four separate rooms. Up to the 1950s, the present car-park behind the pub was a bowling green, with customer-service provided from a hatch at ground level[25].

Photo 8.13
The new Rising Sun, opened in 1904 and here shown about 1915, originally had its own parking recess in the front.

4. The Ball Inn

At the edge of Ranmoor there used to be another public house – the Ball Inn. From at least the 1840s this was at the top of Pitchford Lane, where Tom Lane extends north into Sandygate Road. In the survey leading to the 1805 Enclosure Award, a "house and garden" was on the site, but from 1841 it appears in street

Photo 8.14
451 Sandygate Road, at the top of Pitchford Lane, was the Ball Inn for many years up to the 1880s. Here, in the 1950s, it was a grocer's shop.

directories under "inns and taverns" (rather than "beerhouses"). Around that time it contained a house, pantry (for brewing?) and pigsty. Charlotte Wright was the innkeeper in 1841, a widow of 57 presumably brewing as well as serving her own beer.

Charlotte Wright was still in charge of the Ball Inn at the census of 1861. She was then aged 77 and her resident barmaid was 71. From the mid-1860s and at the census of 1871 the landlord was Joseph Sampson, who was at the same time a grinder. Members of the Sampson family had lived either in the Ball Inn or in the adjacent house since at least the 1841 census, and may have been related to the Wrights. The publican at the 1881 census was Ann Sampson, but soon after then the pub was closed. As shown in Photo 8.14, the building was used as a grocer's shop from about 1917 to the 1970s.

5. The Fulwood Inn

A final pub (number 5 on Map 8.01) opened much later than the others. With the confusing name of The Fulwood Inn (since Fulwood is some distance up the road), this was created in 1999 within one of the area's original "mansions" – Moordale, built in 1863. The story of that building has been presented in Chapter 4 (see number 7 there).

Notes to Chapter Eight

1 Brewing had long been considered "women's work", since it was part of domestic food preparation.

2 To counter that trend, several temperance insurance organizations and friendly societies were established in the 19th century explicitly to provide cover to non-drinkers and to support them in their abstaining life-style.

3 As well as more beerhouses after 1830, the number of fully-licensed public houses also increased for several decades, as magistrates saw less point in restricting those numbers in the face of so many new beerhouses opening beyond their control.

4 It seems likely that some forms of beerhouse existed in previous centuries without formal registration.

5 Up to 1872, beerhouses were permitted to open on weekdays between 5 a.m. and 11 p.m. and on Sundays between 12.30 p.m. and 3 p.m. and then between 5 p.m. and 10 p.m. (There were small changes from time to time.) For licensed public houses there were no statutory restrictions on weekday opening hours before 1864 (when night-time closure became required between 1 a.m. and 4 a.m.), and Sunday hours were similar to those of beerhouses. In both cases, children were allowed to purchase alcohol to carry home to their parents.

6 There was no flat piece of ground large enough for playing cricket near the Bull's Head, and the advertisement probably referred to the Hallam Football and Cricket Club ground opposite the Plough Inn in Sandygate. Albert Slowe, the Bull's Head publican from the late 1880s had been secretary of that club and was still a very active member of it.

7 In some early beerhouses, customers were served in the kitchen – the warmest and best-lit room in the house.

8 Pub characteristics have been described and illustrated (with an emphasis on London) by Mark Girouard in *Victorian Pubs* (London: Studio Vista, 1975).

9 Temperance activities have been reviewed by Lilian L. Shiman in *Crusade against Drink in Victorian Britain* (New York: St Martins Press, 1988). A more detailed account has been provided by Brian Harrison: *Drink and the Victorians* (London: Faber and Faber, 1971).

10 "Montgolfier" was the generic name for a hot-air balloon, invented in France by the Montgolfier brothers in 1783. "Rotary stereoscopic exhibitions" were popular at the time for their three-dimensional presentations of famous buildings and scenes; stereoscopes had been developed in the 1830s.

11 Family life in that period was described in another Gala Day song – "The busy little mother": "She's up in the morning early, she's up in the morning grey; she's washing and scrubbing and nursing and mending the whole of the live-long

day". Furthermore, "the father works quite cheerfully, and she works for him".

12 The Temperance Hall in Townhead Street was taken over by the Sheffield Repertory Company in 1928, and was renamed as the Playhouse Theatre in 1938. After some rebuilding in 1953, it was closed in 1971 when the Crucible Theatre opened. The building was sold in 1973 and was demolished for the construction of commercial offices.

13 The sign "Temperance Bar" is still in place on the front of 377 Abbeydale Road, near to the Abbeydale Cinema.

14 As Chairman of the Health Committee, W. J. Clegg promoted Sheffield's first slum clearance scheme, and led the campaign for a new Town Hall. It was he who laid the foundation stone for the current building in October 1891.

15 See page 288 of L. L. Shiman's book cited in Note 9.

16 In addition, the Plough Inn stands just outside the book's area, on the northern side of Sandygate Road. (See the 1850 map at the front of the book.) The current building was opened in 1930 after demolition of an older one in the previous year. Above the present doorway is a stone carving "BRF 1695", and the pub may have originated well before that year to provide refreshment along what was a pack-horse route.

17 The footpath to the west of the site, from Fulwood Road to Ranmoor Road, was present in the 1790s and was presumably long-established. It was explicitly defined and retained in the Upper Hallam Enclosure Award.

18 The name Highland Laddie might perhaps have referred to the proprietor, but in fact Jonathan Swann was born in Nether Hallam rather than Scotland. Another possibility concerns the travelling salesmen known widely as "Scotch drapers" or "Scotchmen". Those sold from door to door (often on credit) textile and other goods from Scotland and increasingly from parts of northern England. (The Scotsman's Pack pub in Hathersage may be named after this group.) However, Highland Laddie was a common pub name throughout the country at the time, and perhaps it had no more local significance than the Bull's Head that followed it.

19 A planning application by brewers Richdale and Tomlinson of Bramall Lane was granted in 1886 for additions to the Bull's Head; other "additions" were in 1899 and 1903. One of those may have incorporated the adjacent house.

20 Residents of Findhorn in that earlier period also included several other Walker families. Both George Walker and his father were born in Nottinghamshire, but perhaps they still had relatives in the Findhorn area.

21 Alethea Biggin's son Isaac and grandson Joseph were both table-blade grinders. However, by 1876 Joseph was described as a grinder and shop-keeper and by 1883 as a farmer and shop-keeper. From at least 1879 he had a grocer's shop in one of the cottages at the corner of Tom Lane and Fulwood Road (see Chapter 9), and in 1885 he purchased a field to the east of the Rising Sun, perhaps for grazing animals or growing produce for sale. After his death in 1891 or 1892, his wife Catherine continued the shop until at least 1902, when she was aged 63. She lived there until 1910-1911, when the cottages on that corner were demolished to widen Tom Lane.

22 Nationally that name is sometimes said to have been chosen for pubs facing east and receiving early-morning sun. That was the case for the earlier pub on this site.

23 See page 168 of Douglas Lamb's *Last Orders* (Sheffield: Pickard Publishing, 2000). The two forms of baiting had been popular since at least Elizabethan times. A bull or bear was tied to a stake with a rope about 15 feet (4.6 metres) long, and attacked by a succession of dogs. ("Bull dogs" were initially bred for that activity.) Such events would have taken place here only a few times a year, also supposedly in the Ecclesall Rising Sun and Prince of Wales. In addition to spectators seemingly enjoying the spectacle, gambling took place on the probable outcomes. The remains of bull rings are still traceable in several Derbyshire villages.

24 Details of the Town Trust are given in Note 1 at the end of Chapter 2.

25 Land on the Fulwood (west) side of the Rising Sun car-park was filled in around 1960 to build a petrol station.

26 For example, in conjunction with the Church of England Temperance Society, the Vicar of Fulwood opened a small coffee house in Brookhouse Hill in the 1880s. This moved in 1888 to what had been the Blacksmith's Arms in the current Old Fulwood Road.

CHAPTER NINE

Shops and Shopkeepers

For many centuries people bought food and other items from weekly or bi-weekly markets rather than from retail sales-shops of the kind now familiar to us[1]. Shopping expectations were in our terms very limited, since a family often produced much of its own food and made many clothes, and because the range of goods on offer was small. In addition, most people had little money to spend. By the middle ages London and other wealthy towns had acquired distinct shopping districts, and in central Sheffield some retail traders had become grouped in the King Street area close to the market place itself.

The few inhabitants of Ranmoor, Hangingwater and Nether Green in the first part of the 19th century presumably took advantage of those town-centre facilities from time to time, but travel was not easy and purchases had to be carried home for an arduous three miles. By the 1850s, as the local population was starting to grow, a handful of retail shops was available in Ranmoor and in Nether Green. These sometimes originated in the room of a dwelling-house, and were often the responsibility of an artisan's wife as he worked in his primary job. Thus an 1841 street directory (which, like others, listed women only if they were widowed or unmarried heads of household) identifies as shopkeepers in Ranmoor Joseph Howson and James Waterfall, and those are elsewhere described as a blade grinder and a file-maker respectively. In Nether Green, another file-maker (Philip Warbleton) was also a shopkeeper in the 1850s. (In addition, he ran the Rising Sun pub; see Chapter 8). Other directory-listed local shopkeepers in this period were additionally described as a labourer, a carter, and again a grinder.

A shop's kind of business is unspecified in many records, and it may have been a general store selling whatever items were thought likely to be of interest. However, several early shops in the area were explicitly grocers, perhaps selling eggs, bacon, spices, dried fruits, flour, tea, sugar and other provisions. Butter and

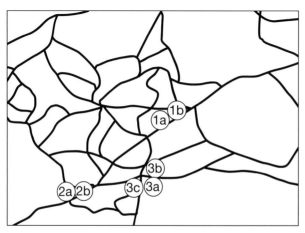

Map 9.01
Shopping centres in Ranmoor,
Nether Green and Hangingwater.
1a, Initial Ranmoor shops.
1b, Later Ranmoor shops.
2a, Initial Nether Green shops.
2b, Later Nether Green shops.
3a, Initial Oakbrook Road shops.
3b, Later Oakbrook Road shops.
3c, Hangingwater Road shops.

cheese were made locally, and grocers sold milk from nearby farms and cured their own bacon.

As well as grocers, the few mid-19th-century shopkeepers in the Ranmoor area included butchers, fish-dealers, boot- and shoe-makers, and also a tailor and draper. Shops of all kinds remained open until perhaps 10 o'clock in the evening, and Saturday evenings were particularly busy after men had received their week's pay. Many people expected to be granted credit when paying for at least part of their purchases[2].

As the number of potential customers increased, running a shop became more profitable and male proprietors no longer needed additional employment. From the late 1870s, street directories provide more detailed information. In addition to two locations on Fulwood Road (in Ranmoor and at Nether Green), a shopping centre developed from the 1890s around the junction of Oakbrook and Hangingwater Roads. Early features of these groups will be considered in three separate sections.

1. Ranmoor Market

Linked to the long-standing importance of markets throughout the country, groups of shops (today called "shopping centres") were often in the 19th century described as "markets". In that way the shops around Deakins Walk in Fulwood Road were for a period known as "Ranmoor Market" (other centres included "Fulwood Road Market" in Broomhill, "Glossop Road Market", and "Nether Edge

Photo 9.01
Isaac Deakin opened Cliff View (376 Fulwood Road, in the right of the picture) as a grocer's shop in 1841. It is seen here in the early 1900s.

Market"). Linked to that name, Marr Terrace (next to the Ranmoor shops) was called Market Place from 1875 to 1904.

Ranmoor's Fulwood Road shops became established in two stages: on the Fulwood side of Deakins Walk from the 1840s, and to the east of Deakins Walk (nearer to Sheffield) in the 1890s. Records up to the 1870s are sketchy, and exact locations are not usually known in that initial period.

Initial Ranmoor shops (1840s+)

The early Ranmoor shops are now numbered 376 to 382 Fulwood Road (1a on Map 9.01). Number 376 was constructed around 1840 or earlier, at least partly as a residential house. It is labelled as Cliff View on the 1850 map at the front of the book, and that name was retained for several decades. Shown as the smaller building to the right of Photo 9.01 (see page 109), it is externally still largely as built (now a wine bar). The adjacent numbers 378-382 were constructed later, when the land's owner (James Waterfall, and then his widow Sarah) made the site available for sale in 1879[3].

An early occupant was Isaac Deakin (1790-1859), who set up his grocer's shop in Cliff View after an 1841 purchase of land near the footpath from Fulwood Road to Ranmoor Road. He had previously been a farmer in Fulwood before working as a grocer near Stumperlowe Hall, and his community activities led to him being elected to several local positions[4]. The path next to his property was in 1922 renamed as Deakins Walk in his memory (see Chapter 3)[5].

Number 376 continued as a grocer's shop long after Isaac Deakin's death, also selling beers and other drinks. Its longest occupancy was by members of the Broughton family. In 1895, William Broughton took over the next-but-one grocery and beer retailers (in number 380, now part of Threshers; see Photo 9.02), and from about 1915 his

Photo 9.02
Broughton's grocer's shop was among the Ranmoor shops in Fulwood Road from 1895 for about 90 years. "Italian Warehousemen" (see the sign) specialised in olive oil, pasta and other imported goods.

Display Box Eleven

NINETEENTH-CENTURY PAWNBROKERS

In the absence of state welfare benefits, many Victorian families had short-term needs for additional cash to cover loss of income through illness or poor trading conditions. (Unemployment allowance was not introduced until 1913.) Pawnbroking flourished to provide easy loans, particularly up to the 1914-1918 war. In the 1880s Sheffield town had some 90 different pawnbrokers and several of those operated two or three separate establishments.

Customers deposited household goods or clothing in return for an immediate cash loan of perhaps one-third of an item's value. On later handing back their "pledge" ticket and repaying their loan with interest, the goods were returned. This simple form of quick credit became firmly established in working-class communities, with basic procedures regulated by the 1872 Pawnbrokers Act. That limited loans to a maximum of £10, and confirmed that goods not reclaimed within a year and one week became the property of the pawnbroker who was then able to sell them.

Interest rates were fixed by the Act, but the actual cost of using a pawnbroker depended on people's frequency of deposit and reclaim, because each deposit incurred its own separate expenditure for the pledge ticket (one half-penny, or a whole penny if the loan was above ten shillings). Frequent visits to the pawnbroker were thus more expensive, even though the interest rate remained the same (effectively about 25% a year). That meant that many families were paying the equivalent of around 100% interest over a year, since short-term loans were very popular from Monday morning (perhaps to pay the rent) to Friday or Saturday (after pay-day). "Sunday best" suits were sometimes pawned to raise temporary cash in that way.[30]

The middle-class residents of Ranmoor, Hangingwater and Nether Green probably made little use of pawnbrokers, but between 1870 and 1910 many less wealthy families moved into the smaller houses that had been built. Some of those people almost certainly pawned goods from time to time somewhere in the town. (No such facilities were available locally.)

Several successful pawnbrokers chose to invest in the area. For example, William Jeffrey, who had premises in Market Street, was one of the trustees of the Storth Crescent Land Society (see Chapter 3), and he and two other pawnbrokers bought all that Society's plots on the eastern (nearer-to-Sheffield) side of the new Gladstone Road. On his plot now stands 6 Gladstone Road, and two plots each were bought by brothers John and Joseph Robert Wright. They built numbers 8 and 10 for themselves on one plot and sold the rest at a profit. The Wright brothers were pawnbrokers together for almost 50 years. Like many others in the trade, they were also silversmiths and jewellers, being able to assess quality and potential resale value as well as working to build up a reliable customer base.

business also occupied Cliff View (376); that accommodated the beer-retailing side of the business. A 1903 invoice describes the company at 380 Fulwood Road as "grocers, corn factors, and provision merchants", with a corn warehouse at 208 Oakbrook Road. Around 1938, the company also acquired number 378, combining that with 376 to form the current single unit (now Threshers wine merchants). William's son Geoff ran the business from about 1950, and Broughton's continued in 376-380 Fulwood Road until Geoff retired around 1985.

Expanding Ranmoor provided good trade for William Broughton and other retailers. Self-service was of course unheard of, and customers were served from behind counters by knowledgeable staff; earlier in period those may have worked a lengthy apprenticeship. Grocers initially blended their own teas, ground coffees and spices, and prepared, packaged and weighed other products themselves. The shops in Fulwood Road used a lane at the rear through which horse-drawn carts brought in supplies. Many customers expected to pay later when presented with a bill or a statement of several bills, and goods were routinely delivered to home addresses.

As indicated above, the current Threshers establishment was previously two shops (378 and 380 Fulwood Road), of which 380 was a grocers from an early date. Number 378 was for a long period a stationer's shop which later became (in about 1890) also a post, money order and telegraph office[6]. The telegraph business required the employment of "telegram boys" who cycled to recipients' homes with messages written out (later printed) from a receiving machine. They also accepted replies (chargeable by the word), which were typed in Morse code into the equipment for return transmission. In about 1936 the post office moved into

Photo 9.03
Until about 1910, three houses remained in the middle of the Ranmoor Market shops (here seen around 1906).

Photo 9.04
George Wildgoose had a butcher's shop next to the Bull's Head for about 20 years from 1878. Seen here around 1910, the shop remained a butcher's up to the 1980s.

number 382 (see below), and the telegraph office appears to have closed[7]. Broughtons grocers then took over number 378, merging that with number 380.

The fourth building in this original group (382 Fulwood Road) became a chemist's shop in 1879 and has remained one ever since with a brief interruption in the 1940s[8]. (A post office shared the shop for about 10 years from the 1930s; see above.) In 1901 James Eardley (born 1856) added number 382 to his three other retail pharmacies (in Fulwood Road, Glossop Road and Upper Hanover Street) and it continued as an Eardley business until 1940 or 1941 (being known as Eardley and Furnival from about 1915)[9]. From the mid-1940s it became the Ranmoor Pharmacy.

Other early buildings in this part of Fulwood Road were initially residential cottages. As shown in the middle of Photo 9.03 (taken around 1906) three of them (numbers 384-388, now an Indian restaurant in a later building) were set back from the road with a small front garden. By 1915 they had all become shops, and the group was demolished around 1962 to create a single grocery store.

Next to the set-back houses, further towards Fulwood, were three retail shops numbered as 390-394. These were built by George Wildgoose in 1877, who also obtained planning permission for stables, a scullery and other buildings (presumably at the rear)[10]. George (born 1828) opened a butcher's shop in number 394 (at the end of the row, next to the Bull's Head Inn; see Photo 9.04), and his brother Benjamin Wildgoose (1820-1884) set up as a grocer in number 392. In the previous (1871) census, those two already had shops of those kinds in the area, probably behind the Ranmoor Inn[11]. George Wildgoose also appeared as a farmer in an 1876 directory. In this period the jobs of butcher and farmer sometimes overlapped, as butchers selected and probably slaughtered their own and others' animals, as well as preparing them for sale[12]. Members of the Wildgoose family continued in 392 and 394 Fulwood Road as grocers and butchers respectively for more than 20 years[13].

Number 392 remained as a grocer's shop for many decades. In 1902, a branch of Burgon and Company (already established elsewhere in Sheffield) moved in; see Photo 9.03. Around 1915 they transferred to a larger shop converted some five years before from two houses (386 and 388 Fulwood Road, see above), and between about 1920 and 1970 number 392 housed a confectioners. From 1948, space was also provided for a sub-post and money order office, which remained the only occupant during the 1970s.

Photo 9.05
A second set of Ranmoor shops was built around 1893. Shown here in the early 1900s, sun blinds of this kind were common for many subsequent decades.

Later Ranmoor shops

A second group of nine shops was established in this part of Fulwood Road in the 1890s (location 1b on Map 9.01)[14]. They are shown early in the next century in Photo 9.05. An 1895 directory listed the four initial occupants as a ladies outfitter, a fruiterer, a confectioner and a butcher (in numbers 364 to 370 respectively). By 1898 the other shops contained a boot-maker, a (horse-drawn) cab proprietor, a cycle agent[15], a plumber and a dealer in glass and china.

The initial (1895) butcher in number 370 (next to Deakins Walk) was Benjamin Brocksopp (born 1867), who had sold meat from the rear of the Ranmoor Inn from

1888. Like many other men at the time, he continued in the trade of his father and grandfather[16]. Shown in Photo 9.06, he remained at 370 Fulwood Road for four decades until 1937. Later butchers in that shop have been John Brown until the 1970s and an ex-employee of his, Alan Howson, since then[17].

In 1977 the nine shops were sold as a block by a member of the Brocksopp family. At some stage Benjamin Brocksopp appears to have become a landlord as well as a shop-keeper.

Photo 9.06
Benjamin Brocksopp's shop next to Deakins Walk (also in Photo 9.05) is still a butcher's today.

Ranmoor shops in the 1950s and 1960s

366 Fulwood Road was occupied between 1957 and 1984 by Ted and Mary Bell, selling fruit, vegetables and flowers. They retired in 1984 both aged 69. Their daughter Pauline has described business activities in that period, also casting light on retail procedures in previous decades:

> One thing that is worth noting is the hugely different style of retailing from that which exists in today's world. Ranmoor was the major food-shopping outlet for most of Ranmoor's residents. Those who were reasonably well off either rang their order in or they brought the list in themselves, and they had a monthly account so even if they called in the shop for something they would have that item booked (added to that monthly account). When you think about it, it was the forerunner of the credit card! Some of the orders were huge, because a lot of people had big dinner parties as a way of promoting or maintaining their businesses and many of those businesses were part of Sheffield's industrial heritage. My father built a reputation on providing melons that were perfectly ripe on the day they were to be served as a starter course at a dinner party. This type of service was demanded of Broughtons [grocers in numbers 376-382] as well as Browns [butcher in number 370] and presumably Shuttleworths [butcher in number 394].
>
> I know that my father spent most of Thursday afternoon (early closing day) and all Friday delivering orders, and it took my mother at least a day each month to send out the bills for the monthly accounts. Everything was of course done on paper with a pen. No computers! There would be an order for every week, odd items etc. to collate, and the whole lot to be added up in order to arrive at the monthly bill that was then posted or hand-delivered with the next order. My mother in her 80s could still add up in her head or with a pen faster than I could do it with the calculator.
>
> It was not unknown for people to ring in the evening and want a lemon delivering because they had forgotten to order it. They would also expect the shopkeepers to get something from one of the other shops and deliver it with the order. So if they only wanted a couple of items from Broughtons they would ask my mother on the phone to get them and put them on the fruit and vegetable order.
>
> When the orders were delivered, my father or brother was expected to take the order down into the cellar and do other odd jobs. I can remember Father telling us about having to blow up balloons for some elderly lady who was expecting her grand-children for Christmas. Trades-people were still regarded as being there to serve.
>
> On the other hand people used to confide quite amazing things to my mother who was a very good listener. She was someone they knew and trusted who was outside the family or immediate circle. There was also something social about shopping. People would stand in the shops talking to friends and neighbours and the staff would be walking round them dealing with other customers. People wanted personal service and attention of a kind no longer on offer because it is too costly in time to provide.

2. Nether Green Shops

The shopping centre further along Fulwood Road at Nether Green was also developed in two stages, but not until the 20th century. Although directories indicate that two or three shopkeepers were somewhere in Nether Green from the 1850s onwards, their locations and trades are generally unclear. However, the Biggin family are known to have worked as grocers from their home at the bottom of Tom Lane.

Photo 9.07
The Nether Green houses in the background of this picture were set back near to Tom Lane opposite Ranmoor Council School until they were demolished around 1910.

Joseph Biggin (c1833-c1895) had been employed as a table-blade grinder up to his 40s, but then he became described as a "shopkeeper and grinder" and by the 1880s he was a "shopkeeper and farmer" (see Note 21 in Chapter 8). With his wife Catherine he ran a grocery business which perhaps offered products from their own farm. They also delivered goods and apparently operated a general carting business;

Photo 9.08
This 1890s picture of Oakbrook Road shows in the background Kensington Crescent of terraced houses and in the foreground Robert Middleton's Kensington Bus Station and Tea Garden.

widow Catherine was described in the 1901 census as both a grocer and an "owner of carts and horses". Their cottage in Tom Lane (Photos 2.11 and 2.12 in Chapter 2) was demolished in 1910-1911 as that road was widened.

On Fulwood Road itself, two sets of Nether Green buildings were established by 1901. Those nearer to Fulwood (numbers 494 to 502; 2a on Map 9.01) were private houses at that year's census. By about 1906 they had become retail businesses – originally a confectioner[18], a tobacconist, a grocer, a greengrocer and a butcher – and have continued as shops to the present time.

Also in Nether Green, numbers 476 to 484 (closer to the bottom of Tom Lane; 2b on Map 9.01) were originally houses rather than shops, apart from number 484 which had become a butchers in the 1890s. They can be seen in the background of Photo 9.07; in the foreground are pupils in their garden at Ranmoor Council School, opened in 1904 – see Chapter 7. These houses were set back from Fulwood Road close to Tom Lane, and were demolished around 1910 as the bottom section of that Lane was widened. The then-vacant site was not developed until about 1928, when the current shops were opened, numbered as 478 to 492 Fulwood Road. Initial occupants were a fruiterer, dyers and cleaners, a confectioner, a chemist, ladies' hairdresser, a dressmaker, a ladies' outfitter, and a grocer.

3. Hangingwater Shops

A third set of local shops became established at the end of the 19th century. Land around Oakbrook and Hangingwater Roads was sold for housing at that time, and a tram route from the city centre was opened in 1901 (see Chapter 11). The area's growth in population was accompanied by the construction of shops in both those roads near to their junction.

First were those on the south side of Oakbrook Road (3a in Map 8.01), developed by Robert Middleton (1845-1918), a file hardener turned builder and

Photo 9.09
In the 1890s this lower section of Hangingwater Road has yet to be developed, and Fulney Road has not been built.

Photo 9.10
Cottages at the junction of Hangingwater and Oakbrook Roads (in the distance here; see also Photos 9.09 and 9.16) became retail shops soon after 1900.

horse-bus operator. He was active in Oakbrook Road from 1887, first building the terrace of houses (171-207) which he grandly named "Kensington Crescent" despite the fact that their line was straight rather than crescent-shaped[19] (Photo 9.08).

He then turned his attention to retail shops, creating those numbered 211 to 217 and 231 to 237. The latter were based on earlier cottages which Robert Middleton remodelled and enlarged in 1900 and 1901. The original buildings are seen from Hangingwater Road in Photo 9.09 and after rebuilding in Photo 9.10[20].

Above the door of number 237 (on the corner with Hangingwater Road, now Oakbrook Pharmacy) is an inscription within a stone crest:

> KENSINGTON
> MARKET
> FOUNDED BY
> R. MIDDLETON
> 1887-1902 AD[21]

The crest can be seen to the right of Photo 9.11 (dated around 1912). Leonard Middleton (one of Robert's sons) was at this time the proprietor, described in directories as a "drysalter &c."[22]. In the early 1900s, "Kensington" (presumably thought to indicate quality) was widely used as a label for all these shops, including Kensington Stores (grocers), Kensington Boot Repairing Depot, and Kensington Tea Garden and Bus Station.

The last of those was another venture of Robert Middleton's, from at least 1898 (see also Photo 9.08). The tea garden (a fashionable idea at the time) was linked to a grocer's shop in number 231, and was in an open space behind the shops. It was aimed at visitors to Endcliffe Park (opened in 1887) and walkers in the Porter Valley as well as local people. By 1901, Robert Middleton had passed the tea garden to Herbert Etchells, and it appears to have closed around 1905[23].

Around the turn of the century Robert Middleton was described in directories as

Photo 9.11
On the corner of Oakbrook and Hangingwater Road is Robert Middleton's stone inscription (above the door). For about five years from 1910 his son Leonard ran the corner shop as a "drug store" (he was not a qualified chemist).

an "omnibus proprietor", and his horses were based in stables he had constructed behind the Oakbrook Road shops. One of his routes was from the Bull's Head in Ranmoor to the Kensington Tea Garden, for example providing onward transport for passengers coming on the horse-bus from Broomhill (see Chapter 11). Photo 8.03 in Chapter 8, dated 1901, shows Robert Middleton and his omnibus outside the Bull's Head on the day this service was terminated, probably put out of business by the electric trams which ran along both Fulwood Road and Oakbrook Road from that year[24].

Shops were also opened on the opposite (north) side of Oakbrook Road in this period. Newly-constructed properties in 1901 (numbers 202 to 208; 3b on Map 9.01) were occupied by a boot maker and repairer, a newsagent, drapers, and grocers respectively. By 1902, the end shop (208, nearest to Nether Green) was rented by the Ecclesall Industrial and Provident Society as its ninth retail outlet.

This local Society had been founded in 1874 as part of a national co-operative movement, itself started in 1844, to provide low-price unadulterated grocery items to workers and their families. Dealing in cash rather than through credit, such societies returned to their members any profits made through "dividends"[25]. The Ecclesall Industrial and Provident Society amalgamated in 1907 with the Sheffield Industrial and Provident Society, forming the Sheffield and Ecclesall Co-operative Society. With a headquarters based in Napier Street (near the city end of Ecclesall Road), this continued trading until the beginning of the 21st century[26].

The Oakbrook Road Co-operative Society shop prospered, and by 1915 the Society purchased spare land nearer to Nether Green for the construction of a larger store. A commemorative plaque was placed on its front above the corner window (Photo 9.14):

C
S   E
S
1915

Photo 9.12
Oakbrook Road shops around 1908 included the Kensington Boot Repairing Depot, next to the left-hand shop here.

Like Robert Middleton's plaque on the opposite corner (see earlier), this inscription remains in place today. The grocery store and its separate butcher's shop closed down in the 1970s, and the property has since been divided into separate retail units.

Another early arrival on the north side was Oakbrook Road's post office, operated by William Dilly and his wife from 1907 until about 1936. William's widow Annie moved the business across the road into number 207 around that year, and their daughters continued there until c1950. The post office returned to its original side (next to its earlier location) in the 1980s and closed in 2008[27].

As part of the area's development around 1900, shops were also opened nearby in Hangingwater Road (3c on Map 9.01). Several started business in 1902-1903 on the western (nearer-to-Fulwood) side of that road (numbers 96-104), and have remained

Photo 9.13
231 Oakbrook Road (currently a delicatessen) has been a grocer's shop since around 1900. It is seen here in the 1940s.

Photo 9.14
In 1915 the Sheffield and Ecclesall Co-operative Society built this substantial branch store on another corner of Oakbrook and Hangingwater Roads. This photograph dates from the 1940s or 1950s.

as retail units since then. Four shops on the other side of the road have since become private houses[28]. Of those, numbers 131 and 133 Hangingwater Road opened in 1902 as a butchers and confectioners respectively. By 1915, both were occupied by Joe Elliott, who had previously lived along the road and been described as a cow-keeper.

As indicated in Chapter 2, the Elliott family had owned land between Hangingwater Road and the River Porter for several decades, including what had been Hangingwater Farm before that became a merely residential property (147

Photo 9.15
Another grocer's in Oakbrook Road was on the corner of Cruise Road, near the centre of this picture. It closed in the 1940s; see Note 27.

Photo 9.16
In the middle of this picture (around 1900) is the shop window of 95 Hangingwater Road. This was a general store for about three decades from 1898.

Hangingwater Road). The Elliotts continued their shop in 131 and 133 Hangingwater Road (see Photo 9.17) until the late 1950s. It later became a ladies' hairdressers, and is now a private house.

A more substantial Hangingwater Road store was built about 1910 nearer to the junction with Oakbrook Road. The occupant was Tom Gillam, who had started in 1901 as a "grocer, provision merchant and corn factor" in numbers 215 and 217 Oakbrook Road. By 1902 he had moved to 237 Oakbrook Road (on the corner with Hangingwater Road) before establishing a new shop at 87 Hangingwater Road (currently Hangingwater Stores). Tom Gillam's shop aimed at more wealthy customers than the other small shops in the area, delivering orders well beyond Hangingwater itself. His business continued until about 1951, and the shop then became a branch of Sheffield-wide grocers Arthur Davy and Sons until around 1969[29].

Photo 9.17
Mary and Nellie Elliott outside the family shop in 131 Hangingwater Road in 1920.

Display Box Twelve

SHOPPING IN SHEFFIELD CENTRE

The development of shops in Ranmoor and other suburbs was accompanied by substantial changes in the centre of Sheffield. Small shops and pubs had for centuries been squashed together around the market and shambles (butchery), near the present King Street and Snig Hill. However, principal streets were remodelled in the latter part of the 1800s, permitting construction of some new and grander buildings. In that period also the Duke of Norfolk (who held the rights to Sheffield markets until 1899) built several imposing new market halls, including the Norfolk Market in Haymarket (1851) and the large Corn Exchange (1881) on the site of the current Park Square roundabout.

These town-centre changes, new construction methods and shopping innovations elsewhere led to the introduction to Sheffield of a new kind of establishment – the department store. The Cole brothers moved their drapery shop (founded 1847) from Fargate to the bottom of Church Street in 1869 with a large and palatial store (Adverts 9.01 and 9.02 on page 124). (That was transferred in 1963 to a new building in Barker's Pool, since renamed as John Lewis.) John Walsh opened a baby-linen and ladies outfitting shop in High Street in 1875, expanding with many more departments in an opulent building opened in 1899. (That was destroyed by enemy bombing in 1940, later rebuilt, and eventually became Rackhams and now T. J. Hughes.) In Angel Street, brothers T. B. and W. Cockayne developed their father's drapery business into a major department store by 1897. (This too was destroyed in World War Two, temporarily rebuilt, and reconstructed in the 1950s; it now houses Argos and other companies.) These large stores aimed to be attractive to lady shoppers, making toilets available and providing refreshment opportunities through comfortable restaurants.

New buildings in Fargate included Arthur Davy's grocer's shop from 1882 (see Note 29). Large retailers moving to the city centre early in the 20th century included two local Co-operative Societies – the Brightside and Carbrook (founded 1868) and the Sheffield and Ecclesall (founded with a different name in 1874) – and T. and J. Roberts (from 1859) and John Atkinson (from 1873), both on the Moor. Marks and Spencer opened in a small way in the Norfolk Market Hall in 1897, before establishing a larger business on the Moor from 1912. Other major stores also became established in succeeding years – Montague Burton, C and A Modes, Littlewoods, Waring and Gillow, Woolworths, and others.

From the early 1920s John Creswick (1882-1967) provided milk deliveries from Manor Farm at the top of Hangingwater Road (number 139). His original deliveries (twice a day) had been from Snaithing Farm (see Chapter 2) with transport as in Photo 9.18 on the next page. After periods farming in Fulwood and Rivelin, he set up in Manor Farm using the vehicle in Photo 9.19.

Photo 9.18
John Creswick started a milk delivery business from Snaithing Farm in Snaithing Lane (see Chapter 2) soon after 1900.

Photo 9.19
John Creswick moved his milk business to Manor Farm (139 Hangingwater Road) in the early 1920s.

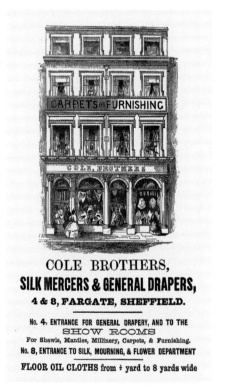

Advert 9.01
The department store Cole Brothers provided a new kind of shopping for Sheffielders. (The Floor Oil Cloths mentioned in this 1862 advertisement were for protection in kitchens and sculleries.)

Advert 9.02
By the time of this 1879 advertisement, Cole Brothers had greatly expanded on what for several generations of local people was "Coles Corner" – opposite the parish church, which became a cathedral in 1914.

Notes to Chapter Nine

1 Early markets were administered by officials of the local Lord of the Manor. He or his ancestors had obtained the market rights from the King, and charged sellers a fee for space, the management of the market, and checks on weights and measures. Sheffield's market was authorized in 1296, and the Duke of Norfolk sold his local rights to the city corporation in 1899.

2 Credit sales were common in this period. Week-to-week credit was available in many shops to customers known to be reliable, usually with selling prices slightly above those charged for cash. Credit was particularly important in times when paid work was scarce. Pawnbrokers also flourished in Sheffield town; see Display Box 11. In many areas "Scotch drapers" – travelling salesmen specialising in textiles and cheap clothing – called at people's homes every couple of weeks or so, usually taking orders on high-interest credit or at inflated prices in return for the convenience of their service.

3 The design and frontage of numbers 378 to 382 reflect later Victorian styles, and they are disproportionately large in relation to number 376, indicating a separate development.

4 Isaac Deakin became parish constable in 1841, a year-long position responsible for the collection of some rates, the supervision of local weights and measures, and certain other administrative jobs. In 1842-1843 he served as one of Upper Hallam's surveyors of highways, supervising the repair of local roads (see Display Box 5 in Chapter 3), and in 1845 he received payments of ten shillings each time he valued new properties for the owners' payment of rates.

5 The road was identified as "Deakin's" Walk (with an apostrophe) until at least the 1970s. Isaac Deakin also owned land in several other parts of Sheffield, and was clearly a respected member of society. In the 1861 census, his widow was described as a "gentlewoman".

6 A post office was in this row of shops until c2002, moving between numbers 390 (c1881-1889), 378 (c1890-c1935), 382 (c1936-1947), 392 (from c1948 to the 1970s), and 384 to c2002.

7 Nationally the telegraph service continued up to 1982, by which time personal telephones were widely available for immediate communications.

8 The date 1879 is still inscribed over the pharmacy's front door. The building was sold in 1883 by Sarah Waterfall (the widow of James, who had bought the land from Isaac Deakin in 1841) to William G. Roper (born c1814), himself a retired chemist long established in Sheffield. However, the first known occupier (in a directory of 1881) was William Jervis (born 1844), who had a chemist's shop in Broomhill from at least the 1871 census and whose father and grandfather had also been chemists in the town. William Jervis was one of the original trustees of the Carsick Hill Land Society described in Chapter 3.

9 Furnival was James Eardley's middle name, probably being his mother's surname before marriage. He was also a mineral water manufacturer, working from Ecclesall Mineral Water Works in Stalker Lees Road. Linked to that, the company designed and made soda siphons for injecting aerated soda water into drinks. A later James Eardley (1924-2007) developed the family business into British Siphon Industries, with wide-ranging interests in steel, engineering and packaging; he lived in 57 Snaithing Lane, Ranmoor, from 1967 to 1990.

10 Those three shops have a single-storey front extension, with an internal floor level lower than the rear of the shop. Photographs indicate that this extension was in place in the early 1900s, and it was probably built as a second stage since its roof obscures the view from upstairs windows.

11 As described in Chapter 8, the buildings at the back of that pub were used by a range of businesses up to the 1950s.

12 Even in the 1920s, Frederick Oates, a butcher at Nether Green, was separately listed as a "slaughterer". His family had also been butchers in Ranmoor since around 1900.

13 After Benjamin Wildgoose's death in 1884, his nephew, George's son Frederick Wildgoose (born 1854), took over the grocery business in number 392 (Benjamin himself had no sons), continuing until about 1899. Frederick then moved into number 390 as a fishmonger and game dealer until c1903. In number 394, George worked as a butcher until about 1895, and with different occupiers that shop continued as a butcher's until the 1980s.

14 The site had been offered for sale by auction in 1879 as "suitable for saleshops". That was a period of economic difficulty, and the land may have remained unsold until later.

15 Cycling clubs had been formed in Sheffield from the 1870s, and cycling became very popular. Retailers sold mass-produced bicycles, but also built their own models which could incorporate customers' particular requirements. Further details are in Display Box 14 in Chapter 11.

16 His father John Brocksopp (born 1835) had been a farmer and butcher with a shop in Broomhill since at least 1871, and his grandfather Henry (born 1801) had been a butcher and cattle dealer in Derbyshire.

17 A stable, carriage house and wash-house were originally behind number 370, with an external hoist to the upper storey of the stable. Those have been demolished and replaced with space for car-parking.

18 On the side of the shop in this group nearest to Nether Green (number 494) is a faded painted sign advertising "Leclerc's Cosy Tea Room". The Leclerc family had a confectionery business at this address between c1910 and c1927. The sign was blocked from view around 1928 as additional shops (476-484; 2b on Map 9.01) were erected in front of it.

19 The southern side of this section of Oakbrook Road was bought by Elias Middleton, Robert's brother, in 1887. Robert commemorated his house-building work on the site by two plaques on the front of houses at each end of his development. Between numbers 171 and 173 is "KENSINGTON CRESCENT AD 1890-6", and between 205 and 207 is "KENSINGTON CRESCENT ERECTED BY R. MIDDLETON AD 1890-6".

20 These were built in the early 1800s, tenanted and from 1817 owned by grinder Joseph Biggin. He extended the original building, and that was converted by Robert Middleton around 1900 into shops on Oakbrook Road. The summary of an 1830 map refers to "three dwellinghouses with an outhouse, yard and gardens" facing onto a lane from Hangingwater Road to Ibbotson Wheel (see Chapter 2). That lane, no longer in existence, was near to the current Fulney Road.

21 As noted elsewhere in the text, "market" was a common name for a set of shops in this period, as in "Ranmoor Market" and "Fulwood Road Market" at Broomhill.

22 A "drysalter" sold salt-based and other chemicals for domestic uses such as preserving, pickling and cleaning.

23 Herbert Etchells (born c1865) had previously been a silver engraver. He continued working as a grocer in number 231 until about 1932.

24 Robert Middleton continued building in subsequent years, being involved with his brother Elias in two houses in Fulney Road and others in Westwood Road. He was on several occasions in dispute with the city council about his failure to conform to building regulations.

25 The success of the co-operative movement was in part due to its exploitation of the retail branch system. Until the mid-19th century, multiple shop trading was unknown, but co-operative societies changed that by opening branches where locally needed. That arrangement permitted large-scale purchasing and the centralised preparation and packaging of goods. Quality standards were centrally maintained, and the salesperson's job was greatly simplified. Linked to multiple outlets, local societies together created their national Wholesale Society, founded in 1855 to help stores "whose small capitals do not enable them to buy in the best markets nor command the services of … a good buyer who knows the markets". See page 281 of *A History of Shopping* by Dorothy Davis (London: Routledge and Kegan Paul, 1966).

26 After several mergers between societies, all Sheffield co-operative societies closed completely in 2008.

27 An earlier closure was number 176, on the corner of Cruise Road nearer to Sheffield. This was built in 1904, and from then was used as a fruiterer's shop and home by Robert and Emily Burrell. (It is near the centre of Photo 9.15.) After Robert's death in the early 1930s, his wife continued the shop until about 1944 when it was converted into two residences.

28 Two of those are numbers 93 and 95. Number 93 was built in 1913 on the corner of Fulney Road, starting as a butcher's shop but soon becoming a greengrocer's (as it was until about 1937). Number 95 was built earlier, in 1898, and operated as a shop from then until around 1930. See Photo 9.16.

29 Founded in the 1860s, from 1882 Arthur Davy and Sons' principal shop (and restaurant) was in Fargate, currently occupied by W. H. Smith stationers. Still visible on the front of that are original stone carvings of a pig and an ox, representing the hams, sausages, potted beef and pork pies prepared and sold by the company.

A factory in Paternoster Row prepared the products for sale, and advertisements describe the company as "the universal food provider" – "ham and bacon curer, the largest maker of polony in the world, and maker of the celebrated tomato sausage." (Polony is a type of pork sausage.) Arthur Davy himself (born 1838) had built Hill Crest in Ranmoor, at the junction of Ivy Park Road and Ranmoor Cliffe Road in 1885. He lived there until 1902. The company continued until 1972.

30 These and other details are explored by Paul Johnson in *Spending and Saving* (Oxford: Clarendon Press, 1985).

CHAPTER TEN

Villas for Victorian Families

The 1860s "mansions" described in Chapter 4 were important both in themselves and because they and their occupants indicated that Ranmoor – until then largely open countryside distant from the town – had become a desirable place to live. Its new residents were clearly prosperous, and many were also top people in Sheffield's public life – mayors, master cutlers, magistrates, town trustees, church burgesses, and even knights of the realm.

The land societies and new roads (see Chapter 3) led to the construction of many less grand but still substantial properties. It became common to describe these houses and vacant plots for sale as "near the mansions recently erected", and by 1872 an advertisement for land to be sold near Snaithing Lane could announce clearly that "Ranmoor is evidently the favourite suburb of Sheffield". The building boom from the 1860s to the mid-1870s was aided by a period of economic prosperity, such that many of the town's manufacturers were able to afford properties previously beyond their means.

This chapter will look at a small selection of those buildings and the people who lived in them in Victorian times. They are indicated by numbers in outline Map 10.01, and are presented in alphabetical order below.

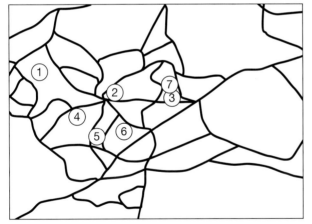

Map 10.01
Some notable Ranmoor houses.
1, Carsick Grange.
2, Cliffe End.
3, Ranmoor Grange.
4, Ranmoor Hall.
5, Storth Oaks.
6, Tylecote.
7, West Lea.

It became fashionable to refer to medium-sized houses on the outskirts of towns as "villas", suggesting a fine building in a country setting[1]. Villas stood in their own grounds, and were already described as either "detached" or "semi-detached" in distinction from terraces of joined-together town houses. The term "villa" gradually became applied extremely widely, even to city-centre terraced rows[2], and the description became less popular by the following century.

1. Carsick Grange, Carsick Hill Drive

Carsick Grange was constructed in 1882 by Elizabeth Hedgeland Birks (1844-1922), who had been a widow for nearly ten years. Her late husband was Edward

Vaughan Birks (1839-1874), a director of the family's brewery, Thomas Rawson and Company, and a town councillor from 1869 until his death[3]. They had lived in Fairfield House in Fulwood Road (later numbered as 274) until Edward's death in 1874, and Elizabeth remained there with her five daughters before setting up home in newly-built Carsick Grange.

The Grange's estate extended for more than two acres across six plots of the recently-formed Carsick Hill Land Society (see Chapter 3). Elizabeth Birks purchased five of those from her brother John E. Bingham of West Lea (see 7 below)[4], and placed her house, stables and main entrance route in the northern section near Carsick Hill Road, with a lodge in Snaithing Park Road at the southern

Photo 10.01
A recent view of Carsick Grange, which was built in 1882 for widowed Elizabeth Birks and her five daughters.

Photo 10.02
Carsick Grange was at the north end of its long estate with a lodge in Snaithing Park Road.

end of a long drive-way. Her initials "EHB" were (and are) carved over the front door. In addition to six bedrooms on the first floor and five bedrooms (probably for servants) on the second floor, the ground-floor rooms and the basement provided considerable space. The Grange is shown in Photos 10.01 and 10.02. Outside were greenhouses, a washing shed, a carriage house and stable, a tool house, a heated potting house, and a cucumber house.

The Birks family employed six domestic servants and a coachman-groom in 1891. Two of Elizabeth's five daughters were married in the 1890s, and others remained at home. (It is not known at what dates, if any, they left.) After Elizabeth's death in 1922, the Grange was bought by Peter Boswell Brown (1866-1948, later Sir Peter), who had lived in 12 Gladstone Road since about 1918. He was joint managing director of the Hadfield steel company, before becoming deputy chairman and then chairman. He was Master Cutler in 1930-1931[5], and lived in Carsick Grange until his death. The house was subsequently converted into apartments, and parts of the grounds have been sold for the construction of houses.

2. Cliffe End, 45 Ranmoor Cliffe Road

A planning application of 8 February 1879 was for "one villa", the property of John Francis Moss. Unusually for the time the application involved a London

Photo 10.03
Cliffe End, at the top of Ranmoor Road, was built in 1879 for John Moss, the Clerk to the Sheffield School Board.

architect, and it gave rise to a building that was not typical of the area – Cliffe End at the junction of Ranmoor and Ranmoor Cliffe Roads (2 on Map 10.01).

John Moss (1844-1907) came from Kimberworth near Rotherham. After being apprenticed as a printer, he moved into journalism and was appointed as chief reporter of the *Sheffield Telegraph* at an early age. When only 26, he successfully applied to be Clerk to the new Sheffield School Board, created in 1870. That was a wholly new post in a new national initiative for elementary education, and he was extremely effective in it, holding the position for the Board's entire existence to 1903. In some documents in that period he was applauded as "the father of education in Sheffield", and his national impact was also considerable through regular advice to government. Details are presented in Chapter 7, with a sketch in Drawing 7.01.

In his School Board role, John Moss worked with several architects in the creation of new schools (no less than 12 in the Board's first three years). A national leader in the field was E. R. Robson (1835-1917), who was chief architect to London School Board between 1871 and 1884. He designed two of Sheffield's Board schools, and later served as adviser in selecting the design for Ranmoor Council School (described in Chapter 7).

Arising from their professional collaboration, it was E. R. Robson who designed Cliffe End[6]. He avoided the more conventional appearance of nearby houses, instead preferring "riotously patterned half-timbering to the first floor, coved eaves, and a big four-flight dormer"[7]. John Moss had probably bought the land when it was offered for sale in 1875, and he sold an adjacent section shortly after that. He and his family lived there until the mid-1880s, when they moved to Ecclesall[8].

Cliffe End was then occupied as a tenant by Henry H. Andrew, being sold to his wife Martha Andrew in 1890. The Andrew family lived there until 1899, when they moved to Snaithing Brook (4 below), at which point Cliffe End was rented out. After Mrs Andrew's death in 1910, the house passed to their two daughters.

Among later occupants was John Lowson Potts (between about 1913 and 1925), who had been an executor of Henry Andrew's will (he died in 1903; see below) and a director of the latter's Toledo Steel Works. The house was bought in 1930 by solicitor Douglas S. Branson (later Sir Douglas), who lived there for more than 30 years[9].

3. Ranmoor Grange, 24 Ranmoor Road

This building (3 on Map 10.01), with its lodge at the junction of Ranmoor Road and Ranmoor Park Road, was constructed by Frederick Edwin Leggoe in 1876. He first demolished an older house near to Ranmoor Road. Known as Ranmoor Cottage, that had been occupied since 1828 by Robert Thompson, an artist and school-teacher in Sheffield, who died in 1868 at the age of 80.

Frederick Leggoe, born in Sheffield in 1833, was an iron and steel trader who moved into accountancy and property development. He also purchased other land in Ranmoor, and in about 1876 built the houses in Marr Terrace (known as Market Place until 1904) next to the Bull's Head pub. These property ventures required substantial borrowing, as did his housing estate in Worksop and perhaps developments elsewhere in Sheffield.

Prior to 1875 he had purchased land to the north of what became Ranmoor Grange, and there built some stables, onto which the Grange itself was later joined. This contained a dining room, drawing room, breakfast room, two large kitchens, six bedrooms, and a billiard room with inlaid oak floor. Behind the house, next to the kitchen garden, were the stables, a carriage house, harness room, gardener's working accommodation, and four greenhouses heated with hot water.

It seems likely that Frederick Leggoe over-extended his activities and mortgages, since he was declared bankrupt in 1881. (Poor economic conditions in the late 1870s may also have contributed to his downfall.) His Marr Terrace properties were sold by creditors in January 1882, and Ranmoor Grange and other local sites were offered for sale as early as May 1879. By the census of 1881 he had moved to Heeley, described by his earlier occupation as an iron and steel merchant, and in 1883 he was running a boarding-house, coffee establishment and skating rink in Matlock Bath[10].

By that year Ranmoor Grange was occupied by William Lockwood, of Lockwood Brothers steel manufacturers in Arundel Street. He was followed before 1890 by John Brailsford of printers Pawson and Brailsford, whose distinctive building in Parade Chambers (built 1883-1885) faced the parish church (a cathedral from 1914) at 1 High Street. John died in his forties, and the Grange was taken over in 1898 by Albert Edward Bingham (born 1867). Son of John E. Bingham of the adjacent West Lea (7 below), he too was a director of silversmiths Walker and Hall in Howard Street.

Albert Bingham left before 1910, and subsequent occupants have included William Hart, Sheffield's town clerk (from about 1916 to 1925) and Anglican Bishops of Sheffield (from the 1940s to the late 70s). Ranmoor Grange then served as a nursing home, before being extended and converted into apartments around 2001.

Photo 10.04
A recent view of Ranmoor Grange, built in 1876 and now converted into apartments.

4. Ranmoor Hall (previously Snaithing Brook), Belgrave Road

On 2 January 1880, William Wheatcroft Harrison submitted to the Council an application to construct a "villa" on the south side of Belgrave Road[11]. He named this "Snaithing Brook" after the stream which flowed southwards along the western edge of the site.

William W. Harrison (1830-1904) had a successful business as a silversmith and electro-plater. Founded by his father John Harrison (died 1863), this employed about 100 men in 1871. He was a justice of the peace and active in charitable work for the Royal Hospital and Cherrytree Orphanage in Totley. In 1884 he had been elected a Conservative councillor, and in 1901 he was appointed an alderman. He lived in Snaithing Brook with his second wife and two daughters until 1899, when he sold the property to Henry Herbert Andrew (1850-1903), principal of the Toledo Steel Works in Neepsend Lane[12].

Photo 10.05
William W. Harrison, seen here around 1890, constructed Snaithing Brook in 1880. The building was renamed as Ranmoor Hall in 1936.

Henry Andrew was Master Cutler in 1895 (see Photo 10.06), by which time he had lived in Cliffe End at the top of Ranmoor Road (see 2 above) for about ten years[13]. After moving into Snaithing Brook, he substantially enlarged the house and outbuildings, placing his initials "HHA" over the front porch. After his changes, the ground floor had a drawing room, dining room, card room, billiard room, library and conservatory, as well as kitchens, a laundry, and rooms for the housekeeper, butler and other servants. On the first and second floors were seven and six bedrooms respectively, with bathrooms, WCs and storage facilities. The owner's substantial collection of paintings was displayed throughout the building, described in a newspaper obituary as "the house of a man of fine taste and most ample means".

Central heating was powered from a boiler in the basement, and outside were stabling for six horses, a carriage house, a harness room, a summer house, greenhouses with vineries, and peach,

Photo 10.06
Henry H. Andrew, here as Master Cutler in 1895, enlarged Snaithing Brook and extended the grounds southwards to Stumperlowe Crescent Road.

Photo 10.07
This recent picture of the rear of Ranmoor Hall shows (to the right) part of the conference centre, which has now been demolished.

rose and orchid houses. H. H. Andrew also extended the site to more than seven acres, running southwards as far as Stumperlowe Crescent Road, and he constructed lodges in Belgrave Road and Storth Lane. The gardens were landscaped to include a small lake receiving water from Snaithing Brook. However, their owner's health had been uncertain for some time. In 1903 he drew up a comprehensive will immediately before leaving on a business trip to New York, and he died soon after arriving there.

Henry Andrew's trustees sold the property to John Kingsford Wilson (1855-1915), the second son of snuff manufacturer George Wilson, the occupant from 1867 of Tapton Hall in Shore Lane (see Chapter 4). John Kingsford Wilson[14] was the proprietor of Spear and Jackson, steel and tool manufacturers employing several hundred people in Aetna Works in Savile Street. He lived with his family in Snaithing Brook until his death in 1915. Subsequent occupants were his wife and son until about 1926.

John Kingsford Wilson was an enthusiastic grouse shooter, as were other members of his family. They owned an extensive area of moors at Moscar, and some of their hunting dogs were kept at Snaithing Brook. Photo 10.08 shows their chauffeur and car, with kennels in the background.

Snaithing Brook was next used as a riding school and horse stables before being purchased in 1936 by Frank Russell, head of General Refractories Ltd[15]. He renamed it Ranmoor Hall, as it has been since. It was a military convalescent home during World War Two, before becoming offices for the newly-created National Coal Board in 1948.

From the 1960s it was used by government departments linked to the Ministry of Labour, which became the Department of Employment and Productivity in 1968 and gave rise to the Manpower Services Commission in 1973. The property was extended as a residential and training centre by the construction of

Photo 10.08
Reg Wyles (1884-1969) was chauffeur in Snaithing Brook between 1903 and 1926. As described in Chapter 11, he later set up his own garage business.

additional buildings and provision of a large car-park. The conference centre was demolished in 2008 prior to residential redevelopment of the southern part of the site, and Ranmoor Hall itself was refurbished.

5. Storth Oaks, 229 Graham Road

This substantial house is located in that part of the Ranmoor storths which remained largely wooded in the 1860s – hence the reference to "Oaks" in its name.

Drawing 10.01
Storth Oaks was the first property to be built (1869) in the upper section of Graham Road, but without that name. Shown here in 1871, it initially comprised two houses.

Drawing 10.02
Storth Oaks was converted into a single residence around 1873, with extensions including a tower over the entrance. This drawing dates from 1885.

It was the first to be built in the new Graham Road (5 in Map 10.01) – in 1869 by Charles D. Pettinger, on the plot he had acquired from the Storth Crescent Land Society when it was formed in 1864 (see Chapter 3).

Charles Pettinger (born 1840) worked (later as a partner and managing director) in the company established by his cousin William E. Laycock (1816-1895), which manufactured hair-seating for domestic furniture, railway carriages and other uses.

W. E. Laycock had lived in Stumperlowe Grange in Fulwood since 1855, was a trustee of the Storth Crescent Land Society, and owned two adjacent plots in the estate (see also Note 28 in Chapter 3).

The property (Drawing 10.01) was originally two semi-detached houses, rented to Frank Turton, a file and steel manufacturer, and J. E. Davis, Sheffield's first stipendiary magistrate[16]. It was bought around 1873 by William Henry Brittain, head of Broadhead, Hall and Company, manufacturers of steel and cutlery products in Barker's Pool, who also acquired the two adjacent plots[17]. He extended the property and converted it into a single residence (Drawing 10.02), naming it "Storth Oaks" and adding a stable and coachman's house. The

Photo 10.09
William H. Brittain remodelled and named Storth Oaks around 1873. He was a major public figure in Sheffield for almost 50 years.

gardens were landscaped by Robert Marnock (see Note 24 in Chapter 4), and William Brittain and his family moved in around 1875. A stained glass window in the new lobby reminded them that "North or South, East or West, Home is Best".

William H. Brittain (1835-1922; see Photo 10.09) was a distinguished Sheffield citizen and politician. He entered the town council in 1871, from 1883 served as an alderman for almost 40 years, and was mayor in 1883 and also 1884. He was master cutler in 1878, became a magistrate in 1885, served as a town trustee from 1880 and later (from 1910) as Town Collector (chairman of the trustees), and he contributed actively to the Mappin Art Gallery, the established church, the freemasonry movement, and the University of Sheffield and its predecessors[18]. He was also an enthusiast for art, literature and antiquities, serving as chairman of Sheffield's Libraries and Museum Committee and president in 1899 of the national Museums' Association. He acquired for Storth Oaks an extensive collection of old oak furniture and books.

Following W. H. Brittain's death in 1922, subsequent owners included manufacturers Frederick Firth and Arthur Winder (Sir Arthur from 1943). The property was offered for sale by auction in 1950, and it became a Royal Infirmary nurses' home in 1957 and a Phoenix House drug rehabilitation centre from 1984[19].

6. Tylecote, 7 Gladstone Road

This house on the western side of Gladstone Road (6 on Map 10.01) was also built within the Storth Crescent Estate. The land was originally (in 1864) bought by Henry Hutchinson, a manufacturer of surgical instruments (see Advert 10.02), who

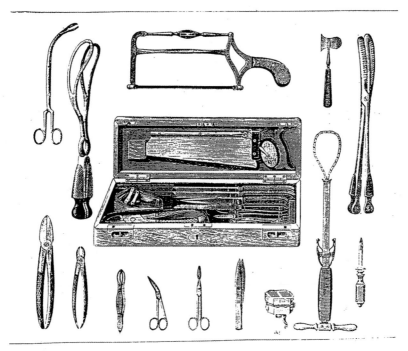
Advert 10.02
Henry Hutchinson – a trustee of the Storth Crescent Land Society – was a successful manufacturer of surgical instruments. The "patent scarificator" in this 1884 advertisement (the box-like instrument at the bottom) was used for blood-letting. It made multiple cuts into the skin, and blood was gathered into a cup, warmed so that a vacuum encouraged its flow.

Photo 10.10
A recent view of Tylecote in Gladstone Road, with an exterior designed in 1880 to be distinct from other houses in the neighbourhood.

was also a trustee of the Storth Crescent Land Society. He also purchased the adjacent plot on the corner of Gladstone and Fulwood Roads.

Henry Hutchinson built for himself Storthwood House on the corner site, and

Photo 10.11
James Dixon, here seen around 1900, lived in Tylecote for nearly 30 years, later moving to Stumperlowe Hall in Fulwood.

in 1885 sold the Gladstone Road plot above that site to James Dixon, a director of his family's firm of silversmiths and electroplate manufacturers. Planning permission for a house there had been granted in 1880, and Tylecote was built in 1880 and 1881. Street directories indicate that James Dixon lived in the house before he became legal owner of the land in 1885[20]. At the time of the 1891 census, he and his wife were there with four children and four servants; by 1901 five of each were with him.

As Photo 10.10 shows, Tylecote is not typical of Ranmoor's Victorian villas. It was designed by architect Herbert Wightman, who was brother of James Dixon's wife Edith, and aimed to resemble what James later described as "many south country houses" through construction with bricks on the ground-floor and a tile-covered upper floor. The design was considered inappropriate by other Storth Crescent Society members but was eventually accepted. South-facing vineries were constructed along the northern wall of the garden.

Like other local residents, James Dixon was usually described as a "merchant and manufacturer". He was born in 1851, one of four grandsons of the James Dixon who in 1806 had founded the Britannia metal company that became James Dixon and Sons in 1833. This was extremely successful, employing around 900 people by

1900 and having a substantial international trade. James's father, Henry Isaac Dixon (1820-1912) lived in Stumperlowe Hall in Fulwood from 1854, and James himself moved there in 1912 after leaving Tylecote in 1909[21]. He and his wife had 10 children, two of whom died in childhood. After retiring from the company in 1919, he moved to the south of England, dying in 1947 at the age of 95.

James Dixon filled many important positions in Sheffield. He was Master Cutler in 1887[22] and later became both a church burgess and a town trustee. He was a magistrate, a town councillor (1890-1894), a guardian of the poor for Ecclesall, a church warden of St John's Ranmoor (1898-1900), and chairman of the Sheffield Deaf and Dumb Association. He was elected a Fellow of the Royal Meteorological Society in 1907, after many years making daily records of the weather at Tylecote, and in 1910 became one of the initial directors of Fulwood Bowling and Tennis Club.

Subsequent owners of Tylecote have included surgeon Douglas Newton (between 1909 and 1920), solicitor Henry Shelley Barker (from 1920 till his death in 1935) and Henry's son Ernest (from c1939 to 1963). Ernest Barker converted the house into two apartments, but it has recently been restored to a single dwelling.

7. West Lea, 5 Ranmoor Park Road

Ranmoor Park Road was created by landowner Frederick Bardwell around 1869 (see Chapter 3), curving northwards from the Ranmoor Inn. Its southernmost plot (7 on Map 10.01) was soon sold, and the road's first house was built in 1870-1871 by George Octavius Cutler (1835-1897), apparently for his own occupation. (He previously lived in Glossop Road.)[23]. (St John's Church, now opposite the site, was not built until 1879.) The house was offered for sale in March 1875[24], already named as "West Lea"[25].

The house was bought by John Edward Bingham (1839-1915), the senior director of cutlery firm Walker and Hall. (One founder of the company, the late Henry Hall, was his uncle.)[26] The company expanded considerably under his leadership, employing several hundred people by the 1890s.

John Bingham served in many public roles. He was Master Cutler twice (in 1881 and 1884), became a magistrate in 1885, and was knighted in 1903. He was earnestly Conservative in his politics, traditional in his Anglican religion, an enthusiastic freemason, and a strong supporter of the part-time military forces, serving as commandant of the Sheffield Engineers Volunteers (see Photo 10.12). His formal later-years title was thus

Photo 10.12
John E. Bingham, photographed in 1910, was an enthusiastic supporter of voluntary military activity. He donated land which became the city's Bingham Park.

Display Box Thirteen

VICTORIAN HOUSE-KEEPING

Managing Ranmoor's early villas was no easy task. Rooms were large and often numerous, and they could be dusty and dirty. The fireplace was a principal culprit in winter, producing soot and ash as well as smoke. To provide some protection furniture was routinely covered with cloths, which themselves quickly became blackened and required frequent washing. Clothes were soon dirty, as were residents' hair and hairbrushes.

Washing and drying clothes, bedding and other items was a hot and steamy business in the kitchen, using water from cooking ranges which were usually burning for the entire day. Soap was the only cleansing agent, as detergents did not appear until the next century. Cooking required extensive preparation, with formal meals often comprising several courses and yielding many utensils and plates to be washed, often in a separate "scullery".

The battle against vermin could be never-ending, especially in the kitchen and in the bedroom, with bugs attracted to mattresses of horse-hair, cow-hair or wool, the three or four blankets on each bed, and probably feather pillows. Mice and rats were common, but particular problems came from fleas, beetles and bugs. Kitchens also attracted cockroaches, which could travel through the house along water pipes. Gaps in walls or between floorboards required frequent treatment with carbolic acid or other types of disinfectant.[29]

Bathrooms in many middle-class Victorian houses had running water (and some flush toilets from the 1870s), but both they and bedrooms required much carrying of jugs and pots[30]. Fireplaces had to be regularly emptied, cleaned, replenished and continually tended.

The expansion of a domestic servant class – mainly young unmarried women recently arrived from the countryside – did of course spread the housework load. Thirty-five percent of the Ranmoor area's 304 households in the 1891 census contained servants who lived in, with those households having an average of two but up to six servants each. In addition, 17% of Ranmoor heads of household in that year had occupations as gardeners, coachmen or similar (often living in the recently-built terraced housing), so that overall more than half the local households included one or more people working as servants.

Recruitment and management of servants could create anxieties for young wives who had to learn appropriate behaviours and domestic routines. Many wives initially had no experience of domestic planning, the management of cooking, cleaning and shopping, and dealing with household accounts[31], and the expectation was that husbands had no part in those tasks. Marital roles were sharply separated, with husbands focusing on their job and provision for the family, and discussion between husbands and wives about household or family matters was often considered inappropriate.

Pressure for extended house-work came not only from the needs of the house itself. In addition, at least in the middle and upper classes the Victorian belief that "cleanliness is next to godliness" spurred on many occupants. Having a carefully presented house was an important part of being viewed as a respectable member of society.

Drawing 10.03
West Lea at the bottom of Ranmoor Park Road, sketched here in 1885, is now the Ranmoor Parish Centre.

"Colonel Sir John E. Bingham baronet". In 1911 he donated to the public an area of land in Ecclesall which became Bingham Park; this was extended to its present size by the city council in 1913 and 1927.

John Bingham (see also Photo 11.13 in the next chapter) had a particular concern for street paving in the centre of Sheffield, and he led local opposition to the use of granite setts. That form of stone-block cobbled surface was favoured by the city's surveyor on the grounds of cost and durability, but John Bingham and others objected that granite was dangerous for horses, which were liable to slip especially on hills or in wet weather[27]. He argued this case vociferously during the 1890s (even patenting his own design for a road surface), and granite was gradually replaced in parts of the town by wooden blocks or tarmacadam. (See also Display Box 5 in Chapter 3.) Other personal crusades by John Bingham included a campaign against excessive smoke in the town (he was active in forming the Smoke Abatement League), and a very public dispute with William W. Harrison and others about the initial introduction of electro-plating into Sheffield[28].

John Bingham made several changes to West Lea. For example, in 1878 he added at the rear a stable and coach house (and what was described as an "ashes place"), and in 1891 he built a billiard room by extending outwards behind the end of the hallway. (Drawing 10.03 shows the earlier appearance, with a greenhouse or conservatory where the billiard room was later built.) After his death in 1915, West Lea was occupied by his widow until she died in 1923. The house was then presented by Sir Albert Bingham (John's son) to the Anglican Church Commissioners to serve as a vicarage, which it did until the late 1970s. It was then purchased by St John's Church itself, and around 1980 was converted into the Ranmoor Parish Centre, with two apartments on the first floor.

Notes to Chapter Ten

1 Their countryside setting was often indicated through names such as Burnside, Dalebrook, Hillside, Meadow House and Moorside – all in the area of this book. Many Victorian villa-dwellers emphasised their closeness to nature by planting imported or ornamental trees in their grounds.

2 For example, plaques on the front elevations of rows of small terraced houses in the Banner Cross district of Sheffield include "Prospect Villas", "Providence Villas" and the intriguing "Cubley Stoop Villas".

3 Thomas Rawson established a brewery in Pond Street in 1758, and it passed through his descendants to spinster Hannah Rawson before it was bought in 1825 by Thomas Birks (1802-1861), who was already linked to the Rawson family through an ancestor's marriage.

4 She also bought five other plots in the Estate around the same time.

5 His wife published an account of that year of office: M. Brown, *Sheffield as Seen by a Mistress Cutler*. Sheffield: Pawson and Brailsford, 1932.

6 The site had been called Cliff End in the 1790s survey leading up to the local Enclosure Award (see Chapter 1) and that name may have originated well before then.

7 See page 270 of the *Pevsner Architectural Guide to Sheffield*, by Ruth Harman and John Minnis (New Haven and London: Yale University Press, 2004).

8 John Moss became a trustee of the nearby Carsick Hill Land Society when it was formed in 1876. He was a long-time freemason, a founder of Sickleholme Golf Club, and a Fellow of the Royal Geographical Society. From about 1900 he became progressively blind, but continued with assistance in his job until his death in 1907.

9 Douglas Branson was active in the Territorial Army, and had been awarded the Military Cross and three Distinguished Service Orders in the First World War. His father, G. E. Branson, had been Commanding Officer of the Hallamshire Battalion of the York and Lancaster Regiment of the Territorial Army up to 1913. (He was closely involved in the purchase of Endcliffe Hall in 1914; see Chapter 4.) Douglas Branson then took over the Battalion until 1925, and was Honorary Colonel between 1940 and 1965.

10 While in Ranmoor, Frederick Leggoe was in frequent disputes with his neighbour, John Bingham of West Lea (see 7 below), about alleged encroachments on the latter's property. Their disagreements included arguments in the Town Council in a period when both had been elected councillors. In 1883 he was involved in a court case about his alleged cruelty to chickens sent from Matlock to a sausage factory in Sheffield. (The magistrates failed to reach a verdict.)

11 He had held a 500-year lease on the site since 25/03/1878.

12 That company had been founded in 1860 by Henry's father, J. H. Andrew (1824-1884), specializing in steel rods and wires, tool steel and mining steel. In 1881 it employed nearly 300 people, and had substantial sales in USA and other countries. Its wires were widely used for the construction of suspension bridges, including the Brooklyn Bridge in New York City. The company was less successful in the 20th century, eventually being developed with different owners as Andrews Toledo.

13 Another of his interests was as a director of the Baslow Hydropathic Establishment. This spa centre and 100-bed hotel had opened in 1881, and Henry Andrew and family were frequent visitors. It ceased operation after World War One, and was demolished in the 1920s.

14 As in other cases throughout the book, his name followed a convention of the time coupling his and his father's surname with that of his mother before marriage – Emily Kingsford (1827-1904). John's two brothers and two sisters were also "Kingsford Wilsons".

15 In that year General Refractories also took over as their Head Office Tapton Park in Tapton Park Road; see Chapter 4.

16 A stipendiary magistrate is a lawyer paid for full time court work with greater power than lay magistrates who work only part-time. J. E. Davis was appointed in 1870 by the Home Secretary in preference to the Town Council's recommended person. He resigned early in 1874.

17 William Brittain also owned property elsewhere in Sheffield. He was a principal developer of the Pinstone Street area of the town centre in the 1880s, close to his works in Barker's Pool.

18 In addition, he served as chairman of the Baslow Hydropathic Establishment. See Note 13.

19 The house's name has been applied internationally by two of W. H. Brittain's descendants. His elder son, Sir Harry Brittain (1873-1974), was a distinguished politician and newspaper director who in 1912 was invited to name two stations on the new Canadian Pacific Railway. One farming community (population about 100) in south-eastern Saskatchewan is now "Storthoaks", and the next station (of similar size) is "Alida" – named after Harry Brittain's wife. W. H. Brittain's other son, Colonel W. Bob Brittain (born 1882), emigrated to New Zealand in the

1920s, and in the 1980s one of his grandsons, Tim Brittain, named as Storth Oaks his cattle stud farm in the North Island of that country.

20 James Dixon had previously rented Ashcliffe, 78 Ranmoor Road, since his marriage in 1873.

21 An insight into the family's life and closeness to the company was given by James Dixon in an article written for the Sheffield Daily Telegraph on 25/08/1933. Describing his 21st birthday celebration in 1872, he wrote that "there were great rejoicings at [Stumperlowe] Hall and at Cornish Place [the factory location, next to the River Don] ... The day began with an old cannon being fired from the pond bank at Stumperlow. At 10 o'clock all the workpeople assembled at Ranmoor, and, headed by the band of the Hallamshire Rifles, walked in procession to the Hall. All assembled on the lawn in front of the house, while the family and a large party of relatives ... stood on the bank at the top of the steps. My uncle, Willis Dixon, as senior partner in the firm, made a speech and proposed my health, and told the workpeople I was taken into partnership that day. I replied, and then Samuel Wood, the senior clerk, presented me with an address. Other speeches followed and I was then suddenly seized by four old women, placed in a chair and carried round ... The rest of the day was spent in the grounds, playing games. At night all the people were entertained at dinner . . . . in five different groups and at five different hotels. My father and I visited each hotel in turn." On the following night his parents also gave a ball at Stumperlowe Hall to celebrate the occasion.

22 Innovations by James Dixon as Master Cutler included the provision of a breakfast for Sheffield postmen at 10 a.m. on Boxing Day, indicated in a newspaper report to consist of "plentiful supplies of beef and ham, pork pies, bread and butter, and tea and coffee". He also arranged a series of free concerts at the Cutlers' Hall, with tickets distributed through clergymen of different denominations.

23 G.O. Cutler was the second of two sons of Hiram Cutler, whose company in Castle Hill was advertised as "merchants and manufacturers of steel, tools, files, saws, cutlery &c". An 1851 census entry for Hiram describes him as a "foreign merchant", and elder son John Edward was listed in 1871 as an "American merchant"; the company had a substantial export business. George Cutler was seemingly not involved in that work, being described in the 1861 and 1871 censuses as a "gentleman" and an "annuitant" respectively. An 1864 directory included "F.R.S.L." after his name – a Fellow of the Royal Society of Literature. By 1881, he had moved to Warwickshire, living off "land and dividends".

24 An 1874 plan for the Ranmoor Crescent Land Society (Map 3.04) shows the occupant as F. E. Leggoe (see Ranmoor Grange, above). It is not known whether he was then a tenant or the owner.

25 The sale details described how the house was "replete with stoves, chimney pieces, and fixtures of the best class. Hot and cold water pipes are laid throughout." A bathroom and a water closet were installed on the first floor.

26 The company was founded about 1845 by George Walker who was joined by Henry Hall in 1848. An advertisement around 1860 made it clear that the company's business then involved more than manufacture: "Parties wishing to have their Dinner, Tea and Coffee Services, Candlesticks, Spoons, Forks and other articles plated or replated can have them done at [Electro Works in Howard Street] at about ONE THIRD OF THEIR ORIGINAL COST" (capitals in the original).

27 On 13/12/1889, the *Sheffield and Rotherham Independent* reported that "Mr J. E. Bingham JP . . . . last evening was pitched from his dog-cart while driving down Glossop Road, alighting on his head. He was unconscious for some time." This episode may have contributed to his concern about road surfaces.

28 See Geoffrey Tweedale's chapter "The electroplate controversy" in *Aspects of Sheffield 1*, edited by Melvyn Jones (Barnsley: Wharncliffe Publishers, 1997).

29 In *The Victorian House* (London: Harper Collins, 2003) Judith Flanders cites one contemporary writer who emphasized that, unless the battle was waged unceasingly, bugs would "multiply till the kitchen floor at night palpitates with a living carpet . . . . and the beetles would collect in corners of the kitchen ceiling, and hanging to one another by their claws would form huge bunches or swarms like bees towards evening, and as night closed in swarthy individuals would drop singly on to the floor, or head, or food" (page 76).

30 In working-class districts bathing required a tin tub in front of the kitchen fire even into the 20th century.

31 Domestic how-to-do-it manuals became very popular in this period. For instance, Mrs Beeton's *Book of Household Management* was published in 1861 and sold 30,000 copies in its first three years. This emphasized how the mistress of the house was like "the commander of an army or the leader of any enterprise"; "her spirit will be seen through the whole establishment". The book covered issues troubling to many a middle-class Victorian wife, such as the duties of each category of staff, how to receive morning calls, how to seat guests at dinner, and how to dress, as well as containing recipes and cooking suggestions.

Moving Around

Up to the 19th century, travel was almost always on foot, even over long distances. However, during the 1800s innovations in transport were made possible by technical advances (new materials, electricity, the internal combustion engine, and so on) and a steady population growth to create more customers. In turn, transport improvements encouraged the outward spread of towns, creating suburban homes for people who worked in the centre; previously it had been necessary to live close to a place of work.

First to become established in Sheffield were horse-drawn cabs, buses and trams, followed by electric trams and motor-cars around the end of the 19th century, with motor-buses becoming available from 1913. Bicycles were also popular from the 1880s. Those developments will be considered in turn.

First however, let's not forget that travel by any means requires suitable routes. For centuries, the Ranmoor area had been criss-crossed by footpaths and lanes, only some of which remain today. The lanes were in effect footpaths that had become heavily used. They may or may not have been edged with walls or bushes, but they certainly lacked hard surfacing of the kind we now expect.

Existing local routes from medieval times, such as Darwin, Snaithing, Storth and Tom Lanes, have been widened considerably in the past two centuries and now look much the same as later roads. Some footpaths have been preserved in narrow gennels (sometimes called ginnels or snickets) that run between 19th century developments[1]. Early maps also show several paths that no longer exist[2]. These were supplemented or obliterated in the 1860s by roads constructed by the freehold land societies and others, as described in Chapter 3.

Photo 11.01
Horse-cabs wait for passengers outside the Ranmoor Inn in the early 1900s. Trams (see the left of the picture) reached the area in 1901.

Horse Cabs and Buses

Hackney carriages (horse-drawn cabs for hire) were popular in towns from the 17th century[3]. By the early 1800s they were common in Sheffield centre, seeking business in the narrow streets. After Sheffield's incorporation as a borough in 1843 their operation became regulated, and licenses were required as in other towns. Official cab-stands (as many as 31 by the late 1870s) were established for passengers to board, and from that decade shelters for waiting cab-men were also provided.

An 1879 Directory told its readers that "the cabs and 'hansoms'[4] of Sheffield are superior to those of most other towns and number about 260". It seems likely that the wealthy residents of Ranmoor were among the more frequent cab users, and cabs waited for business outside both the Bull's Head and the Ranmoor Inn (see Photo 11.01).

At least some of their horses were stabled nearby. For example, one cab proprietor around 1881 was also the Ranmoor Inn landlord who used buildings at the rear of the pub, and J. Whitaker Collis stabled horses in those buildings from 1898 (and possibly earlier) to about 1910. Stabling was continued there by cab proprietor John Bowling until at least 1913 (see Photo 11.02). Another cab proprietor (Harry Hobson) lived nearby in 356 Fulwood Road between c1898 and c1910, with "Hobson Brothers Blacksmiths" also at that address for part of that time.

Personal transport was also available for people with money. Several local residences had their own coach-house, and in the larger houses domestic staff often included a coachman or groom. A number of local people drove their own "gigs" or "dog-carts", small two-wheeled vehicles that held only one or two passengers[5]. Two examples are shown in Photos 11.03 and 11.04.

Arrangements had to be made for "parking" a horse and carriage when making visits in the town. Sometimes, use might be made of one of the town-centre livery stables which provided accommodation and food for horses and storage for vehicles (also offering facilities for travellers stopping briefly in Sheffield). Horses and vehicles of all kinds were also available for rent, perhaps for the summer only or when one's animal became ill or died (also providing temporary replacements for cab and other proprietors)[6].

Horse buses, widely described as omnibuses[7], were introduced in Sheffield in 1838, with an early route being from town to the then-expanding Broomhill[8]. By the 1860s there were more than 25 scheduled horse buses each day from the railway station (originally in the Wicker) or the Market Hall to

Photo 11.02
Cab proprietor John Bowling stabled his horses at the back of the Ranmoor Inn. He lived at 45 Ranmoor Road for almost 30 years from 1898.

Photo 11.03
*This privately-owned two-horse "dog-cart"
was photographed in August 1905. It was
probably driven by the family's coachman.*

Photo 11.04
*Joseph Lowe, here outside St John's Church
around 1900, was an agricultural agent in
Nursery Street.*

Broomhill and back, at a one-way fare of three pence[9]. The fare to Ranmoor was initially four pence, with four daily bus services from about 1856, six in the 1860s, and nine in the 1870s[10]. By 1895, horse-buses from the city to Ranmoor were every half-hour between eight in the morning and 1 p.m. and then every 15 minutes until 10.15 p.m.

A separate shorter service was introduced from Broomhill to Ranmoor (about a mile, 1.6 kilometres), with the licence held from the 1870s by Reuben Thompson, who also operated several other services throughout the city[11]. From 1890 J. Whitaker Collis[12] acquired the Broomhill to Ranmoor licence, with a terminus outside the Bull's Head as shown in Photo 11.05.

Photo 11.05
This two-horse bus provided transport between Broomhill and the Bull's Head in Ranmoor.

Photo 11.06
Travellers from Sheffield to Ecclesall around 1890 might have used this vehicle operated by Reuben Thompson.

Although a town bye-law required that "every driver or conductor of any omnibus shall be sober and cleanly and neatly dressed and shall conduct himself in an orderly and respectful manner", problems were not unknown. Drivers routinely waited for departure times inside a nearby public house, not always making proper arrangements for care of their vehicle[13]. Buses were sometimes dirty, and horses were not always fit for climbing the hills of Sheffield. For instance, in 1871 two omnibus companies were separately summoned for working unfit horses. Witnesses described how buses travelled so slowly that they sometimes had to get off to lighten the load. In addition, conductors were occasionally accused of diverting fare money to their own pockets[14], and formal protests were common[15]. From 1871 the town council had parliamentary approval (via the Sheffield Improvement Act of that year) to inspect and license all buses, drivers and conductors annually, and the first licences were issued in July 1872. By the mid-1870s, 44 different companies had horse-bus licences in Sheffield, although 20 of those had only one licensed vehicle.

As shown in Photos 11.05 and 11.06, omnibuses were usually about 14 feet long (c4.3 metres), with space for around 16 passengers inside and perhaps another ten on top, where no protection was available against bad weather. They were usually drawn by pairs of horses, but a few larger ones (including those on the Sheffield-to-Broomhill route) were "four in hand" requiring twice as many horses[16]. Fixed bus stops were not introduced until the 1890s, so passengers were at first picked up or dropped as required[17].

The interior of horse buses (lit by oil lamps when necessary) was rather spartan, reflecting the fact that many passengers were travelling to or from their work-place in dirty clothes. An 1872 bye-law required that "suitable mats" be provided on the floor, but "clean straw may be used in wet and cold weather". However, the Broomhill and Ranmoor services, with their middle-class users, were noted for their greater comfort and cleanliness.

During the 1890s, Robert Middleton operated a bus service from Moorhead to his Kensington Bus Station at the junction of Oakbrook and Hangingwater Roads (see Chapter 9). Travelling through Hunter's Bar and Rustlings Road (which was built about 1888), this was indicated in one account to be drawn by ponies rather than horses. In addition, he used a small vehicle to carry passengers on a short local route – from Kensington Bus Station to Ranmoor and back. Definitely not

BOROUGH MEWS, BEDFORD STREET,
(OPPOSITE THE INFIRMARY,)
CEMETARIANS, or Superior Family Funeral Saloon Omnibuses, with Black and Grey Horses. Neat One Horse Omnibus for Children's Funerals.

JOHN WING UNWIN,
OMNIBUS AND CAB PROPRIETOR,
Licensed to let Horses, Gigs, Phætons, Dog Carts, &c.
254, SHALESMOOR,
AND
BOROUGH MEWS. BEDFORD STREET,

Advert 11.01
Like other bus and cab proprietors, John Wing Unwin was also an undertaker.

luxurious, that is shown outside the Bull's Head in Photo 8.03 of Chapter 8. Both of his services (and many others) became uncompetitive after the introduction of electric trams – see below.

Many omnibus companies operated more than buses, in addition hiring out horse-cabs and providing vehicles for weddings and other events. Several also acted as undertakers[18]. For example, around 1890 Reuben Thompson was described as a bus operator, a cab proprietor and an undertaker, with about 180 horses in total. John Heath's company was established in 1880 and soon provided both private omnibus and undertaker services with as many as 130 horses and 100 vehicles. By the early 1900s Joseph Tomlinson had a large central stable block, a construction and repair works, and several depots around the city, operating cabs, omnibuses and carriages and also offering services as an undertaker. That joint activity is illustrated in Advert 11.01, in which John Unwin Wing is shown to operate "cemetarians" as well as being an "omnibus and cab proprietor"[19]. Elsewhere, he advertised "Furniture &c removed with light Spring Dray".

During the latter part of the 19th century there were many thousands of horses in Sheffield providing personal transportation and working on commercial activities of all kinds[20]. Precise numbers are not available, but London is known to have had about 80,000 horses at any one time in the 1890s. All these required stabling, feeding, shoeing and other forms of care, employing many people as well as requiring considerable expenditure[21].

A smithy is shown on 1890s maps next to the Rising Sun in Fulwood Road, and another one was up the hill in what is now Fulwood Old Road. Several drinking troughs for horses were also present up to the early 1900s. For instance one was placed in Fulwood Road above Carr Bank Lane (near the current petrol station) and another was close to the entrance to Thornbury (on the opposite side of the road). Other troughs were part-way up Hangingwater Road towards Ecclesall (near the current number 120) and set into the wall at the bottom of Storth Lane (opposite number 11)[22]. Horse numbers gradually declined as new forms of power became established, but some horse-drawn vehicles were still being used in Sheffield into the 1930s.

Horse and Electric Trams

Trams[23] had been running in Sheffield since 1873 – pulled by horses. Running on tracks, those had the advantage over omnibuses of permitting a smoother ride. They were also slightly larger, and by the 1890s horse trams ran from the town centre on routes to Brightside, Carbrook, Heeley, Hillsborough and Nether Edge (with none towards Ranmoor)[24]. Their track was owned by Sheffield Corporation, but the Corporation was legally prohibited from running tram-cars. That was the responsibility of the Sheffield Tramways Company, and there were many disputes between the Corporation and the Company about the maintenance of tracks and payment for such maintenance[25].

At the end of the Company's lease in 1896, the Corporation took over operation of the city's horse-tram system. At that point they reviewed arrangements in other towns and countries, and decided that an electric tram network should be created, extending more widely than before. Despite the necessary disruption of laying miles of track and installing overhead cables for power transmission, progress was very rapid. Twenty-six different lines were planned, and the first of those came into use in September 1899. A dedicated power station was built at Kelham Island.

Two electric routes reached the Ranmoor area in 1901. One came along Fulwood Road (Photo 11.07) and terminated near the bottom of Storth Lane (Photos 11.08 to 11.10), and the other (Photo 11.11) was via Oakbrook Road from Hunter's Bar. The Hunter's Bar trams initially went no further than just past the junction with Hangingwater Road, since motor power and braking capacity were inadequate for the steepness of Nethergreen Road. Subsequent engineering developments allowed trams by 1904 to reach the new Ranmoor Council School on Fulwood Road (see Chapter 7)[26], and in 1909 the line was continued a little further up to the Rising Sun. (Fulwood Road was being widened in that period.) Subsequently (from 1923) some trams on both routes went as far as Canterbury Avenue near Fulwood Church.

The fare on all other routes from the city centre was one penny irrespective of distance, but it was initially set at double that amount on these two new routes. However, public opposition to the higher rate led to it being reduced to the standard one penny in October 1902[27]. The Corporation's electric tram service was extremely successful, and passenger numbers increased rapidly. By the 1920s trams were frequent on most routes, for example reaching Hunter's Bar every two

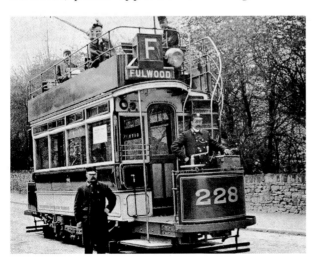

Photo 11.07
Two electric tram routes reached Ranmoor and Hangingwater in 1901. The "Fulwood" sign on this tram (sometime between 1904 and 1909) refers to Fulwood Road; the line did not reach Fulwood itself for two more decades.

Photo 11.08
Another early (c1905) tram ready to leave for Sheffield along Fulwood Road.

Photo 11.9
Outside seats were popular on this day around 1903. The tower in the distance is that of Ranmoor College (see Chapter 5).

Photo 11.10
This c1910 view shows a conductor using the customary bamboo pole to reverse the direction of the trolley pole, for the return journey to Sheffield. (Automatic reversers were introduced from 1915, but the bamboo pole continued to be carried in case of emergency.)

minutes. Popularity was aided by the low fares – lower than in comparable cities.

A vehicle's route was for the first few years indicated by large letters on its front: T for Tinsley, NE for Nether Edge and so on. Early trams along Fulwood Road displayed the letter F (e.g., Photos 11.07 and 11.08) and those along Oakbrook Road to Nether Green showed NG (Photo 11.11). Later trams – with an enclosed top deck – showed the destination in words. From 1902 to 1939 post-boxes on late-evening trams (marked as "postal cars") were available for mailing letters and post-cards[28]. Weekend services in the 1930s were especially popular with walkers, who travelled by tram to a terminus such as at Fulwood and set off on foot into the neighbouring countryside.

Photo 11.11
The "NG" sign on this tram (sometime between 1904 and 1908) indicates that its route was to Nether Green, along Ecclesall and Rustlings Roads. (Firth's Alms Houses are to the right of the picture; see Chapter 5.)

Parallel sets of driving controls were provided at each end of a tram, requiring insertion of a key which also determined the direction of travel. Some early models had only a single deck (and thus less weight) so they could cope with steep hills or pass under low bridges, but most (all after 1921) were double-deckers. Comfort was not great by later standards, and upper passenger decks remained without a roof until changes were introduced from 1904 (see Photos 11.07 to 11.09 and 11.11). Most trams had roofs by 1907, but some remained uncovered until 1913. Drivers had no protection at the front of a vehicle until after 1906. Seats were wooden until the mid-1920s, with sitting space provided for up to around 50 people (depending on the model, increasing to 62 in the final vehicles), and only after the 1939-1945 war was passenger comfort close to a level we would now expect.

Motor Buses

As the city continued to expand outwards, motor-bus services were introduced to supplement the tram system. Buses (both single-decker and double-decker) were purchased from 1913, and by 1916 the Corporation was operating those on as many as ten different routes.

In the early years motor-bus routes mainly extended outwards the tram network, rather than running along the same routes. For example, the first service (in 1913) was from Broomhill to Lodge Moor Hospital, later becoming the 51 route from the city centre. In 1936 the tram service along Fulwood Road was replaced by the number 60 bus (now the number 40) and the Nether Green tram (which continued running to Fulwood) was replaced in 1952 by the 88 bus (now 86). Another local bus route from 1931 to about 2006 was the Outer Circle (number 2), which ran (in part) from Ecclesall along Oakbrook Road, Gladstone Road (see

Photo 11.12
In 1932 this Leyland bus was working on the Outer Circle route, here at the top of Gladstone Road.

Photo 11.12) and Ivy Park Road onward to Rivelin Valley Road. (Up to about 1970, route number 3 ran in the opposite direction.) Sheffield trams ceased operation altogether in 1960, until Supertram started in 1994.

Motor Cars

Transport for private individuals also gradually came to depend on the internal combustion engine[29]. Car ownership in the city grew slowly at first, from about 20 vehicles in 1900 to perhaps 1400 in 1914. At least ten manufacturers were producing cars in Sheffield up to 1920[30]. The city's first motor show was held in 1900, and societies such as the Sheffield and District Automobile Association were formed soon afterwards, providing advice and information for members and organizing trips into the countryside. Taxi cabs also gradually moved from horse-power to petrol engines, and larger petrol-driven passenger vehicles for hire began to appear locally from 1906[31].

Repair facilities for private cars soon became established around the city. For instance, Reuben Thompson (previously a horse-vehicle operator; see above) established a motor engineer's business in Broomhill from 1907 (also running a taxi business – see Photo 11.13 – and providing other vehicles for special events), and in 1919 the Broomhill Motor Company was opened in Peel Street, continuing as Rolls-Royce dealers until the 1960s. The Ranmoor Motor Company was set up in Sandygate Road in 1928 by Reginald Wyles (previously chauffeur at Snaithing Brook; see Chapter 10), moving to its present site in what was previously a blacksmith's premises in Old Fulwood Road in 1934. At the corner of Nethergreen and Fulwood Roads, the Nether Green

Photo 11.13
A 1905 Sheffield taxi, with horse-drawn vehicles in the background. Operator Reuben Thompson is talking to Sir John Bingham, both standing on granite setts of the kind Sir John so strongly opposed for horse travel (see Chapter 10).

Display Box Fourteen

EARLY DAYS OF CYCLING

The first steerable pedal cycle was invented around 1861. Later developments were the "penny farthing" (with one large and one small wheel) from the mid-1860s[34], and spoked wheels, chain drives and pneumatic tyres during the 1870s and 1880s. Originally expensive, bicycles were at first largely used for competitive road racing, but, as mass production brought down prices, people were increasingly attracted to cycling as a leisure activity. That became immensely popular from the 1880s.

Bicycle touring was mainly restricted to men, although some independent-minded women cycled in "bloomers" – a divided trouser-like skirt – instead of the bulky dress which was conventional at the time. Bloomers had been popularized in the 1850s and 1860s in USA by Amelia Jenks Bloomer, a temperance and social reformer who published her ideas widely and energetically.

Although factory-made bicycles became common, small makers also set up in business – six in Sheffield by 1888. Among shop-holders in Fulwood Road (at number 358) from about 1898 was John Staniforth, originally described as a "cycle agent" but between 1902 and 1910 as a "cycle maker". No doubt he also carried out repairs, presumably drawing customers from around the neighbourhood. In this period Sheffield directories listed several dozen people in the city employed in the cycle trade, as makers, dealers, repairers or agents.

Cycling clubs became popular in this period, in part to provide mutual support against the anti-cyclist drivers of horse-buses and carriages and later of cars and charabancs. First in Sheffield was the Sheffield Bicycling Club, formed in 1872. Lessons and practice opportunities were provided on the Sheffield Bicycling Grounds in Sharrow Vale[35], and group rides took place to Baslow, Ladybower and other Derbyshire destinations. Some clubs retained an interest in racing (for instance at the annual Charity Tournament held from 1888 at Bramall Lane)[36], and by 1906 there were 20 cycling clubs in the city, often with their own uniforms and berets. Officials marshalled riders during an outing, in the early years perhaps with the club's bugle. Wider social activities were also undertaken – dances, dinners, concerts, football matches and so on, although the active members were for many decades predominantly men. ("Ladies Day" outings of the Sharrow Cycling Club, founded in 1887, originally required their lady participants to travel by coach.)

Although some initial societies were short-lived, others lasted for years. However, from about 1910, and especially after the 1914-1918 war, cycle-club membership gradually declined.

Garage opened (as "motor car agents") around 1929. With several proprietors, this continued for several decades.

Instead of the "carriage houses" constructed by early residents of Ranmoor to store their horse-drawn vehicles, planning applications were now made for "motor houses" (or sometimes "motor sheds") – the first in Oakbrook House in 1904 and soon afterwards for smaller properties in Fulwood, Gladstone, Graham and other Roads. (Some residents no doubt used existing carriage houses for their new cars.) The term "motor garage" came into local use around 1910. Cars were often maintained and driven by a family's chauffeur, who may in the early period have worked previously with horses as a groom or coachman. For some years horse-drawn and engine-driven vehicles operated in parallel[32], but by the 1930s cars had taken over, and several sets of garages were constructed for individual rental especially in the Hangingwater area[33].

THE "SHEFFIELD" BICYCLE,

Made in THREE QUALITIES, on the Celebrated "STANLEY" Principle, with all THE LATEST IMPROVEMENTS.

PRICE LISTS ON APPLICATION.

We have great confidence in recommending our No. 3 MACHINE, as being THE BEST MACHINE IN THE MARKET, AT THE PRICE.

MANUFACTURED BY

F. H. ANDERTON, 43, 45, 47, COPPER ST., Gibraltar St.

Advert 11.02
At the forefront of 1879 cycling technology, this bicycle was said to contain "all the latest improvements".

Notes to Chapter Eleven

1 Still-existing gennels include the narrow route alongside the Bull's Head pub, which then continues north beyond Ranmoor Road at its junction with Ranmoor Crescent. The remnants of other paths lead from Nethergreen Road to Armthorpe Road, from Snaithing Lane to Belgrave Road, and from Fulwood Road (next to the petrol station) uphill to Carr Bank Lane.

2 For instance, one no-longer-existing path ran from the bottom of what is now Gladstone Road to Storth Lane (then called Water Lane) a little to the north of the later-constructed Fulwood Road. This path previously also continued westward through Nether Green to Tom Lane. Another path cut

through fields where now stand Firth's Homes (see Chapter 5), continuing beyond Hangingwater Road to Ibbotson Wheel on the River Porter (see Chapter 2). The precursor of Belgrave Road used to extend in a south-westerly direction on the other side of Tom Lane towards Stumperlowe Hall.

3 "Hackney" derives from the type of light horse particularly suited to pulling these vehicles. Early "Hackney cabs" usually had two wheels and a single horse with the driver to the rear, but four-wheeled, two-horse models were also used. (Present-day Sheffield taxis are still officially known as "Hackney carriages".) "Cab" is short for "cabriolet", a French word for a small coach.

4 "Hansom cabs" were named after Joseph Hansom's 1834 design, although that was soon substantially modified by others.

5 Information about these personally-driven vehicles is largely derived from accounts of disaster. For example, in 1879 Charles Henry Firth of Riverdale House was driving his dog-cart in Haymarket when a wheel struck against the axle of a cab. He was thrown out, much bruised and received three broken teeth. In 1884 Alfred Dearman, of Ashcliffe in Ranmoor Road, was being driven in a four-wheeled phaeton (see Note 19) in Glossop Road when the horse bolted after hitting another vehicle, and he was killed. In 1889, John Bingham, of West Lea in Ranmoor Park Road, was thrown from his cart (again in Glossop Road), "alighting on his head" in the words of a newspaper report.

6 Individuals operating substantial horse-rental business were widely known as "job-masters". Stables providing for travellers were referred to as "bait liveries", where "bait" was the contemporary word for a stop or break during a journey.

7 From the Latin word "omnibus", meaning "for all".

8 Long-distance coaches had operated from Sheffield since the previous century, and smaller vehicles provided horse-drawn transport for paying customers to Rotherham from about 1800.

9 A turnpike toll-bar (established in 1821) was in place at Broomhill until 1852. Buses before that date terminated before the bar in part to avoid having to pay a toll.

10 Details of many local developments are provided in C. C. Hall's *Transport in Sheffield*, published in 1977 by the Transport Publishing Company of Glossop. He describes how principal horse-bus operators on the Ranmoor route up to the 1880s were the Sheffield Carriage Company, Charles Thompson, and William Henry Haigh. 20-century developments are covered by Kenneth Gandy in *Sheffield Corporation Tramways*, published by Sheffield City Libraries in 1985.

11 During the 1880s Reuben Thomson was on several occasions accused of running dirty and poorly-maintained vehicles and of poor time-keeping. After disputes with the Council, he withdrew from horse-bus activities in the early 1890s, later turning to petrol-driven vehicles (see the section on Motor Cars). Both Reuben's father (Thomas Thompson) and his uncle (Charles Thompson) had been substantial cab and omnibus proprietors in the 1860s and 1870s. Charles Thompson's horse-bus routes included those to both Broomhill and Ranmoor. When he retired from that business in 1873, he sold no less than 110 horses and nearly 20 vehicles. After retiring, Charles built Whiteley Wood Grange off

Hangingwater Road in 1878-9 (see Chapter 2).

12 J. W. Collis was born around 1850 and lived in Glossop Road; his business employed about 15 men. In 1876, he became a trustee of the Ivy Crescent Land Society (see Chapter 3), and he was noted in the district for giving public readings from the American humourist Artemus Ward.

13 In a much publicized case in 1890, a bus was left unattended in Broomhill one evening while the driver had a drink in the York Hotel and the conductor was away buying tripe for his supper. The horses set off towards town, taking three passengers with them. The bus hit another vehicle, the horses bolted, and one lady was killed. The driver and conductor were fined for leaving the bus unattended.

14 Ticketing procedures were at first primitive, with no provision for cancelling those that were issued; re-issue was thus possible. Some companies sold tokens – a form of prepayment which ensured travel with only that company. For example, one of the Broomhill services in 1852 provided "tokens that will pass for threepence each and may be had at the office in the Angel Inn, from the driver, or from Mrs Woolhouse's grocer in the Haymarket". See page 10 in C. C. Hall's book cited in Note 10.

15 For example, the *Sheffield and Rotherham Independent* of 25 October 1889 described a deputation to the City's Watch Committee "to complain of the character of the omnibus traffic to Broomhill and Ranmoor". It was alleged "that the horses were utterly incompetent to perform the work required of them, that gross cruelty was constantly used to force them to do their journey, and that the condition of the horses led to a great want of punctuality".

16 According to J. Edward Vickers, the drivers of these larger vehicles "were the cleverest handlers of reins to be found. Coming down to town on snow- and ice-covered roads, the men kept their horses on their feet with marvellous skill . . . . It was very rare for a horse to be down or a bus to overturn" See page 11 of J. E. Vickers's *From Horses to Atlanteans* (Sheffield: JEV Publications, 1972). Related information is provided in Chapter 6 of that author's *A Popular History of Sheffield* (Sheffield: Applebaum Publications, 1978).

17 Some reports describe journeys making between 10 and 15 stops on the way from town to Broomhill, but the typical number is unknown. The round-trip journey from the city to Broomhill was scheduled to require an hour, including time for the horses to rest at the terminus.

18 An advertisement in the late 1860s by Charles Thompson "omnibus and cab proprietor" covered "party carriages, waggonnettes, excursion omnibuses, and every description of vehicle on

hire", as well as "wedding equipages of an elegant character". His Funeral Department offered "hearses and mourning coaches, large and small omnibuses, suitable for family or children's funerals".

19 A "phaeton", mentioned in the advertisement, was a sporty horse-drawn carriage, named after the mythical Phaeton who had a disastrous chariot accident when speeding across the sky. The company was "licensed to let" these and other vehicles, being a precursor of present-day car-rental companies. Another company advertised in 1862 "carriages and horses let out for hire by day, month or year".

20 Even in the mid-1800s, occupants of Stumperlowe Hall in Fulwood – James Dixon (see Chapter 10) and his father – travelled on horseback to their works in Cornish Place next to the Don.

21 *The Horse World of London*, written by W. J. Gordon in 1893, contains many details of animals and procedures which would have been familiar in Sheffield as well as London. The text is available on-line at http://victorianlondon.org; follow "Publications" in the list on the left side of that screen, and then "Social Investigations".

22 Horse troughs required natural supplies of water. The trough near Thornbury was adjacent to the Oak Brook (by the late 1800s culverted under the road), and Storth Lane ("Water Lane" until 1886) had a stream running along it in this section. Other troughs were probably fed by springs.

23 "Tram" is derived from a Scandinavian word for "beam" used in several European countries. Continuously-joined wooden beams were used from the 17th century or earlier to provide tracks in coal-mines and other settings, before becoming available in metal form in the 1800s. Original terms for passenger transportation included "tram-ways" and "tram-cars", rather than merely "trams", since that word initially referred only to the track along which vehicles moved.

24 The use of horses with trams was expensive. Figures quoted on page 40 of J. E. Vickers's book *From Horses to Atlanteans* indicate that food, bedding, shoeing, harness, stabling and other costs were more than three times as great as wages paid to staff.

25 One contentious issue concerned the space between the tracks. Was that the responsibility of the Company because their vehicles used the tracks, or payable by the Corporation because the central area belonged to them and was also used by the general public?

26 The 1904 building works included public conveniences at what became the tram terminus. That building, set into the wall near the Rising Sun, is currently being converted into a workshop and retail unit.

27 The one penny fare was doubled throughout the city in December 1919.

28 In the early part of the 20th century there were six postal deliveries in Sheffield each day, with the first at 7 a.m. and the last at 7 p.m. From Ranmoor Post Office 11 collections were made between 5 a.m. and 9.15 p.m.

29 English car-making started in the 1890s. For instance, the Daimler Motor Company dates from 1893, AC Cars from 1901, and Rolls-Royce and Rover from 1904.

30 For example, the "Hallamshire" car was made by Sheffield engineers Durham Churchill and Company between 1900 and 1905. Particularly well-known was the Sheffield Simplex Motor Company established in Tinsley in 1907. This explicitly set out to rival Daimler and Rolls-Royce. It later also produced motor cycles, and opened a factory in Kingston-on-Thames before coming to an end sometime in the 1920s.

31 Sheffield's first petrol-driven "waggonnette" for hire was introduced by Joseph Tomlinson in 1906, having transverse seats for 27 passengers. It is notable for a 1907 accident at Moscar with three fatalities. On that journey it had previously been overtaken by a two-horse carriage, and its speed was generally very slow. Engineering and design improvements led to increasing numbers of waggonnettes and "char-à-bancs" in succeeding years.

32 Related trades also continued in parallel. For instance, a 1905 Sheffield advertisement by William Wilson and Son was primarily as "carriage builders and harness makers", but it also indicated that "motor car bodies, canopies and wheels" were available and "motor repairs a speciality".

33 For instance, there were rows of garages available for rent in Fulney Road and in the yard behind 49 Nethergreen Road.

34 Sheffield's Kelham Island Museum contains a "bone-shaker" "penny farthing" constructed around 1869 by John Crowley and Company of Kelham Iron Works. See also Advert 11.02 from an 1879 directory.

35 A town-centre "cycle ground" for individual learning and practice had been opened in 1868, also visited by spectators who paid to watch this novel activity. Advertisements in the 1880s indicate that cycle retailers provided riding lessons and that the purchasers of a cycle could receive lessons free of charge.

36 Around 1891, the *Football, Cricket and Cycling World* was published weekly in Sheffield, placing cycling among other competitive sports. Racing success for particular cycle models was important in advertising and selling those models.

Index